Drawing on their numerous years' experience as counsellors, tutors and writers, **William Stewart** and **Jan Sutton** introduce readers to the basic principles that underpin counselling practice; provide insight into various counselling approaches; clarify the nature of counselling and the role of the counsellor, and assist readers to develop a repertoire of key counselling skills and qualities, such as active listening, genuineness, unconditional positive regard, empathy, goal-setting, etc. They also address the important issues of ongoing supervision to enhance counselling practice, and counsellor self-care to reduce the risk of burnout.

William Stewart is author of *An A–Z of Counselling Theory and Practice* and Jan Sutton is author of *Healing the Hurt Within*.

LEARNING TO COUNSEL

COUNSEL

HOW TO DEVELOP THE SKILLS, INSIGHT AND KNOWLEDGE TO COUNSEL OTHERS

William Stewart & Jan Sutton

ROBINSON

ROBINSON

First published in Great Britain in 1997 by How To Books Ltd

This revised and updated edition published in 2017 by Robinson

10 9 8 7 6 5 4

A CIP catalogue record for this book
is available from the British Library.

ISBN: 978-1-47213-849-1

Typeset in Garamond by TW Type, Cornwall

Printed and bound in Great Britain by Clays Ltd, Elcograf S.p.A.

Papers used by Robinson are from well-managed forests and other responsible sources.

Robinson
An imprint of
Little, Brown Book Group
Carmelite House
50 Victoria Embankment
London EC4Y 0DZ

An Hachette UK Company
www.hachette.co.uk

www.littlebrown.co.uk

How To Books are published by Robinson, an imprint of Little, Brown Book Group.
We welcome proposals from authors who have first-hand experience of their subjects. Please set out the aims of your book, its target market and its suggested contents in an email to
howto@littlebrown.co.uk

Contents

Foreword

William and Jan have much to take credit for in the education and training of the aspiring counsellor. It is satisfying to see that they are committed to the 'Ronseal' philosophy that determines the contents do exactly as it says on the tin. It can be frustrating to read counselling books that purport to be able to deliver the finished practitioner by the final chapter but William and Jan are far too open and honest to claim such a thing. They realise that counselling is an art, a science and a practice. All those who wish to become proficient practitioners are required to have a comprehensive knowledge of basic counselling concepts and theories, on-the-job counselling practice and a discipline of self-critical reflection, which can be found in clinical supervision.

A brief look at the contents page will reassure the reader that they are going to be offered a comprehensive and logical journey of learning, which will open up this subject to them in digestible chunks and provide them with the tools required to make good judgments about how they and counselling are best suited to each other – what models work for them and which may not be quite so congruent with their personalities. What comes through the whole book is the re-enforcement of the message through the respect the authors have for their readers – it is not easy in the written word to convey concepts like empathy, compassion and valuing but your authors, by being authentic in their own practice, deliver this fundamental moral purpose in spades.

The book is begun and ended with two very important issues in practice. The first is how do we make clients feel safe in our care and this is very much about a way of 'being' and of 'being there' for them on their journey to healing. The ending is about your own self-care – 'who cares for the carers' – this job should distress you and you need to have a place where you can yourself find healing so that you do not suffer 'burnout' and can be there for your clients in their need. That is why 'practice supervision' is essential to safeguard the practitioner and client.

As the practice of counselling and therapy becomes ever more sophisticated, it seems to be moving away from its foundations of actually 'Helping the Client' and towards using advanced techniques that take counselling out of the reach of 'The Skilled Helper' (Egan), making it a lofty profession. This book is refreshing because it stays within the foundations of counselling and therapy and so is within everyone's understanding.

We highly recommend this book to you and hope that you enjoy the many insights that these very experienced counsellors have committed to share with you – *Learning to Counsel* is a lifetime's achievement distilled for your understanding and growth as a student or proficient practitioner.

Simon Carr (Principal Tutor and General Manager)

Neil Morrison (Chief Executive and Principal)

Institute of Counselling

Preface

Being invited to produce a fourth edition of what has proved a popular book is very satisfying, and writing it has been a stimulating and rewarding experience for both of us. Since publishing the first edition in 1997, *Learning to Counsel* has proved such a success that it has taken us by surprise, and we have been greatly encouraged by the positive feedback received from both students of counselling, and tutors.

The book is based on our experience as counsellors and of running counselling workshops and lecturing. It is not intended to serve as a substitute for hands-on experience, which is crucial to effective practice. However, it is our belief that the skills presented here can enhance all human relationships.

We have thoroughly revised the fourth edition, reworked and updated most of the chapters and new material has been added. New case studies have been included and some of the original case studies have been developed. And a new chapter has been added, which introduces four counselling approaches to add to the repertoire of counselling skills. We have also included more links to appropriate websites.

Finally, to add a touch of warmth, some inspirational quotes and poems have been added to the chapters.

Written in a clear, concise and jargon-free style, and with its wealth of case studies, examples of skills in practice, and practical exercises, this new edition is an ideal text for those contemplating embarking on a counselling or psychotherapy course, trainee counsellors, counselling tutors to use in training, professionals working in the area of health care, management and education, and counsellors working in the voluntary sector.

The framework of the book is based firmly in the person-centred approach of Carl Rogers, and the skills-based approach of Gerard Egan. Carl Rogers suggested that if counsellors can plant the core conditions necessary for growth

– genuineness, unconditional positive regard, empathic understanding and warmth – these enable a healthy and nurturing relationship between counsellor and client to flourish. He believed that these conditions were sufficient to bring about growth and change in clients, enabling them to move towards fulfilment of their own potential.

Gerard Egan suggested that in addition to providing the core conditions, counsellors may need to help clients make decisions, clarify and set goals, and to support them with implementing their action. In his three-stage model, Egan analyses the skills that the counsellor needs to develop and use for each stage of the model.

To become a professional counsellor takes years of training and supervised counselling practice, and we would not presume to suggest that by reading this book you will have at your fingertips all that it takes to become an effective counsellor. A knowledge and understanding of the major theories of counselling is important, and a sound knowledge of psychology. However, counsellors can benefit from a model to guide them in their work, together with a repertoire of skills, and a careful study of the principles outlined here will provide a basis for counselling practice.

The book has been arranged in a logical sequence and we recommend that you work through the case studies and exercises in the sequence presented. Please ensure you have a pen and notebook handy to write down your responses to the exercises. Throughout several chapters, we follow five fictitious clients to demonstrate the skills.

We hope this new edition will provide you with some understanding of what is involved in counselling; will help you achieve some insight and appreciation of counselling, and will help you develop the skills you need to counsel more effectively.

To avoid the clumsy formula of he/she we have used them interchangeably throughout the book.

Finally, we would like to thank Giles Lewis and Nikki Read at How To Books, for their continued support for our work.

Jan Sutton has authored numerous personal development books including *Healing the Hurt Within: Understand Self-injury and Self-harm, and Heal the Emotional Wounds,* How To Books Ltd, third (revised) edition (12 Nov 2007). Because of ill health, Jan has retired as an independent counsellor after more than two decades working in the counselling profession.

William Stewart has spent a lifetime in the field of mental health in nursing and psychiatric social work and for four years was a student counsellor/lecturer at a college of nursing in London. He has been a tutor with the Institute of Counselling in Glasgow since 1992. He has published many counselling and self-help books in hard copy and on Kindle.

Jan Sutton

William Stewart

CHAPTER 1

Exploring Counselling

*Nature gave us one tongue and two ears so we could hear twice
as much as we speak.*

Epictetus (Greek philosopher)

This broad-ranging first chapter covers considerable ground on the multifaceted
topic of counselling. It opens by defining counselling, illustrating the differences
between counselling and other forms of helping, and examining whether
a distinction can be made between counselling and psychotherapy. It then
addresses the extensive range of counselling approaches currently practised,
and outlines five widely used approaches: psychodynamic counselling, person-
centred counselling, cognitive behavioural therapy (CBT), eclectic counselling
and integrative counselling. Next, it draws attention to transference and
countertransference (a psychoanalytic concept) and clarifies that psychodynamic
counselling is different from psychoanalysis. The issue of confidentiality is then
discussed, followed by a review of future climate changes in the profession,
and the potential impact of these. The broad work areas where counsellors
are employed, a debate on the opportunities of full-time paid employment
for counsellors, what motivates people to seek counselling, barriers to seeking
counselling and the elements required to counsel effectively draw the chapter to
a close.

DEFINING COUNSELLING

Counselling, often described as 'talking therapy', is a process aimed at providing
clients with the time and space to explore their problems, understand their
problems and resolve, or come to terms with their problems, in a confidential
setting. The British Association for Counselling and Psychotherapy (BACP)
define counselling and psychotherapy as 'umbrella terms that cover a range
of talking therapies. They are delivered by trained practitioners who work
with people over a short or long term to help them bring about effective

change or enhance their wellbeing.' http://www.bacp.co.uk/crs/Training/whatiscounselling.php.

Dictionaries usually define counselling as giving advice or guidance.

Advice is mainly one-way, based on giving an opinion, making a judgment and/or a recommendation, and tends towards persuasion.

Guidance is mainly one-way, based on showing the way, educating, influencing and instructing, and tends towards encouragement.

Counselling is a two-way collaborative exchange, a supportive relationship that enables clients to explore their problems so that they have more understanding and develop skills to resolve or come to terms with their problems.

To lay the foundations for building a trusting relationship, counsellors:

- Provide a safe and supportive setting, free from intrusions and distractions.

- Respect client confidentiality.

- Respect the client's principles, ethnicity and coping resources.

- Refrain from being judgmental.

- Avoid stereotyping or labelling.

- Shelve personal prejudices.

- Maintain impartiality, integrity and reliability.

> *If you judge people, you have no time to love them.*
> Mother Teresa of Calcutta

Through the counselling process, clients are helped to:

- Adapt to situations that cannot be changed (e.g. terminal illness, death of a loved one).

- Consider aspects of their lives they want to change.

- View their situation from a different perspective.

- Create positive changes.

- Develop coping strategies.

- Develop their full potential.

- Find their own solutions to their problems.

- Gain insight into their thoughts, feelings and behaviour.

- Grow and develop.

- Let go of painful secrets.

- Make informed decisions.

- Manage life transitions and crises.

- Resolve personal and interpersonal conflicts.

- Set and achieve goals.

- Take control of their lives.

For counselling to prove an empowering experience, the client must be self-motivated and committed to change. Being coerced into participating to satisfy someone else's needs is likely to be met with resistance, or a reluctance to cooperate.

CLARIFYING WHY COUNSELLING IS NOT ADVICE-GIVING

Giving advice frequently means telling people what they *should* do or *ought* to do. This conflicts with the true meaning of counselling. Certainly, counsellors help clients look at what is *possible*, but they avoid telling clients what they should do. That would be the counsellor *taking control* rather than the client *gaining* control.

The counsellor who answers the question 'What would you advise me to do?' with 'What ideas have you had?' is helping the client to recognise that they have a part to play in seeking an answer. They help the client take responsibility for finding a solution that feels right for them.

Advice may be appropriate in crises; at times when clients' thoughts are clearly confused or they feel overwhelmed following a traumatic event. At such times, the counsellor will exercise greater caution than when clients are fully responsive and responsible. Advice offered and accepted when in crisis, and then acted upon, could prove to be, if not 'bad advice', not very apt to meet the client's needs. When people are in a state of shock or under stress, they are vulnerable. For all those reasons, counsellors are wary about responding to a request for advice.

Advice is generally considered inappropriate in person-centred counselling and most humanistic and holistic approaches. It may be more appropriate and acceptable when working with the very young, with people who are disturbed or helpless or on essentially practical issues.

One of the basic assumptions in any counselling is that clients are helped to work towards their own solutions. This is why it is important to explore as many different avenues as possible; and it is in this area that the concept of advice appears to create conflict. It is how we present alternatives or point out the legal consequences of certain actions, which must give some bias; but provided that we leave with clients as much initiative as they are capable of exercising and give them every opportunity to discuss whatever they wish, then we do no violence to the principle of self-responsibility.

Whenever you are asked for advice or inclined to give advice, be sure that you are well informed about the situation.

- Do you have enough information and expertise to advise another competently?

- Ask yourself what might be the end results of this advice giving. Is it likely to make the counselee more dependent?

- Can you handle the feelings that might come if your advice is rejected or proven wrong?

If you then do give advice, offer it in the form of a tentative suggestion, give the counselee time to react or talk through your advice, and follow up later to see the extent to which the advice was helpful.

Not offering advice can sometimes prove difficult for even the most seasoned counsellors. For example, if a client is suffering from tension the counsellor may suggest relaxation techniques to help reduce stress levels. Even though the given 'advice' might be offered with the client's best interests at heart, the choice should always remain with the client as to whether it is pursued.

> *He that gives good advice, builds with one hand; he that*
> *gives good counsel and example, builds with both; but he that*
> *gives good admonition and bad example, builds with one hand*
> *and pulls down with the other.*
> Francis Bacon, Sr., English lawyer and philosopher (1561–1626)

EXAMINING WHY COUNSELLING IS NOT PERSUASION

Counselling is not about persuading, prevailing upon, overcoming the client's resistances, wearing the client down or 'bringing the client to their senses'. Persuasion is in direct conflict with at least one principle of counselling, self-direction – the clients' right to choose for themselves their course of action. If the counsellor were to persuade the client to go a certain way, make a certain choice, there could be a very real danger of the whole affair backfiring in the counsellor's face and resulting in further damage to the client's self-esteem.

This concept of self-direction, based on personal freedom, is the touchstone of the non-directive approach to counselling but is present in most others. The basis of the principle is that any pressure that is brought to bear on the client will increase conflict and so impede exploration.

EXPLORING WHY COUNSELLING IS NOT EXERCISING UNDUE INFLUENCE

Some people believe that successful counsellors are those who are able to suggest solutions to clients' problems in such a way that the clients feel they are their own. This is commonly called 'manipulation', behaviour from which most counsellors would recoil. However, situations are seldom clear-cut. There is a fine line between legitimate influence and manipulation. Manipulation always carries with it some benefit to the manipulator. Influence is generally unconscious. In any case, suggesting solutions is not part of effective counselling. There is a difference between exploring alternatives and suggesting solutions and manipulation. Manipulation invariably leaves the person on the receiving end feeling uncomfortable, used and angry.

The dividing line between manipulation and seeking ways and means to resolve a problem may not always be easily seen, but the deciding factor must be *who benefits?* Is it you, or is it the other person?

Case study of manipulation

An example of manipulation, taken from a training session, illustrates the point. Joe was going through a difficult time with his girlfriend. The trainee counsellor, in the belief that it would be best for Joe to end the relationship, introduced a whole gamut of moral issues, which left Joe feeling so guilty that he said he would sever the relationship. This would have been inappropriate and would have left both Joe and the girlfriend feeling resentful. That is manipulation.

COUNSELLING SKILLS VS. COUNSELLING PER SE

Counselling skills are used by a range of professionals and volunteer helpers. Examples of counselling skills in practice include the doctor who listens attentively to his patient without interrupting before prescribing, the psychiatrist who pays thoughtful attention to the symptoms being described by a patient before making a diagnosis, the priest who helps an anonymous parishioner accept God's grace and forgiveness from behind the curtain of the confessional box, or the life-coach who allows time and space for a client to explore any roadblocks that are hindering achieving a desired goal.

The dividing line between using counselling skills and counselling per se is often blurred. Managers, nurses, social workers and other health practitioners may apply counselling techniques to help their clients, patients or employees, and may have undertaken a counselling skills training course. In effect, they use counselling skills as a part of their role, but counselling is not their main career or how they earn a living.

Counselling, in contrast, is a distinct occupation which requires extensive training, supervised practice to reflect on one's own performance and maintain high standards of professionalism, keeping abreast of changes in the field, and an ongoing commitment to personal growth and professional development. It entails a sound understanding of theories of human development and counselling theory and its applications to practice. Furthermore, it is a mandatory requirement of many counselling training courses for trainees to undertake personal therapy, the aim of which is to address personal issues that arise through their counselling work, to foster personal growth and to experience what it feels like to be in the client role.

Counselling is a contractual agreement – client and counsellor have agreed to work together. The client may have attended an initial assessment interview to determine if counselling is appropriate and counsellor and client may have negotiated a time-limited contract (typically between six and twelve sessions) or an open-ended contract (no set limit on number of sessions). (*See* Chapter 4 for an example of a counselling contract and further discussion on the topic.)

COUNSELLOR AND PSYCHOTHERAPIST: IS THERE A DIFFERENCE?

The terms counsellor and psychotherapist are often used interchangeably and, just as distinguishing between using counselling skills and counselling per se is not straightforward, so it is with attempting to differentiate between counselling and psychotherapy. Some would argue that there is no difference, or that the disparity is minimal. In contrast, others would advocate that a distinction can be made on the basis that psychotherapy is more in-depth and longer term and that a psychotherapist receives more extensive training than a counsellor.

What we are talking about is a matter of degree, not difference. We have to acknowledge that there are people who are more qualified to deal with those who are severely disturbed – these people are psychiatrists, and therapists who have specialised in this line of work. At the same time, there are many people who operate at the other end of the dimension – the problems of daily living – who are more likely to come the way of the counsellor, rather than be admitted to psychiatric care in hospital, or some other place. As one moves from 'Daily living' through the dimension towards 'Psychoses', counsellor involvement will invariably lessen. At the same time, the involvement of the psychiatrist is likely to be very little in the problems of daily living.

DAILY LIVING	⟶	PSYCHOSES
	Mild anxiety, depression, severe anxiety, bi-polar, obsessions, schizophrenia	
Counsellor involvement less serious		Psychiatric involvement more serious

DIFFERENT COUNSELLING APPROACHES

An overwhelming array of counselling and psychotherapy models exists. The list below is by no means an exhaustive one. What is important to emphasise is that a particular approach, method or model does not necessarily make an effective counsellor. What will make more of a difference is the relationship between client and counsellor rather than technique. Thus, developing relationship skills must rate very highly. In behavioural or cognitive counselling, for example, there might not be as much emphasis on the counsellor working within the client's frame of reference (a key concept in person-centred counselling that is further discussed in Chapter 2), yet the relationship can be just as rewarding and the outcome equally positive.

- Adlerian therapy
- Behaviour therapy*
- Bibliotherapy
- Brief therapy
- Client-centred counselling
- Cognitive analytical therapy (CAT)
- Cognitive behavioural therapy (CBT)
- Cognitive therapy
- Creative therapies – art, drama, music, dance, movement
- Dialectical behaviour therapy (DBT)
- Eclectic counselling
- Emotional freedom techniques (EFT)
- Existential counselling
- Eye movement desensitisation and reprocessing (EMDR)
- Gestalt therapy*
- Humanistic psychotherapy
- Integrative counselling
- Logotherapy
- Multicultural counselling
- Multimodel counselling
- Narrative therapy
- Neuro-linguistic programming (NLP)
- Person-centred counselling
- Primal therapy
- Psychoanalysis
- Psychodynamic counselling
- Psychosynthesis*
- Rational emotive behavioural therapy (REBT)
- Re-birthing
- Sensorimotor psychotherapy
- Solution-focused brief therapy
- Systemic therapies
- Transactional analysis*
- Transcendent counselling
- Transpersonal therapy

Those with an * are developed in Chapter 11.

Descriptions of some, but not all, of the approaches can be found on the BACP website at http://www.bacp.co.uk/seeking_therapist/theoretical_approaches.php.

The roots of many approaches are based on the psychoanalytic, person-centred and cognitive or behavioural traditions. Five widely used approaches: psychodynamic counselling, person-centred counselling, cognitive behavioural therapy (CBT), eclectic counselling and integrative counselling are discussed next.

Psychodynamic counselling

A psychodynamic approach (derived from psychoanalysis) is the systematised knowledge and theory of human behaviour and its motivation. Inherent in this is the study of the functions of emotions. Psychodynamic counselling recognises the role of the unconscious, and how it influences behaviour. Further, behaviour is determined by past experience, genetic endowment and what is happening in the present.

In psychodynamic counselling the counsellor is far less active than in many other approaches, and relies more on the client bringing forth material, rather than reflecting feelings and inviting exploration; and what the client discloses will be interpreted according to the psychoanalytic model. Just as in psychoanalysis, where the patient is expected to report anything that comes to mind, so in psychodynamic counselling. Hesitation to reveal is interpreted as resistance, which must be worked through before progress is achieved.

Insight

While feelings are not ignored – for to ignore them would be to deny an essential part of the person – feelings are not the emphasis; insight is, and that insight relates to the functioning of the unconscious. For the underlying belief is that it is the unconscious that produces dysfunction. Thus insight, in the psychodynamic model, is:

- getting in touch with the unconscious, and

- bringing what is unconscious into the conscious.

Although insight is usually worked towards in those approaches which focus on feelings, in the psychodynamic approach it is considered essential. You achieve insight when you understand what is causing a conflict. The premise is that if insight is gained, conflicts will cease. Insight is often accompanied by catharsis, which is the release of emotion, often quite dramatic.

On the one hand, the development of insight can elicit excitement. It brings clarity, awareness and understanding to complex situations – like stepping out of a fog and seeing things more clearly. Insights may be sudden and experienced as a flash of inspiration, like a light has suddenly been switched on, or that 'eureka moment' when one realises something for the first time. Insight may be accompanied by a sense of relief or element of satisfaction – 'now I understand why I am like I am, why I have these feelings about . . ., why I behave as I do towards . . .'. In contrast, insight gained too early in the therapeutic relationship can elicit distress by providing lucid recognition of the painful truth about a previously repressed experience that is not ready to be faced – 'that can't be how things really were . . .', 'She wouldn't have allowed that to happen to me'.

Insight, rather than dawning spontaneously or springing unexpectedly, more usually develops stage-by-stage as the client develops the psychological strength to deal with what is revealed. It may linger for days or weeks, gradually working away in the client's subconscious mind, figuring in their dreams, or revealing itself in flashbacks (unwanted brief snapshots or scenes from the past). From initially seeing things through frosted glass and with a lack of detail, shape slowly takes place, ultimately revealing a picture or image that doesn't filter out the truth that lies beneath.

The skilled psychodynamic counsellor will recognise when traumatic insight is being gained prematurely, and will slow the pace down until the client has achieved sufficient ego strength to cope with information that is filtering through from the unconscious to the conscious.

Understanding why psychodynamic counselling is not psychoanalysis

Psychodynamic counselling is derived from psychoanalysis, generally believed (although this is sometimes disputed) to be 'the baby' of Sigmund Freud. What is important to establish is that psychodynamic counsellors are not analysts, and counselling is not psychoanalysis. The principal difference between psychoanalysis and counselling is that psychoanalysis deals more, but not exclusively, with the unconscious and the past, while counselling deals more, but not exclusively, with the conscious and the present – the here-and-now and the very recent past and how to live in the future. Counselling cannot ignore the past, for it is the past which has made us the way we are now. It is inevitable that things from the past will creep through into the conscious present. Nor can counsellors ignore the unconscious. The past and the present are bound together with cords that cannot be broken and it is inevitable that things from the past will filter through into the conscious present. When this happens, the client will usually be aware of it. As previously mentioned, flashes of insight can carry with them a degree of exhilaration, or the possibility of pain if they bring forth traumatic memories. The counsellor's ability to hold a client safely through the coming to light of traumatic insights is paramount to the client's movement forward in the healing process.

Exploring the past

We do not want to give the impression that exploration of the past has no place in counselling or that probing is inappropriate and unnecessary. We have said that the past and the present are inseparable and if this is so then the one cannot be examined without some part of the other emerging; it is all a matter of degree and emphasis.

The past will show its influence quite clearly; and if dealt with when appropriate, will yield fruit. Too much emphasis on the past can detract from the present.

If the counselling relationship helps clients to learn to do their own exploring, they will have acquired a valuable tool, which they can put to good use in the future.

Solving problems

Sometimes counsellors will enable clients to look at problem-solving strategies, but we cannot solve clients' problems. If we attempt to do this, it would put the client in an inferior position. The client would become dependent. The aim is to help clients explore what the problem is, then together client and counsellor work out how the client might go about resolving the problem. However, some problems may never be solved, but clients can learn strategies to manage them more effectively.

Counsellor and client have come together for a specific purpose and however satisfying the counselling relationship is, it will end. Both counsellor and client will go their separate ways, possibly never to meet again. The client will have experienced something unique, and the counsellor will have contributed something to the good of humankind, and in turn, the client will have something he or she can offer to someone else.

Transference and countertransference

Before moving on from the topic of psychodynamic counselling and psychoanalysis, we consider it important to address two additional key concepts in the psychoanalytic school of thought, i.e. the phenomenon of transference and countertransference. Simply put, transference refers to the client's unconscious transfer of feelings, attitudes and desires projected on to the therapist that are associated with significant relationships from the client's past (parents, grandparents, siblings, teachers, doctors, authority figures, etc.). Client transference reactions can be affirmative (positive feelings towards the therapist) or negative (hostile feelings toward the therapist).

Transference allows old conflicts to resurface and to be worked through. The therapist is careful to avoid responding to the displaced feelings and behaviour. Negative transference will interfere with therapy. It shows in direct attacks on the therapist or, by acting out negative feelings rather than exploring them, an unwillingness to work through resistances. Intense positive transference may make excessive emotional demands on the therapist and prevent exploration of feelings.

One of the principal indicators of transference is that the client seeks to change the relationship from a professional to a personal one and does not respect the boundaries.

If the counsellor reacts to these projected feelings, this is called 'countertransference'. For example, if the client is angry with the counsellor, *as if the counsellor is the perceived parent*, transference is taking place. If the counsellor then reacts by relating to the client in an authoritarian manner, in a parental way, that is countertransference. We are more likely to experience countertransference when something being related by the client resonates within us, possibly because of some unresolved part of our life. We may detect this transference by wanting to take action on behalf of the client, even though that would be inappropriate.

Counsellors, in contrast to psychoanalysts, do not deliberately foster transference. In psychoanalysis, much use is made of transference and of working through it. Nevertheless, counsellors should be aware that clients may be investing feelings in them that would be more appropriately directed toward another person. These feelings are more likely to develop in psychoanalysis than in counselling, partly because of the depth at which analysts work, but also because of the greater frequency of contact. To acknowledge these may be sufficient. By so doing, the counsellor is opening the way for clients to discuss their feelings at that moment. This supports the point made earlier that counselling deals more with the present than with the past and more with the conscious than with the unconscious.

Person-centred counselling

A broad distinction can be made between the psychodynamic and person-centred approaches. The psychodynamic approach works with insight related to unconscious material, whereas the person-centred counsellor works with insight related to the client's feelings. If in the process unconscious material is elicited, so be it, but the unconscious is not the focus. According to Carl Rogers (1902–1987), founder of the person-centred approach, four core conditions are crucial to facilitating therapeutic growth: genuineness, unconditional regard, empathic understanding, plus non-possessive warmth. These conditions (also referred to as personal qualities) are discussed in detail in Chapter 2.

Rogers, believing that diagnosis, planning and interpretation are more for the analyst than for the clients (called patients), started to think about what it meant to be a client and to see things from the client's perspective, rather than try to get the client to conform to some theory.

The aim of person-centred counselling is to engage clients in an equal partnership. The counsellor provides a supportive, non-judgmental understanding atmosphere, but will not advise, interpret or direct the client.

The person-centred approach emphasises clients' capacity and strengths to direct the course and direction of their own counselling. They have the ability to solve their problems, however massive they seem. The more the counsellor understands what something means *to the client*, the deeper the relationship in which they experience the core conditions, the more in charge clients feel. And the more empowered they feel the more able they are to tackle whatever difficulties they are experiencing.

When clients feel that their thoughts, feelings and behaviours are being received without judgment, at that moment; when they feel accepted, and when they feel safe enough to explore their problems and gradually come to experience those parts of themselves they normally keep hidden – from yourself and others – at that moment clients will know that they are being listened to and understood.

Essential characteristics of the helping relationship

Necessary features of the counselling relationship, as defined by Carl Rogers (Rogers, 1961), highlight the following questions that counsellors should consider:

- **Trustworthy.** Can I be in some way that will be perceived by the other person as trustworthy, as dependable or consistent in some deep sense?

- **Congruent.** Can I be expressive enough as a person so that what I am will be communicated unambiguously?

- **Warmth.** Can I let myself experience positive attitudes towards this person, attitudes of warmth, caring, liking, interest, respect?

- **Separateness.** Can I be strong enough as a person to be separate from the other?

- **Secure.** Am I secure enough within myself to permit the client to be separate?

- **Empathic.** Can I let myself enter fully into the world of the client's feelings and personal meanings and see these as they do?

- **Accepting.** Can I be accepting of each facet of this person that he presents to me?

- **Non-threatening.** Can I act with sufficient sensitivity in the relationship that my behaviour will not be perceived as a threat?

- **Non-evaluative.** Can I free this client from the threat of external evaluation, from his or her past and my past?

CASE STUDY

Joan is terrified of retiring (William speaking)

Introduction

I have chosen this case study because it illustrates the counselling process from referral to final evaluation and because it is based mainly on a person-centred foundation. As with the other case studies that follow, it is not presented as an ideal, but as how it actually happened.

Fundamental to the person-centred therapy is the relationship established between therapist and client, based on the core conditions of empathy, genuineness or congruence, non-possessive warmth and unconditional positive regard.

Person-centred therapists prefer to talk about attitudes and behaviours and creating growth-promoting climates. Their view of their clients is that they are intrinsically good, capable of directing their own destinies, and the concept of self-actualisation is at the centre of person-centred counselling, in common with other humanistic therapies, philosophies and approaches; the focus is on engaging the client's frame of reference and in understanding and tracking precisely what something means to the client.

The therapist's task is to facilitate clients' awareness of, and trust in, self-actualisation. The therapeutic process is centred on the client and it is the client's inner experiencing that controls the pace and the direction of the relationship. When clients are accepted and when the core conditions are present, they feel safe enough to explore their problems and gradually come to experience the parts of themselves they normally keep hidden from themselves and from others.

The aim of person-centred counselling is to engage clients in an equal partnership. The counsellor provides a supportive, non-judgmental understanding atmosphere; will not give advice, interpret or direct; but will constantly seek to understand what something means to the client. The more the counsellor understands what something means to a client; the deeper the relationship in which clients experience the core conditions, the more in charge they feel. And the more empowered they feel, the more able they are to tackle whatever difficulties they are experiencing.

Finally, being person-centred not only means having the client at the centre of the counselling relationship, it also means having one's self at the centre. This does not mean being self-centred or egotistical, it means that the core conditions reside deep within and find expression in our relationship with others. If, for example, we are not genuine within, how can we be genuine with clients? In order to accept clients as *they* are, we must accept ourselves *we* are, although this might involve change. Can we really listen to the feelings of other people, or track the meanings of their messages, if we do not understand ourselves?

Introduction to Joan

One year previous, Joan had surgery for the removal of a benign tumour from her abdomen. She has been attended by her GP for many years and over the past year, he has been concerned for her well-being.

The GP wrote to me:

Dear William

I have referred Miss Joan— to you for therapy. Since her operation one year ago, I have seen a gradual ebbing away of her zest for life. She is not on any medication at present, and generally, her health is fine. I think she has some emotional problems she needs to explore. I would appreciate a follow-up report from you at some stage. Joan is aware of what I have written.

The Client

Joan, a head teacher, is approaching retirement age. She is unmarried and lives alone in a fashionable part of the town. She has no relatives living, although she has many friends and acquaintances. She is a regular churchgoer and is Secretary of her local Conservative Party.

Therapy

The initial session

Joan: I feel much better about talking, although it hasn't come easily. What do you think about me, how long do you think I should be coming?

William: Now would seem an appropriate place to start to explore the counselling contract with you.

Joan: Heavens! That sounds very formal.

William: Yes, I suppose it does. You sounded quite put off then.

Joan: Well, in a way, yes. I just thought we'd have a cosy chat. But that's being a bit naive, I suppose. Go on, William, please.

William: One of the first things we should deal with is, I generally recommend that we meet weekly, here, for about fifty minutes. I also recommend that we set a contract for six sessions.

Joan: And then that's it?

William: Not necessarily. On the sixth session we will review where we are, then renegotiate further sessions. On the other hand, we could have an open-ended contract, with no specified length. How does that sound?

Joan: Oh, I don't think so, thanks. I don't think I could cope with something as indefinite as that. I like to work towards something definite. So, six sessions to start with would suit me fine. And how much will this cost?

William: My normal fee is . . . although I do work to a sliding scale for people who have difficulty meeting that fee. How does that sound to you?

Joan: That's fine, no problem. I already feel it will be money well spent. I must admit, though, to some nervousness. I have some idea of your style from today, but does it mean probing into my deep unconscious, into the hidden parts?

William: You mean like some interrogation? No, my way of working is that I will try very hard to listen to you and to understand what it means to you. I'll try not to probe into areas you're not ready to look at. I hope I shall be sensitive to your needs and also what is happening between us. However, if at any time I don't understand it from your point of view, will you tell me, please?

Joan: That doesn't sound at all like I was expecting. It's more like a partnership.

William: Yes, it is. So that means that we both have to be honest and open with each other. Now that may take time, to build the relationship. But we've already started doing that.

Joan: I'm a bit hesitant about saying this, but I know the doctor has written to you, and has asked for some sort of report, at some stage. What will you tell him?

William: I sense a fear there, Joan, that perhaps what we discuss will not be kept confidential. Let me explain. What we discuss will be kept strictly between us. That is a strict ethical point in counselling. Yes, I will be contacting the doctor at some stage. Would you prefer it if we constructed the letter between us?

Joan: Well, that's really partnership. Thank you, I feel good about that.

William: Can you think of any exceptions to the rule, Joan?

Joan: If I confessed to some crime, like murder, or was involved in a drug ring or something like that. That sounds awful and not like me at all. *[Both laugh.]*

William: Yes, although it's not likely, something like that, where someone else would be put at risk. But even then, I would feel it essential to discuss it with you before I took action.

Joan: And then I can hop on a plane and be out of it.*[Both laugh.]*

William: There's one point I ought to raise about confidentiality. I meet regularly with my supervisor to talk about my clients. He helps my development as a counsellor. How do you feel about that?

Joan: He wouldn't know my name, would he?

William: Not if you don't want him to. I shall refer to you as Miss A. How about that?

Joan: Certainly, so long has he can't identify me. I'd hate to bump into him in Church!

William: So far, we've tied up the number of sessions, the fee, confidentiality and my own supervision. At the end of every session we'll spend a few minutes reviewing what has taken place, seeing where we've come from and possibly what to focus on next time, although that can never be hard and fast. I also like to start the next session with a few minutes reflecting on the last session. Generally, I'll say something like, 'Has anything occurred to you arising out of the last session?' I find that this allows us both to be tuned in. How does that sound?

Joan: I'm impressed. There is order, yet a great sense of freedom in what you say.

William: That's how I like to think of it. When we get to the end, whenever that is, we may like to carry out a formal evaluation, and I have a pre-printed questionnaire that I find useful, although it can be as formal or informal as we wish. The last thing to talk over is the goals.

Joan: Ah, that's not so easy. I've already told you some of my feelings about retiring, and I suppose if I put them all together, I want to feel happier about retiring. At the moment, the prospect seems too awful to face. It's as if I'll have no identity of my own. All these years my identity has been wrapped up in being a teacher.

William: So your goal would be to accept this new phase of your life and learn to live life in a different way? It's possible that as we go on, other areas will become known that you feel you need to work on. Let's leave it there for now, though we can always look at the contract again.

Exploration

Joan had been talking about not feeling in control of her life.

William: So then, if we look at that a bit closer, you feel that something is, or has been, controlling you.

Joan: Mmm. I suppose you could say that. Thinking about that, it's this worry, isn't it? Silly really, letting something like that take control.

William: Like a tyrant. Almost like keeping you in prison.

Joan: That is very accurate. In fact, over the past year I have felt like a prisoner. If I didn't have my job to go to, and all the other things, I wouldn't want to go out. I mean, I'm all right when I am out, as if I've escaped, but it's when the door closes, then I feel trapped.

William: As if the cell door clangs behind you?

Joan: *[Her lip trembling.]* Yes, as if I've committed some terrible crime. And I feel so alone.

William: Isolated and cut off from all human contact.

Joan: *[Reaching for a tissue.]* Silly isn't it? Why should I feel like this? I mean, so isolated, yet I keep very busy.

Speaking of her work, Joan says:

Joan: *[Crying.]* I don't want it to end. My whole life has been teaching. I've had hundreds of children, even though they weren't mine. If only . . .

William: If only?

Joan: Yes, if only. Could this be connected? It's not something I talk about, and it happened a long time ago.

William: You seem to have made a connection between how you feel now and something in your past life, yet you are hesitant about expressing it.

Joan discloses that several years before she had had an affair with a married man, who had died in a climbing accident. This had been gnawing away at her over the years, the more so as she was friendly with the widow, and godmother to the daughter. Much of what then takes place relates to Joan's need to forgive herself, as well as talking through her anxiety about retirement.

At no time in these brief extracts do I go beyond what Joan is talking about. No probing questions are asked, no interpretations, just a constant seeking of clarification *of what it means to Joan*.

For the terminal evaluation, see Chapter 9.

Cognitive behavioural therapy (CBT)

Aaron T Beck (the founder of CBT, born 1921) was influenced by the philosophy of Epictetus, who placed prominence on the belief that 'Men are disturbed not by things, but by the view which they take of them' (*The Enchiridion*, first century AD). CBT focuses on how a person thinks, and how thinking influences behaviour – what you think, you become, is the basic premise upon which the CBT approach is built. Emotional or behavioural problems are considered the consequences of faulty learned thinking and behaviour patterns. The aim of CBT is to change faulty thinking and behaviour patterns by having the client learn new patterns, to learn decision-making and problem-solving skills as part of the process of thinking and behaviour rehabilitation.

Clients are helped to challenge the discrepancies between their thoughts, feelings and behaviours within and outside of counselling. False logic and irrational beliefs contribute to faulty thinking, thus one particular challenge is that of replacing irrational thinking with rational. Changing behaviour and self-defeating beliefs is the focus, rather than trying to find the root cause. CBT is a collaborative endeavour – the client–counsellor relationship being more like that of tutor and student. It is typically short-term, structured, directive and goal-oriented. Completion of homework tasks by the client in between sessions forms a significant component of treatment. CBT is used widely to treat depression, anxiety, panic attacks, phobias, obsessive-compulsive behaviours, eating difficulties, etc.

CBT is different from many other forms of therapy; it is:

1. *Pragmatic* – helps identify specific problems and then an attempt is made to solve them.

2. *Highly structured* – rather than talking freely about one's life, client and therapist will discuss specific problems and set goals for the client to achieve. As part of this, clients may be given homework in the form of activities that they should try to complete before the next therapy session.

3. *Concerned with the present* – unlike some other therapies that attempt to explore and possibly resolve past issues, CBT is mainly concerned with how we think and act now.

4. *Collaborative* – the CBT therapist will not tell clients what to do; they will work with them in order to help them improve their situation.

Some clients and some counsellors do not relate well to CBT. Because CBT focuses more on cognition (thinking) than on affect (feeling), the whole process can feel alien. Counsellors who relate to the person-centred approach may find themselves uncomfortable with the more directive and structured approach of CBT. The same applies to certain clients; yet these are the very clients who would probably benefit from CBT.

Some of the most common cognitive errors are:

1. *All-or-nothing thinking*: Placing experiences in one of two opposite categories (e.g. flawless or defective, immaculate or filthy, saint or sinner).

2. *Overgeneralising*: Making sweeping inferences (e.g. 'I can't control my temper') based on a single incident.

3. *Discounting the positives:* Deciding that if a good thing has happened, it couldn't have been very important (e.g. refusing to take pride in earning a degree because 'Everyone goes to university these days').

4. *Jumping to conclusions*: Focusing on one aspect of a situation when forming a judgment or deciding what the 'data' means (e.g. 'I haven't received a phone call from the team because they think I'm useless and they don't want me to play for them').

5. *Mind reading*: Believing one knows what another person is thinking with very little evidence (e.g. 'I know she dislikes or disapproves of me because she's never spoken to me').

6. *Fortune telling*: Believing one knows what the future holds, while ignoring other possibilities (e.g. 'I haven't heard back about the job interview. It means I really messed it up and will never get a job').

7. *Magnifying/minimising*: Evaluating the importance of a negative event, or the lack of evidence of a positive event, in a distorted manner (e.g. a woman assumed her best friend didn't really value her, when she invited a relative to be the godmother at her son's christening).

8. *Emotional reasoning*: Believing that something must be true, because it feels like it is true, (e.g. 'I can just feel she's going to walk out on me – It's not anything she's said or done, specifically').

9. *Making 'should' statements*: Telling oneself one should do (or should have done) something, when it is more accurate to say that one would like to do (or wishes one had done) the preferred thing (e.g. 'I should have got up in

time to catch the bus, and then I wouldn't have driven and been involved in an accident').

10. *Labelling*: Using a label (bad mother, idiot) to describe a behaviour – and then imputing all the meanings the label carries.

11. *Inappropriate blaming*: Using hindsight to determine what one 'should have done', even if one could not have known the best thing to do at the time. Also, ignoring mitigating factors or ignoring the role that was played by others in a negative experience or event (e.g. 'I shouldn't have gone off on holiday, and then I would have been there when my father had a heart attack and died').

For more on CBT, see

http://www.mind.org.uk/information-support/drugs-and-treatments/cognitive-behavioural-therapy-cbt/#.VpYB9P_nmic

http://www.aliceboyes.com/free-cognitive-behavioral-therapy-cbt-youtube-videos/

http://www.bing.com/videos/search?q=youtube+cbt&qpvt=youtube+CBT&FORM=VDRE

Eclectic and integrative approaches: are they two sides of the same coin?

While some counsellors choose to remain loyal to their original model of training, others elect to spread their wings and offer an eclectic or integrated approach. Understanding the difference between eclecticism and integrationalism can be a bit like wading through treacle as often there appears to be an overlap – what they share in common is the belief that no one approach or theory suits all.

The fundamental difference between the two can perhaps be explained on the premise that while eclectic counsellors are most likely to have one core framework, psychodynamic or Rogerian, for instance, they tailor their interventions to suit the client's particular needs by adopting techniques from other models, whereas, in contrast, integrative counsellors weave together or draw on the strengths of multiple theories, such as CBT, psychodynamic and humanistic, to develop a model that best suits their personality and style of working.

A counsellor using an eclectic or integrated approach may use a *psychodynamic* approach to bring unconscious drives and/or defences into conscious awareness. *Behavioural* therapy may be appropriate if a particular behaviour pattern is inhibiting, e.g. if the client has a specific sexual difficulty. *Cognitive* therapy could help if the messages from the client's earlier life are leading to self-defeating or self-destructive thought patterns or behaviours. Most counsellors using an eclectic approach work with the person-centred core principles.

For example, in *person-centred* counselling, the counsellor works with being warm, accepting, genuine and real. In *psychodynamic* counselling, the counsellor interprets unconscious motivation from a theoretical base, not from what something means to the client, as in person-centred counselling. In *transpersonal* counselling, working with the body, through touch and movement, may be acceptable. In *imagery*, the counsellor works with the meaning of symbols to tap into the client's deeper feelings. In *Christian* counselling the focus is on helping the client explore the spiritual aspect within a psychological framework.

(For more on eclectic counselling, see http://teachereducationguidanceandcounsellin.blogspot.co.uk/2011/03/eclectic-counseling.html.)

UNDERSTANDING CONFIDENTIALITY

Counselling is a highly confidential relationship. The preservation of confidential information is a basic right of the client and an ethical obligation upon the counsellor. If you were asked what is your understanding of 'confidentiality', you would probably say that you didn't want the details of what you disclosed gossiped about or discussed with people who didn't have to be involved. You would probably agree that the counsellor, where necessary, would be free to discuss broad details with professional colleagues, but only after your prior consent had been obtained.

Most counsellors at some time in their careers have been faced with the painful decision of whether to respect confidence or, for the good of society or to prevent something disastrous happening, to break it. Whatever is decided, no action should be taken without discussion with the client.

Confidentiality is two-way. Just as the counsellor respects the client's privacy, there is an obligation on the client to respect the counsellor's privacy and whatever the counsellor discloses about him or herself, or what the client gleans about the counsellor from the relationship. What the client tells other people about the counselling is the client's prerogative provided it does not break the confidential relationship with the counsellor.

The BACP lays down a strict code of ethics for its members, although not all counsellors are members. (Membership of this or any other body is not yet a legal requirement in Britain.) Confidentiality provides the client with safety and privacy, and any doubts about confidentiality will seriously interfere with what the client reveals.

Nothing the counsellor says, writes or in any way communicates to a third party should identify who the client is. When writing to another professional, such as a doctor, then we suggest that the content of the letter is discussed with the client, and a copy given to the client. The counsellor should have a copy of the BACP *Ethical Framework for the Counselling Professions* (2016) available for clients to peruse.

(Taken from Stewart, W. & Martin, A. (1999). *Going for Counselling*. Used with permission of the authors.)

Counselling touches human lives intimately, possibly more so than any other helping relationship. The counsellor is frequently the observer, and often the recipient, of confidential material about people, their life situations and intimate details of their families. Confidentiality is both an ethical consideration and an element in the counselling relationship. At first glance, it is deceptively simple.

- Confidentiality means not passing on secret details about another person disclosed during counselling.

- Everything said in a counselling interview is confidential; not everything is secret – what are secrets?

- The private secret is that which, if we reveal it, would libel, injure or cause great sadness to the person concerned.

- The pledged secret is when one person shares something with another and is assured that it will remain in confidence.

- The entrusted secret is the explicit or implicit understanding that the confidant will not divulge the information.

- A belief that everything the client says must never be shared with anyone else can lead to problems.

- If it becomes imperative that some information must be passed on, full discussion with the client is essential.

- The professional counsellor is bound by certain ethics, which are not applicable in their totality to people using counselling skills as part of their repertoire of work skills. People who use counselling at work, as distinct from independent counsellors, must consider the rules of professional conduct of their organisation. It is helpful to ask, is this information concerned mainly with the client as a person within the organisation? Purely personal material, unless it impinges on the client's working life and influences performance, is of no concern to anyone else. The dividing line between 'personal' and 'organisational' is finely drawn. Only after a weighing up of all the pros and cons will we realise why the balance is tipped the way it is and so make our decision to keep something or pass it on.

- Wherever possible agreement to disclose should be received, to avoid feelings of betrayal.

- Feelings as well as facts should not be shared indiscriminately.

- Confidentiality is limited by

  Whose needs predominate?

  Who would be harmed?

  The organisational needs.

  The needs of the wider society.

Counsellors need to be quite clear what information gleaned during counselling they may pass on and to whom. Some clients need to be reassured of confidentiality and counsellors should take time to clarify precisely what the client understands by confidentiality.

While it would be breaking confidentiality to relate to someone what the client said, it would not be wrong to relate your feelings and professional opinion about the client's mental and emotional state, or to give an opinion.

The person's right to secrecy is never absolute. Counsellors may be required by a court to disclose secret information. Failure to do so may lead to imprisonment for contempt of court (Stewart, 2013).

Applying the principle – Jenny feels betrayed

Jenny was a single woman in her mid-thirties, regular in attendance at the local church. Her job in Inland Revenue provided her with a secure income. But Jenny was troubled, and sought out one of the women of the church, not a counsellor. Through her tears, Jenny 'confessed' that she was deeply in love with one of the elders, a happily married man, with three children.

No, she assured her friend, there was nothing going on. The man probably didn't even know. Yes, he was kind, and so was his wife, and frequently had Jenny round for meals and social evenings.

The friend, without Jenny's knowledge, approached the man in question, and his wife, and advised them to reduce the contact with Jenny. This led to a strained atmosphere, though Jenny never knew why. The couple no longer had Jenny round to their house, and in the end Jenny left that church, hurt. Eventually she discovered the reason, not from her confidante, not from the couple, but from someone else to whom her friend had repeated the tale 'in strict confidence.' Jenny felt that something precious had been stolen from her.

(Adapted from Stewart, William, *An A–Z of Counselling Theory and Practice* (5th edition) Cengage Learning, page 400 and used with permission.)

(See the BACP Ethical Framework http://www.bacp.co.uk/ethical_ framework/ETHICAL%20FRAMEWORK%20(BSL%20VERSION)/ Respectingprivacyandconfidentiality%20.php.)

CONFIDENTIALITY AND YOUNG PEOPLE

In counselling, the counsellor might be on the horns of a dilemma, if, for example, the young person, who might be under the age of sixteen, discloses sexual activity, or worse, sexual abuse. Should the counsellor override counsellor/client confidentiality or keep the disclosure within the counselling relationship? The argument could be put that if a young person comes for counselling on her own, then she has achieved *a sufficient understanding and intelligence to understand fully what is proposed.* If, however, she is accompanied by her parent (even though the parent might not be present during the session), then it could be argued that maybe the client should confide in her parent. If the disclosure is of a serious nature, such as rape or sexual abuse, then the counsellor has a duty of care to help the young client understand all the implications of telling her parent(s), and/or the police. However, if the young person is over the age of eighteen, then the rules of disclosure do not apply.

Instead, the counsellor's role would be to support the client if she decides to report what has happened.

Against that is the argument that if children of a very young age are choosing to take contraception without parental knowledge, then they are also old enough to make the decision of whether or not to involve their parents.

Above all, the counsellor has to avoid persuading the young client either way; and this is one instance where scrupulous records should be kept.

Assuring confidentiality with young people seeking counselling can be particularly fraught with problems. To feel supported they need to be aware at the outset when the counsellor is bound to breach confidentiality. Many agencies working with young people apply the 'Gillick Principle'. If the young person is considered 'Gillick competent', access to counselling or medical treatment without parental consent or knowledge may be permitted. For a discussion of a child's legal rights, which includes Gillick competency, see the NSPCC page, http://www.nspcc.org.uk/ preventing-abuse/child-protection-system/legal-definition-child-rights-law/ gillick-competency-fraser-guidelines/.

WHERE DO COUNSELLORS WORK?

Counsellors are employed in various settings: independent practices, schools, colleges, universities, hospitals, GP practices and other mental health services, and charitable and voluntary organisations. Some are paid a salary, hourly or sessional rate by their employing body, some (typically in the independent sector) charge a set fee, or offer a sliding scale depending on the client's financial circumstances. Others (typically in the voluntary sector) provide their expertise as a 'labour of love', receiving no financial reward, although they may receive free training and supervision from the employing agency (Relate, Cruse and the Samaritans, for example).

PAID EMPLOYMENT AS A COUNSELLOR

Getting a foothold in the door to paid full-time employment as a counsellor is no easy feat, because full-time positions, although slowly increasing, do not match the number of professionally trained counsellors. Moreover, potential employers are becoming increasingly insistent on counsellors being accredited by the British Association for Counselling and Psychotherapy (BACP), or well on the pathway to achieving accreditation. See the BACP website (http://www. bacp.co.uk) for further information about careers in counselling and the BACP accreditation scheme.

WHAT MOTIVATES PEOPLE TO SEEK COUNSELLING?

People frequently seek counselling at times of crisis or change. They may have reached the end of their tether, or cannot see a light at the end of the tunnel and are struggling to cope. A current precipitating event such as a major life event (e.g. from married to widowed or single, coming to terms with a terminal illness, a pending change in career direction) may spur a person to seek help. Equally, the motivation might stem from deeply rooted unresolved traumatic experiences such as child abuse, loss, neglect, abandonment or issues of attachment, which are interfering with a person's ability to cope and function in the present. The desire to change self-defeating thinking patterns, or self-harming behaviours such as a compulsion, phobia, addiction, an eating disorder or self-injury could be the driving force. Interpersonal relationship problems, intimacy problems, sexual problems or work-related issues are other potential reasons. Thoughts, feelings and emotions that the person cannot make sense of such as feeling emotionally overwhelmed, emotionally numb, debilitating depression, unrelenting anxiety or stress, feelings of hopelessness, helplessness or despair, or suicidal thoughts may be the final straw that fuels the desire to seek help.

BARRIERS TO SEEKING COUNSELLING

The road to the counsellor's door may have been a long one. Attempts to sort out one's problems alone may have proved futile and talking with a partner, friends, family members or colleagues may have been unfruitful. Embarrassment, pride, shame or strongly held beliefs ('I should be able to sort this out myself', 'asking for help is a sign of weakness', 'I could never tell anyone . . .', 'what would they think of me . . . ?') can also serve as a strong deterrent from reaching out for help. Furthermore, although the benefits of counselling are becoming more widely recognised, there is still an element of stigma attached to it in some circles, and unhelpful comments from prejudiced or unenlightened others such as 'counselling is a waste of time and money', 'they do more harm than good', 'it's for the self-indulgent', 'why can't you just pull yourself together?' can put hurdles in the way. Just such an attitude is superbly illustrated in the following poem taken from Sutton, J. (2007: 398–9) *Healing the Hurt Within*.

Take my advice (why don't you?)

Go and get a life I say
just tell your hurt to go away.
I don't like it when you are low,
I want the 'old you' back, you know.

It's not healthy to be depressed,
you're getting really self-obsessed,
get out of the bed and face the day,
put on a smile; it's better that way.

There, there, dear, I know how you feel,
but it's all in the past so what's the big deal?
Go find a job: you could learn how to knit,
I think that you should stop dwelling on it.

Aunt Maud says her neighbour Miss Wood
thinks all this counselling really does you no good,
And my friend Beryl (her sister's a nurse)
says she's read in the paper that they just make you worse.

And I'm not being nasty, but can you not see
how your nervous breakdown is worrying me?
You know that I love you, you know that I care,
but I really do think you're being unfair.

And then there's the children, they still need their mum,
so pull up your socks and get off your bum.
I know what you're thinking, I'm nobody's fool,
emotional blackmail's a powerful tool.

So take my advice and block out the past,
live for today and put on your mask,
try not to cry, try not to feel,
who really cares if you're not being real?

What does it matter, what small price to pay,
to take who you are and lock it away?
So please stop this nonsense, do it for me,
I know that you're hurting, but I don't want to see.

—*Stephanie*

LEARNING TO COUNSEL

To draw this chapter to a close, we highlight the three basic elements required to counsel effectively.

1. **Knowledge and understanding.** This involves:

● Gaining knowledge of the theory of personality development and the underlying principles of the counselling approach adopted.

● Gaining knowledge of common psychological processes, for example bereavement and loss and relationship interactions.

2. **Developing skills.** This involves:

● Changing behaviour, which can feel very uncomfortable to begin with. However, in time, and with practice, the skills feel more comfortable and counsellors start to use them without even thinking about them – they become part of your style.

3. **Personal development.** This involves:

● Being able to separate your own feelings from the feelings of the client. This means increasing self-awareness: the more self-awareness gained, the more you are able to understand your clients.

SUMMARY

In this chapter, we have explored counselling from several standpoints. First, we defined counselling, highlighted the distinction between counselling and other forms of helping, and discussed the ambiguity surrounding the terms counselling and psychotherapy. We then drew attention to the wide-ranging counselling approaches presently practised, outlining five common approaches, explained the meaning of transference and countertransference and demonstrated the difference between psychodynamic counselling and psychoanalysis. Next, we focused on the important topic of confidentiality. Other topics featured have highlighted the numerous settings in which counsellors work, addressed counsellors' current prospects for full-time paid employment, and identified the diverse reasons that prompt people to seek counselling and potential barriers that can serve as a deterrent from seeking help. To conclude, the key elements required to counsel effectively were emphasised, and the primary focus of this book clarified.

Our next task is to explore essential counsellor qualities.

*Advice is seldom welcome; and those who want it the most
always like it the least.*

Philip Dormer Stanhope (Fourth Earl of Chesterfield)

REFERENCES

McLeod, J. (2013). *An Introduction to Counselling*, 5th edition. Maidenhead: Open University Press.

Rogers, C. (2004). *On Becoming a Person: A therapist's view of psychotherapy.* Robinson.

Royal College of Psychiatrists, resources list http://www.rcpsych.ac.uk/info/glosTreats.htm

Stewart, W. & Martin, A. (1999). *Going for Counselling.* Oxford: How To Books.

Stewart, W. (2013). *An A–Z of Counselling Theory and Practice*, 5th edition. Cengage Learning.

Sutton, J. (2007). *Healing the Hurt Within: Understand Self-injury and Self-harm, and Heal the Emotional Wounds.* 3rd revised edition. Oxford: How To Books.

Exploring Essential Counsellor Qualities

In Chapter 1, we introduced you to a broad range of topics related to counselling. In Chapter 2 the emphasis is on counsellor qualities (attitudes), considered by Carl Rogers as vital for therapeutic change: empathy, genuineness, unconditional regard and non-possessive warmth. Also referred to as 'the core conditions', these qualities are essential to building a therapeutic relationship (a collaborative client–counsellor relationship – strong bond – growth-promoting environment). We also accentuate the importance of responding appropriately to help clients feel accepted, heard and understood.

Developing self-awareness is another crucial aspect in the personal and professional development of a counsellor. This topic is discussed in Chapter 3. In this, and subsequent chapters, exercises designed to increase your self-awareness are included, so be sure to keep a notebook handy from here on.

ELABORATING ON ESSENTIAL COUNSELLOR QUALITIES

Fundamentally, the counsellor qualities mentioned are relationship qualities that are embraced in most therapies, and deemed crucial in person-centred counselling. Briefly, they include the counsellor's ability to:

- *Convey a deep level of empathic understanding:* the ability to step into the client's world – *as if* you are in their shoes and without losing the *as if* quality.

- *Demonstrate genuineness:* being oneself (open, transparent) in the relationship, not hiding behind a mask of professionalism (also known as congruence, realness or authenticity).

- *Show unconditional positive regard:* acceptance of the client without judgment or conditions attached (also referred to as caring, valuing, prizing, respect).

- *Convey warmth:* appropriately and without any desire to possess.

LOOKING CLOSER AT THE CORE CONDITIONS

Empathy

Empathy is the ability of one person to step into the inner world of another person and to step out of it again, without becoming that other person. An example is the singer or actor who genuinely feels the part he is performing.

It means trying to understand the thoughts, feelings, behaviours and personal meanings from the other's internal frame of reference. For empathy to mean anything, we have to respond in such a way that the other person feels that understanding has been reached or is being striven for. Unless our understanding is communicated, it is of no therapeutic value.

Empathy is not a state that one reaches, or a qualification that one is awarded. It is a transient thing. We can move in to it and lose it again very quickly. Literally, it means 'getting alongside'.

Empathy is the central core condition of the person-centred approach, although therapists from a wide range of approaches rank empathy as being one of the highest qualities a therapist can demonstrate.

Levels of empathy are related to the degree to which the client is able to explore and reach self-understanding. It can be taught within an empathic climate.

Primary empathy works more with surface or stated facts and feelings; advanced empathy works more with implied facts and feelings.

The difference between empathy and identification is that in identification the 'as if' quality is absent. We have become the other person.

Genuineness or congruence

Genuineness is the degree to which we are freely and deeply ourselves and are able to relate to people in a sincere and non-defensive manner. For example, we may not approve of an aspect of a client's behaviour, and may aim to find a way to sensitively point this out to the client. Also referred to as authenticity, congruence or truth, genuineness is the precondition for empathy and unconditional positive regard.

Effective therapy depends wholly on the degree to which the therapist is integrated and genuine. In person-centred counselling, skill and technique play a much less important role than relating to the client authentically. Genuineness encourages client self-disclosure.

Appropriate therapist disclosure enhances genuineness. The genuine therapist does not feel under any compulsion to disclose, either about events, situations or feelings aroused within the counselling relationship.

An essential element in genuineness is that it is not a role adopted specially for the counselling relationship. If it were, then it would be false. This means that in all our relationships we strive to be genuine.

We can aid genuineness by not taking refuge in the role of counsellor; by being spontaneous, tactful, respectful and natural; by avoiding being defensive; and being open with no hidden agenda.

Being genuine means being truthful, and not pretending. It means agreement between what we feel and what we say. Betty telephoned William. 'I want you to see my husband. He's being perfectly silly, says he wants a divorce – after all these years! Talk some sense into him, will you?' Betty was irate when, several weeks later, Dennis did go ahead with the divorce. Betty considered William had failed, but he refused to work to any hidden agenda.

We would not be genuine if we took on a client we did not feel competent to work with. We are not being genuine if we feel angry at something the client says, and we attempt to hide our feelings.

For example, Derek at one stage was sounding off about women, and being really sexist. William felt his anger rising, and said so, adding that sexism and racism do stir him up. He said to Derek, 'I fully acknowledge that these are my feelings, and that I need to discuss those at supervision, but had I not voiced them here and now, they could seriously affect our relationship.'

Derek would have sensed William's change of feelings and attitude – for feelings influence attitudes – and not known why. William's openness helped them both deal with the here and now. Anything less and Derek would have been quite justified in questioning William's sincerity.

Admitting that we do not understand what the client is saying, or cannot identify the feelings, or something is unclear, is being genuine. It certainly does not mean that we lose face; in fact, it produces the opposite effect. Admitting that we are not perfect will enhance the relationship; it makes us real people, not cardboard cut-outs of some idealised counsellor.

Unconditional positive regard (UPR)

This is a non-possessive caring and acceptance of the client, irrespective of how offensive the client's behaviour might be. The counsellor who offers unconditional positive regard helps to create a climate that encourages trust within the counselling relationship. It is where we communicate a deep and genuine caring, not filtered through our own feelings, thoughts and behaviours.

It is about valuing and respecting the client as a unique human being.

Demonstrating unconditional positive regard facilitates change.

Positive regard helps clients feel safe. Knowing that they are accepted, and that whatever they are or whatever they say will not affect the counsellor's regard for them, is like an anchor in the midst of a storm.

Above all, positive regard is not filtered through the counsellor's feelings and values; it is not conditional upon what is happening in their own life. Neither is it conditional upon clients complying with what the counsellor wishes them to be. (Adapted from Stewart, W. & Martin, A. (1999), *Going for Counselling*. Used with permission.)

Conditional regard, on the other hand, implies enforced control and compliance with behaviour dictated by someone else.

Showing non-possessive warmth

Non-possessive warmth is genuine. It springs from an attitude of friendliness towards others. A relationship in which friendliness is absent will not flourish. Showing non-possessive warmth makes the client feel comfortable. It is liberating, non-demanding, and melts the coldness and hardness within people's hearts.

Possessive warmth, on the other hand:

- Is false
- Makes us feel uncomfortable and wary
- Is more for the needs of the giver than for the receiver
- Is smothering and cloying
- Robs us of energy.

Warmth is conveyed by:

- Body language: posture, proximity, personal space, facial expressions, eye contact
- Words and the way we speak: tone of voice, delivery, rate of speech and the use of non-words – all these are 'paralinguistics'.

All the indicators of warmth – the non-verbal parts of speech and body language – must be in agreement with the words used; any discrepancy between the words and how we deliver them will cause confusion in the other person.

Warmth, like a hot water bottle, must be used with great care. Someone who is very cold, distant, cynical, mistrustful could feel threatened by someone else's depth of warmth. A useful analogy would be to think how an iceberg would react in the presence of the sun.

WAYS OF COMMUNICATING WARMTH

Conveying warmth

We convey warmth by:

- Body language – posture, proximity, personal space, facial expressions, eye contact
- Words and the way we speak – tone of voice, delivery, rate of speech
- All the indicators of warmth – the non-verbal parts of speech and body language – must be in agreement with the words used; any discrepancy between the words and how we deliver them will cause confusion in the other person.

Warmth and physical contact

It is worth digressing a little here to examine physical contact. Touch can convey a powerful message of unconditional acceptance, if used sparingly and appropriately. However, not everybody is comfortable with touch, so it is crucial to check out the client's views about being touched. With a distressed client, a simple question such as: *'What would you like me to do?'* can guide the counsellor to responding appropriately.

For survivors of child abuse, touch can be a particularly difficult issue – some are not comfortable with any form of touch as it can open the doorway to unresolved wounds, or re-activate painful memories – *so please tread cautiously.*

(Sutton, 2007) Even shaking hands or an innocent pat on the client's shoulder may trigger an adverse reaction in some clients. Physical contact should never be forced on clients.

But warmth can be controlled – too much can be threatening to some people. Some of us enjoy physical contact; others shrink from it. People who are in distress might reach out for human contact, others move away from it. Judging when it is right to reach out – even a hand – is often fraught with difficulty. Some counsellors do not even greet their clients with a handshake, being of the opinion that even this can be an infringement on the professional relationship.

When a person is crying, we may feel the urge to hug, but that may not be an appropriate response. Doing so might be a response from the parent within us to a child in distress and that might be inappropriate. Yet letting the client cry the grief out is often difficult to observe. Such was the case with Janice.

CASE STUDY

Janice feels worthless (William speaking)

Janice sat opposite me, talking about her feelings of worthlessness, of being rejected by her father after her parents divorced. Slowly the tears came, great big tears that fell from her eyes like waterfalls. I have never seen such tears. She did not reach out and take one of the tissues from the box, and I wondered what her tears were saying. The front of her dress was wet when eventually her tears shuddered to a stop. 'I'm glad for that,' she said, 'and I'm glad you just let me cry. I was getting rid of all the tears I couldn't cry all those years ago.' That for me was a salutary lesson of just staying with the client and not letting my own needs and feelings take precedence.

On the other hand, there was Ted. Ted had been talking about the break-up of his marriage, and the feared loss of his home and children. Ted's crying was that of a child, gasping for breath, who has been crying for a long time. Sensing the terror Ted felt, I leaned over and held his hand. He pulled me to him, and as I held him, the sobbing slowly eased.

In the case of Janice, I was aware (this awareness came via experience) that I wanted to hold her, to ease her pain. Those were *my* needs, the parent within me. For Ted it was different. *His* needs were uppermost. If Ted had pushed me away, then I would know I had it wrong.

When the core conditions are present – and appropriately expressed – a climate is created in which a positive therapeutic outcome is likely. When clients are in a relationship in which the core conditions are demonstrated, they will learn to relate to themselves with respect and dignity.

Criticism of the core conditions centres more on their efficiency than their necessity. Some theorists argue that, while the core conditions must be present, by themselves they are insufficient. Other interventions are necessary.

There is a body of opinion that neither a 'relationship' nor a 'skills' approach is sufficient. Both are needed. This would depend on the nature of the problem and the personality of both client and counsellor. Counsellors generally choose an approach or method that suits their personality.

DEMONSTRATING ACCEPTANCE

Inherent in the idea of demonstrating acceptance is that the counsellor does not judge the client by some set of rules or standards. This means that counsellors have to be able to suspend their own judgments. Acceptance is a special kind of loving that moves out toward people as they are, and maintains their dignity and personal worth. It means accepting their strengths and weaknesses; their favourable and unfavourable qualities; their positive and negative attitudes; their constructive and destructive wishes, and their thoughts, feelings and behaviours.

Understanding what acceptance means

Communicating acceptance means we avoid pressurising the client to become someone else. We do not take control, and we avoid judging, criticising or condemning. We do not attach 'if' clauses; *e.g.* 'I will love you if . . .'. Clients will test the counsellor's unconditional acceptance, until they sense that the counsellor accepts them as they are, without approval or disapproval, and without making the client feel less a person.

When counsellors accept clients just as they are, clients accept counsellors just as *they* are, with *their* strengths and weaknesses, with their successes and failures. The degree to which we accept other people is dependent on the degree of our own self-awareness. Only if we are well grounded psychologically can we work with other people to mobilise their feelings and energies toward change, growth and fulfilment.

When we feel accepted as we truly are, including our strengths and weaknesses, our differences of opinions – no matter how unpleasant or uncongenial – we feel liberated from many of the things that enslave us.

Acceptance is client-centred

Acceptance is directed to the needs of the client, rather than to the counsellor's own needs. Acceptance recognises the potential of the client for self-help, and it encourages the promotion of growth of the client. Acceptance contains elements of the counsellor's thoughts (knowledge, psychological grounding), feelings (use of self) and behaviour (which must be congruent with what we say).

The qualities of acceptance

- caring
- concern
- compassion
- consistency
- courtesy
- firmness
- interest
- listening
- moving toward
- prizing
- respect
- valuing
- warmth.

Obstacles to acceptance

There are numerous obstacles that can get in the way of acceptance. One major obstacle is stereotyping.

Stereotyping explained

Stereotyping – also described as labelling, classifying, typecasting, pigeon-holing, categorising, putting in a mould, pre-judging or making assumptions – occurs when we allow ourselves to be influenced by preconceived beliefs about people or groups of people. Stereotyping allows no room for individuality, and is generally negative. It stems from our deeply embedded, and often conditioned, conviction about others, and may be due to fear or a lack of understanding about people different from ourselves.

Stereotyping can have a damaging effect on the therapeutic relationship. To remain neutral, and to prevent putting a barrier in the way, counsellors need to listen to themselves carefully for any signs of 'putting their client into a niche'.

Other obstacles to acceptance

- Lack of knowledge of human behaviour.

- Blocks or blind spots within self, for example, conscious hidden agendas, or unconscious unresolved conflicts.

- Attributing one's feelings to the client.

- Biases and prejudices, values, beliefs.

- Unfounded reassurances, unwillingness to explore.

- Confusion between acceptance and approval.

- Loss of respect for the client.

- Over-identification with the client, which may be an unconscious blind spot, or a conscious hidden agenda.

The case study that follows uses some of the eight 'obstacles to acceptance' outlined above.

CASE STUDY

Bruno demands obedience

Bruno, aged fifty, born in Italy, married to Kath, an Englishwoman, says, in highly belligerent tones, 'I'm the boss in the home, that's what we agreed when we married. She promised to love, honour and obey, and that's what she'll do. I'll have none of this equality business. Women are there to do what men want and say.'

Counsellor says, 'You shouldn't feel like that, women should be respected as people in their own right. That attitude belonged to the Victorians. You clearly do not respect your wife.'

Suggested obstacles to acceptance

Attributing one's own feelings to the client, coupled with confusion between acceptance and approval. Not taking cultural influences into account.

DEMONSTRATING A NON-JUDGMENTAL ATTITUDE

Being non-judgmental is yet another important facet of acceptance. Judgment is to do with law, blame, guilty or innocent, and punishment. Clients may engage in self-judgment and will need to work through this if healing is to take place. Although counsellors are entitled to hold their own values, these should not be imposed on the client, and the counsellor must strive not to make judgments about their clients.

Understanding judgmentalism

Judgmentalism takes no account of feelings. It is critical, and condemns others because of their conduct or supposed false beliefs, wrong motives or character. Judgmentalism is arbitrary, without room for negotiation or understanding, and is an evaluation and rejection of another person's worth. The result of judgmentalism is that it dims, divides and fragments relationships.

Judgmentalism seeks to elevate one person above another. Within it are the characteristics of self-exaltation, self-promotion and the determination to be first on every occasion.

Judgment often attacks the person rather than the behaviour. Judgmentalism creates massive blind spots in our relationships. We cannot counsel people effectively while we are judging and condemning them. When we are troubled we need help, not judgment.

When we pass judgment upon others, if we examine ourselves, we will find that the very thing on which we pass judgment is also present within ourselves in one degree or another.

Detecting judgmentalism

Judgmentalism can often be detected by such words as:

- should
- ought
- must
- got to
- don't

and by such phrases as:

- in my opinion
- I think . . .
- this is what you should do.

Why counsellors should avoid being judgmental

Judgmentalism is moralistic. It is based on norms and values, warning, approval/disapproval, instruction, and it induces inferiority. Judgmentalism evokes inhibition, guilt and distress. It is often associated with authority, control, hierarchy, rules and regulations that impose standards of behaviour. Judgmentalism is the opposite of acceptance. Judgmentalism paralyses: acceptance affirms and encourages action.

A judgmental response has a tendency to indicate that the counsellor has made a judgment of relative goodness, appropriateness, effectiveness, rightness. In some way, the counsellor implies, however grossly or subtly, what the client might or ought to do. The responses imply a personal moral standpoint, and involve a judgment (critical or approving) of others.

Being non-judgmental is a fundamental quality of the counselling relationship. Demonstrating a non-judgmental attitude is based on the firmly held belief that assigning guilt or innocence, or the degree to which the client is responsible, or not, for causing the problem has no place in the counselling relationship.

Clients who are nurtured within a non-judgmental relationship learn not to pass judgment upon themselves. Within this relationship, they find the courage and the strength to change.

Being non-judgmental

'Non-judgmental' does not mean being valueless or without standards. It does mean trying not to mould others to fit into our value systems. Our values may be right for us; they may be very wrong for other people.

Being non-judgmental means recognising and understanding our own values and standards in order that we can suspend them and so minimise their influence on the way we respond to other people. Counsellors must remain true to their own values and standards. They are not human chameleons. Whenever we speak, we communicate the unspoken judgment that lurks within our hearts.

When we feel non-judgmental, that feeling is communicated. No words can convey a non-judgmental attitude if it does not reside within the heart of the counsellor. Counsellors may not like all clients, but it is their duty to strive to be free from prejudices that will lead them into being judgmental. Being non-judgmental means holding within the heart respect for other people's opinions. Very often, we are judgmental over trivial issues.

Developing a non-judgmental attitude

We can develop a non-judgmental attitude by:

- recognising and carefully scrutinising our own values and standards; we may decide to abandon some of them

- trying to see the world from the client's frame of reference

- not jumping to conclusions

- not saying, 'I know how you feel'

- not comparing the client to someone else

- not becoming over-involved.

To formulate a non-judgmental response involves:

- being receptive and accepting

- concentrating on what the client's experience means, not on the facts

- being interested in the person, not just in the problem itself

- demonstrating sincere respect for the client as a person of worth

- facilitating, not interpreting unconscious motives

- trying to understand what it means to be this particular client

- getting into the client's inner world; their frame of reference

- not rushing to answer

- being aware of your own values

- hearing, then responding to, the client's expressed and implied feelings

- accepting that clients know more about their inner world than you do.

Empathic understanding

Empathic understanding is primarily a subjective experience on the part of the counsellor. It means having the ability to perceive the client's world as the client sees it – to grasp it from their frame of reference – and being able to communicate that understanding tentatively and sensitively. Demonstrating empathy means:

- being able to step into the client's shoes, and being able to step out again

- being able to stand back far enough to remain objective, rather than standing too close and risk becoming enmeshed in the client's world

- being close to, yet remaining separate from – it doesn't mean we become the other person.

Empathy works within the conditional framework of *as if* I were that other person. It taps into the listener's intuition and imagination.

Is there a difference between empathy, sympathy and pity?

Sympathy and pity are frequently confused with empathy, yet they are not the same. Sympathy could be defined as feeling *like*, or sharing in another's feelings, 'I know exactly how you must be feeling.' Pity, on the other hand, could be defined as feeling *for*, 'There, there, don't upset yourself so . . . it hurts me to see you crying.' While appropriate in certain situations, such as comforting someone who has recently experienced bereavement, there is little room for sympathy and pity in counselling. Counselling is essentially about facilitating change. Expressing sympathy or pity can hinder this process by keeping the client stuck, or wallowing in their current situation.

For empathy to mean anything, we have to respond in such a way that the other person feels that understanding has been reached, or is being striven for. It means constantly checking for inaccuracies, for example:

- 'Would I be right in thinking that . . . ?'

- 'I think I understand what you mean . . . but can I just recap to be sure?'

- 'What you seem to be saying is . . . how does that sound?'

It means being *genuine* if we don't understand, for example:

- 'I'm not quite clear what you mean . . . perhaps you could give me an example?'

- 'I'm getting a bit confused about . . .'

- 'I'm trying to get a picture of your situation but it's a bit fuzzy. I wonder if you would mind going over what you just said.'

Levels of empathy are related to the degree to which the client is able to explore and reach self-understanding. It can be taught within an empathic climate.

The three parts of empathy

1. **Thinking** (cognitive) – an intellectual or conceptual grasping of the feeling of another.

2. **Feeling** (affective) – a mirroring or sharing of the emotion with the other person.

3. **Behavioural** (doing) – assuming in one's mind the role of the other person.

Empathy is also communicated non-verbally through facial expression, eye contact and a forward leaning of the trunk, reducing the physical distance between counsellor and client. Non-empathic body language weakens the spoken message, however deeply empathic it may be.

Empathy is not a gift from the gods; it is a skill we can all develop. For some of us, we might have to work very hard at it, for others it might come easier. If you find it difficult to pick out feelings and respond to them with empathy, try not to feel too discouraged. Keep plugging away at it, and find a sympathetic friend on whom you can practise.

Love is empathy

A mother took her five-year-old son shopping at a large department store during the Christmas season. She knew it would be fun for him to see all the decorations, window displays, toys and Santa Claus. As she dragged him by the hand, twice as fast as his little legs could move, he began to fuss and cry, clinging to his mother's coat. 'Good heavens, what on earth is the matter with you?' she scolded impatiently. 'I brought you with me to get in the Christmas spirit. Santa doesn't bring toys to little cry-babies!'

His fussing continued as she tried to find some bargains during the last-minute rush on 23 December. 'I'm not going to take you shopping with me, ever again, if you don't stop that whimpering,' she admonished. 'Oh well, maybe it's because your shoes are untied and you are tripping over your own laces,' she said, kneeling down in the aisle to tie his shoes.

As she knelt down beside him, she happened to look up. For the first time, she viewed a large department store through the eyes of a five-year-old. From that position, there were no baubles, bangles, beads, presents, gaily decorated display tables or animated toys. All that could be seen was a maze of corridors too high to see above, full of giants moving about on legs as large as trees.

These mountainous strangers, with feet as big as skateboards, were pushing and shoving, bumping and thumping, rushing and crushing!

She took her child home and vowed to herself never to impose her version of a good time on him again. *(Source unknown)*

CASE STUDY

Sandra (William speaking)

Here is one way to analyse a case. Sandra, aged seventeen, has been sexually assaulted by her boyfriend. She cannot tell her parents because they are friends with the boy's parents. She writes to the counsellor for advice and says, '*I never thought he was like that, well you know. He just seemed to lose control and went crazy. I hit out but he just laughed. I feel so, I don't know how I feel. God, if only we hadn't gone to the party. I know my parents won't understand, but do you understand, I love him.*'

Here is my analysis: blame, shame, guilt, anger, brutalised, humiliated, betrayed, dirty, defenceless, numb, used, violated, conflict, helpless, a target for anger/aggression, confused, trapped, mocked.

Other words that *rape* victims have used to describe their feelings and themselves: anguished, bedraggled, cheapened, desperate, distressed, frantic, guilty, helpless, humiliated, pathetic, pitiful, shocked, slut, tart, torn apart, troubled, unfortunate and worthless. The case study says 'sexually assaulted' and not 'raped,' but these additional feelings might help to focus a bit more.

Essential points of this case study:

- Not to skate over the sexual abuse, but not to assume that it is rape.

- To work through the client's statement bit by bit.

- To reflect feelings in a tentative way.

- To work with the feelings of self-blame, but not to look for reasons for the assault. Not to blame alcohol or drugs, for example.

- To notice her declared love, not to attack her boyfriend but to point to the possible conflict.

- To reflect the conflict of not being able to tell her parents, and the feelings attached to that.

Appropriate response:

Sandra, I sense how distressed you are. The sexual assault by the man you trusted has left you feeling betrayed and disgusted. What started out as an evening of adventure turned into a nightmare of horror and pain, and now you feel ashamed, angry and guilty. What he did terrified you, and left you feeling bewildered, as if you were seeing a complete stranger, someone who had taken leave of his senses. It also seems that you regret ever going to the party, and that has something of self-blame in it, like you feel responsible in some way. Even when you tried to stop him he mocked you and thought it was one big joke, and you were powerless to prevent what happened, and now you feel belittled and cast aside as something worthless. I also hear a conflict, a sort of tug of war, between what happened and your feelings for him. Part of you, the head, says this shouldn't be, and the other part, the heart, still holds on to the love you feel for him, and so you feel confused and scared. I also hear another conflict, between keeping it to yourself or to tell your parents, fearing they will judge you, misunderstand, possibly condemn, and all this isolates you from them at a time when you need them a lot.

Note: If this had been an interview I would probably have added, *what has happened is a serious assault and you may want to consider if the police should be involved. The second issue is what do you think about getting one of our female doctors to examine you? She will be able to advise you and answer any of your questions.*

STAYING IN THE CLIENT'S FRAME OF REFERENCE

The frame of reference is a two-part concept that is emphasised in person-centred counselling. Table 2.1 gives an example of the internal frame of reference of a client (the client's inner world).

Table 2.1: Internal frame of reference: The inner world of the client

Cultural influences	Experiences
Beliefs and values	Memories
Meanings	Feelings, thoughts and emotions
Sensations	
Perceptions	Behaviours

External frame of reference: 'the inner world of the counsellor'

The contents of the counsellor's frame are similar to the client's frame, and therein lies a danger. When the experiences of one person are akin to someone else's, it is tempting to 'know' how the other person feels. This knowing cannot come from our experience. It can only make sense as we listen and try to understand what things mean to clients from their own frame of reference. The external frame of reference is when we perceive only from our own subjective frame of reference and when there is no accurate, empathic understanding of the subjective world of the other person.

Evaluating another person through the values of our external frame of reference will ensure lack of understanding. When we perceive accurately another person's experiences solely from within their internal frame of reference, that person's behaviour makes more sense. The principal limitation is that we can then deal only with what is within the consciousness of the other person. That which is unconscious lies outside the frame of reference.

Examples of *external* frame of reference responses:

● I'm interested in what's going right for you, not what's going wrong.

● You should always respect your parents.

● My advice to you is to drop him.

● You have troubles. Let me tell you mine.

Examples of *internal* frame of reference responses:

● Though you don't like to show it, you've been feeling very depressed recently and even contemplated suicide.

● You are thrilled that you've just been promoted and can't believe your good fortune.

- You are pretty scared at the thought of being unemployed.

- You have mixed feelings about the wedding ceremony and will be glad when it is out of the way.

Communicating with another person's frame of reference depends on:

- Careful listening to the other person's total communication – words, non-verbal messages and voice-related cues.

- Trying to identify the feelings that are being expressed and the experiences and behaviours that give rise to those feelings.

- Trying to communicate an understanding of what the person seems to be feeling and of the sources of those feelings.

- Responding by showing understanding, not by evaluating what has been said.

The ultimate proof of active listening is effective responding.

Building a bridge of empathy

To understand the frame of reference of the client, the counsellor needs to build a bridge of empathy in order to enter the client's world; encourage the client to communicate; understand the personal meanings from the client's perspective and convey that understanding to the client.

Lack of self-awareness impedes the ability to enter someone else's frame of reference. The more we feel able to express ourselves freely to another person, without feeling on trial, the more of the contents of our frame of reference will be communicated.

LISTENING WITH UNDERSTANDING

More than any other communication skill, responding with understanding helps to create a climate of support and trust between two people or among the members of a group. There are three basic ways of responding:

1. **Evaluating: which is often our first instinct.** Whenever we evaluate others, we *decide* whether they are right or wrong. The process of evaluating and judging doesn't draw people closer together; it sets them farther apart.

2. **Hollow listening: listening without responding.** Listening is hollow if it consists merely of listening and nothing more.

3. **Responding with understanding.** The most effective, yet the least used response in interpersonal communication. Responding with understanding in counselling entails making a real effort to 'hear' the client's feelings and responding in such a way that the client feels truly heard and understood. *The ultimate proof of genuine listening is effective responding.*

CASE STUDY

Ali (William speaking)

The Client

Ali was a Hindu schoolteacher. He had been away from India for many years and had done well in England. He came for personal therapy as part of the self-development requirements of his counselling training. We had developed a trusting relationship over several months, when he brought news that his father had died.

A rift in the family resulted in Ali not being told of his father's death until after his father had been cremated. The basic belief in Hindu religion is that the cremated body returns to its elements of fire, water, air and earth, and is thus reunited with God. The eldest son lights the funeral pyre, while mantras and sacred texts are recited by the priest. Then follows a period of ritual where gifts of food are left for the soul of the departed. When this period is over, the bones of the deceased may be buried. Hindus believe in reincarnation (transmigration), which is the rebirth of the soul in one or more successive existences, which may be human, animal or, in some instances, vegetable.

Although not the eldest son, Ali was thrown into a deep depression of sadness and guilt that he had not been there to say goodbye to his father. Only as I explored with him the importance of that ceremony did I appreciate his feelings of betrayal and desertion. Viewing all this from his frame of reference was enlightening for me, and explaining it helped Ali to start to come out of his depression.

Discussion

This would not be the place to discuss all the religions and how the faith of the therapist might conflict with the client's; what does seem more helpful is to show how it is possible to transcend particular faiths to arrive at one way in which client and therapist could stand on common ground.

Working with Ali and trying to understand what this meant to him from his perspective – from the internal frame of reference – meant that I had to risk stepping out of my – external – frame of reference. This is a challenge for any therapist because the more we get into the client's inner world, the more danger there is of losing one's grip of one's own world. So it is a case of always remaining attached to our own world; like walking with a dog on a stretch lead. Yet, although engaging in therapy at this level is risky for the therapist, this is when the most productive therapy is achieved.

SUMMARY

Two key themes have been highlighted in this chapter: the importance of developing the counsellor qualities of genuineness, unconditional regard and empathic understanding to build a firm client–counsellor relationship and facilitate the client's personal growth, and striving to respond accurately so clients feel truly heard and understood. Additionally, we have drawn attention to the significance of increasing self-awareness – an understanding of our inner world – our beliefs, attitudes and values. Grasping the legacy of our past, cultivating self-knowledge and self-acceptance, brings self-enlightenment and the ability to assist others on their journey to raised self-awareness. This topic is taken up in Chapter 3.

> *The first step to change is awareness.*
> *The second step is acceptance.*
>
> Nathaniel Branden (Psychotherapist and author)

REFERENCES

Sutton, J. (2007). *Healing the Hurt Within: Understand Self-injury and Self-harm, and Heal the Emotional Wounds.* 3rd revised edition. Oxford: How To Books.

Developing Self-Awareness

In Chapter 2, we blended the essential ingredients of counsellor qualities – genuineness, unconditional regard, empathic understanding and warmth – with strategies designed at responding accurately. These basic elements are the finest we can offer to clients to begin building a solid base of trust and to foster therapeutic progress. A further important 'seasoning' skill that can enhance the client–counsellor relationship and advance the client's journey to personal growth and self-empowerment is the counsellor's commitment to increasing self-awareness, which is the aim of this chapter.

In order to maximise learning, we examine three pivotal, well-recognised and straightforward models to improving self-awareness, namely:

1. Psychiatrist Adolf Meyer's *Life Chart*.

2. Professor in psychology Abraham Maslow's *Hierarchy of Human Needs*.

3. *The Johari Window* created by American psychologists Joseph Luft and Harry Ingram (hence the name).

Three exercises based on these models, specifically aimed at enhancing self-awareness, are provided. Additional exercises to promote increased self-knowledge are given using the psychoanalytic technique of free association, and exploring your internal frame of reference.

EXPLORING THE MEANING OF SELF-AWARENESS

The basic components of self are:

- I am one person.
- I am the same person now as I was yesterday and as I will be tomorrow.
- I can distinguish between myself and the rest of the world as being not me.

- I know that I am thinking, feeling and doing.

- I have an accurate mental perception of my body.

- I have positive standards, ideals and ambitions that form my conscious goals.

To become effective counsellors, we need constantly to strive to increase our self-awareness – to discover what makes us tick – to monitor what goes on within us: our thoughts, feelings, sensing, intuition, attitudes, beliefs, and how these manifest themselves in our behaviour. Burnard (1997) – in his enlightening book dedicated to raising self-awareness – defines self-awareness as '. . . the continuous and evolving process of getting to know who you are.' If we don't know *'who lives in here'* and feel at home with ourselves, it's likely that our ability to help others will be impeded. A lack of self-knowledge means there are areas that are unknown or invisible to us. By increasing our self-understanding, we enhance our ability to be genuine and empathic, and our understanding of what makes other people tick. Developing a skill without the necessary grasp of the principles would be like an engineer trying to build a house without having the ability to read a blueprint, or being able to understand what was meant by stresses and strains. As far as counselling is concerned, the development of insights and self-awareness is crucial, if anything worthwhile is to be achieved.

Self-awareness is being aware of our physical, mental, emotional, moral, spiritual and social qualities, which together make us unique individuals; they are all working together to help us towards our fullest potential.

Self-awareness hinges on our ability and willingness to explore our own inner world. It is doubtful if any of us truly *knows* who we are. Life is a constant discovery about parts of us that have, until that moment, remained hidden from our conscious knowledge. There is always more to learn. Every new relationship gives us the opportunity to discover more about ourselves. Indeed many of us would rather be thought of by others in a way other than as our true self. Yet this, by itself, can put us under great pressure. Generally it is less stressful to be true than to be false. There is no guarantee that being self-aware will bring 'happiness' – a transient feeling – however, it will bring a certain sense of wholeness. You can never say, 'I have arrived.' But you can say, 'I am arriving.'

The quest for self-knowledge is the backbone to a counsellor's personal and professional development. Self-knowledge facilitates deeper understanding of the issues that clients present with in counselling – it is to counselling as the glove is to the hand.

Exercise 3.1

Using your life chart to develop self-awareness

This activity is based on the 'life-chart' theory of Adolf Meyer (1866–1950), an influential Swiss–American psychiatrist, much of whose teaching has been incorporated into psychiatric theory and practice. This exercise will take some time, and you may find it easier to spread it over several sessions.

1. Start from your birth date, and, chart your life up to the present. You might not remember your birth! But what were the circumstances surrounding that momentous event? Were you a 'wanted' or 'unwanted' child? Where do you fit in the family?

2. Record anything significant, such as illness, presents, changes in the family, school, college or university, first boyfriend/girlfriend, marriage, children, and so on.

3. Pay particular attention to recalling your thoughts, feelings and behaviours associated with the events. This can be considered in two strands: as you were at the time, and as you now feel about them.

4. Use the chart as a basis for deeper exploration of your past life. You may find it helpful to talk to your family about specific happenings. They might be able to fill in some of the details.

As you progress through life, you can use this chart to add to your self-awareness. As you explore the various stages of your life, don't rush over them; use free association (see Exercise 3.5) to plumb the depths of what hitherto might only have been vague memories. **Be cautious about with whom you share the intimate details of your life chart!**

Creating a visual timeline chart

For people who think in pictures, or have a poor memory for dates, an alternative to the method described above is to create a visual timeline chart of significant life events. This can prove useful for *seeing* the high and low points and significant dates in chronological order.

For example, you could record your childhood illnesses, and the effect they had on you; highlights of your schooldays; your career; your relationships; your peak experience; your major disappointments; your experience of grief and loss; the positive and happy events, such as your wedding, the birth of your children, and so on.

CASE STUDY

James reconstructs his life chart – the first eight years (William speaking)

James had one advantage over some people; he kept a diary, and had done so for years. Thus, it was relatively simple for him to reconstruct his life chart. He said to me, 'This is going to be easy. It's all there.' But although the details were there, at least from the age of eight, filling in the gaps before that age, and then tapping into the feelings, proved far from easy.

Writing of his birth, he said, 'I was a replacement child, my parents having lost a child, run over at the age of five. Thinking about my birth I feel privileged, but also a weight of responsibility. Although I never knew John, I feel that I miss him.' He then went on to say how even thinking about his dead brother filled him with longing, as if a part of him was missing. This led him to make links with the way he related to people. He needed other people, but he was always afraid they would be taken from him.

The next significant event was his mother being taken ill when James was about four years old. He recalled his father being anxious, and very short-tempered, which was nothing unusual. He recalled the ambulance taking her away, and the feeling of emptiness in the house. 'Mum was the one who kept the home going,' he wrote. 'As I'm writing this now, I feel tearful. Am I tapping into the feelings I had then?' Then he wrote of the joy when his mother came out of hospital. Then he had a flash of insight: 'Is that why I'm terrified if Jenny complains of not feeling well? Am I afraid of losing her?' He went on to relate that with the birth of each of his two children he hadn't felt afraid. 'For that wasn't an illness.'

James liked school. Disciplined for stealing a penny from one of the other pupils and sent to the head teacher with feelings of disgrace and guilt, he wrote. 'Is this tied up with my wanting to blame other people, and always needing to judge them?'

The next incident was when James himself was taken to hospital with meningitis. He spoke of a bleak time, painful memories – physical and emotional – and a near-death experience.

'I felt an obligation to serve God. This created great conflict between good and evil within me. That's the first time I've ever said that, even to myself. Good and evil. Two sides of the coin? Two parts of me? I'll have to work on that!'

USING MASLOW'S HIERARCHY OF HUMAN NEEDS TO ENHANCE YOUR SELF-AWARENESS

Abraham H Maslow (1908–70), a US psychologist and philosopher best known for his self-actualisation theory of psychology, proposed that the primary goal of psychotherapy should be the integration of the self. Maslow postulated that each person has a hierarchy of human needs that must be satisfied.

The theory is that only as each need is satisfied are we motivated to reach for the next higher level; thus, people who lack food or shelter or who cannot feel themselves to be in a safe environment are unable to concentrate on higher needs.

Our drive for self-actualisation may conflict with our rights and duties and responsibilities to other people who are involved.

While I might be high on self-actualisation today, tomorrow something could happen that would change that, and thrust me back into satisfying the basic needs. For example, if my job were made redundant, then however much I might want to continue the upward climb toward reaching my potential, my primary concern is likely to be trying to find another job to meet the security needs. If I were flying over the desert and the plane crashed, and I survived, my immediate needs would be very basic: food and water, not self-actualisation.

Another way of looking at Maslow's model is that rather than moving on from stage to stage, as in climbing a ladder, all five needs are being met simultaneously, to some degree. It must also be remembered that full self-actualisation is never reached.

Maslow's hierarchy of needs is frequently presented as a pyramid encompassing five levels of needs. According to Maslow, the four lower levels of the human needs are 'D-needs' (deficiency needs), which means that individuals do not suffer providing these needs are met, but may experience anxiety if they are unmet. Maslow originally developed his five-level Hierarchy of Needs model in the 1940s and 1950s. Over the years the hierarchy of needs has been adapted by others to include cognitive needs (the pursuit of knowledge), aesthetic needs (the appreciation of beauty) and transcendence needs (spiritual needs); however, Maslow's original five-level hierarchy remains the definitive resource for understanding human motivation.

THE HIERARCHY

Self-actualisation

This is the capacity of human beings to grow and develop toward emotional and psychological maturity and self-fulfilment. This level of personal growth may be met through the challenge of creativity or demanding greater achievement. Self-actualising behaviours include risk-taking, seeking autonomy and freedom to act.

Ego-status – esteem needs

These are met through status within a group, responsibility, ambition and a desire to excel –the ego-status needs will motivate the person to display competence in an effort to gain social and professional rewards; meeting status needs depends on the willingness and ability of other people to respond appropriately.

Belongingness and love needs, through family, friends, workgroups

The need of relationship with others, to be appreciated and accepted – met through family ties and membership of groups.

Safety – protection

Security, orderliness, protective rules and risk avoidance – met by salary, law and order, insurance policies, alarm systems.

Basic

Biological and physiological and survival needs – met by air, food, shelter, clothing, sex.

For more details of the hierarchy, see http://www.simplypsychology.org/maslow.html

Exercise 3.2

Using Maslow's theory to develop your self-awareness

1. Where do you think you are now on the needs hierarchy?
2. Which of your basic needs are being met?
3. Which of your basic needs are not being met?
4. How secure do you feel with yourself and your environment?
5. What could you do to enhance your need for security?
6. How satisfied are you with your need to belong?
7. What could you do to nourish your need for love and affection?
8. On a scale of one to five (one being the lowest and five being the highest) where would you rank your current level of self-esteem?
9. What could you do to boost your esteem needs?
10. What gifts and talents are you blessed with that you could make better use of?
11. What could you do to ensure your gifts and talents are utilised to their full potential?
12. What other steps could you take that will help you on your journey to self-actualisation?

INTRODUCING THE JOHARI WINDOW

Derived from the work of Jo Luft and Harry Ingram (1955) and named after them, the Johari Window focuses on the dynamics of interpersonal relationships and human interactions. It is usually diagrammatically presented in the form of a four-paned 'window'. The four quadrants:

1. known to all
2. blind region
3. hidden region and
4. unknown region

represent the whole person and different levels of awareness.

The theory suggests that through the process of self-disclosure and constructive feedback from others, the 'known to all' area expands, and the three other areas are reduced, thus increasing self-knowledge and self-awareness and integration. The model is a simple and effective tool for developing self-awareness.

For more details, see http://www.selfawareness.org.uk/news/understanding-the-johari-window-model

Quadrant 1: Known to all

The quadrant 'known to all' can be viewed as our fully open window, or public region. It is the aspects of us that we choose to show, or that cannot remain hidden from others, for example our height, body size and shape, skin colour, attitudes, beliefs, morals, opinions, behaviour, hobbies. The 'known to all' area of our window can be enlarged by self-disclosure (revealing more of ourselves).

Quadrant 2: Blind region

The 'blind region' refers to aspects of us that others can see but that we are oblivious to, for example, mannerisms, habits and other aspects of our behaviour that we remain unaware of. The 'blind region' of our window can be expanded by listening to, and being receptive to hearing, what other people observe (feedback). Constructive feedback is designed to help not to condemn. Becoming aware of the impact of our behaviour and actions on others offers the opportunity for change – if we choose to.

Quadrant 3: Hidden region

The 'hidden region' refers to aspects of us we know about but choose not to disclose (typically out of fear, guilt or shame, or because they might hurt others if revealed) –for example, watching pornography, sexual addiction, self-injury, child abuse, unacceptable traits, fear of public speaking. The 'hidden region' of our window can be increased by opting to come out from behind our façade and reveal hidden aspects, our fears or closely guarded secrets, with safe and trusted others. The process of disclosing intimate details about ourselves with a trusted other can result in increased openness and intimacy for both.

Quadrant 4: Unknown region

The 'unknown region' refers to aspects of us not yet discovered by ourselves or known to others – that which remains unconscious, repressed, denied, disowned or split off from our awareness – our dark side (or in Jungian terms our 'shadow' side). In psychoanalytic language, this is the region of the unconscious, seething with repressed desires, thoughts, feelings and wishes, which influence our current thoughts, feelings and behaviour. Unconscious material often contains negative or painful experiences that are deemed too difficult or perilous to face. Safely accessing our unknown regions usually requires help, support and sensitive feedback from a qualified counsellor or psychotherapist.

Exercise 3.3

Creating your own Johari Window

For this activity, you are advised to use a large sheet of paper divided into four quadrants.

1. In the *known to all* quadrant, record the parts of yourself that you and others are aware of.

2. In the *blind region* quadrant, record things about yourself that have been brought to light through feedback by others.

3. In the *hidden region* quadrant, record what you know about yourself that others don't know.

4. You may not be in a position to record anything in the *unknown region* quadrant unless you have had, or are currently in, therapy. However, if you have gleaned any personal insights about yourself through individual or group therapy, for example, record them in this quadrant.

Peruse your Johari Window then consider the following questions:

1. What could you do to enlarge your *known to all region*? What would you like others to know about you?

2. How could you expand on your *blind region*? What aspects of yourself or your behaviour would you appreciate feedback on? Who do you trust to provide you with constructive and accurate feedback?

3. How many items did you list in your *hidden region*? Are you surprised at the number of things you keep hidden from others? What is the personal cost

to you of keeping these aspects of yourself hidden? If you marked them on a scale – assuming there is more than one – which hidden aspect would be the least threatening to disclose? Which would be the most? If you decided to reveal the least threatening aspect as a starting point, who would you consider most trustworthy to tell?

4. Are there any aspects of your life of which you are dimly aware, but can't shed light on? Do you have any significant memory gaps in your personal history? Do you sometimes experience a strong emotional reaction to certain events and can't grasp why? Do you get recurring dreams or flashbacks that you can't make sense of? It's possible that these could indicate material stored in the unknown (unconscious) region of which you are unaware. Unravelling unconscious material requires extremely careful handling, and is best left in the hands of therapy professionals.

5. How different would you like the quadrants of your Johari Window to look in a year? Five years?

LIMITATIONS TO SELF-AWARENESS

Being self-aware does not mean we are as transparent as the purest glass. Being aware of self means just that; striving to know who we are, our faults and failings, our good points and strengths. It also does not mean that we have nothing to hide from other people; it means that we are selective about what we reveal and to whom. It does not mean that we have worked through all our problems and difficulties; it does mean that we still have foibles and quirks, but that we are seeking to understand them and how they influence our lives and our behaviour.

Becoming aware of self means that we are prepared to dip into the regions of our personal underworld. It may mean that we have to fight with fearsome feelings and memories which influence our lives. But it may also mean us getting in touch with what is beautiful and worthy. For rarely is our quest solely concerned with discovering the dark. One of the functions of the psyche is to help us transform the bad and the ugly into the good and beautiful.

Exercise 3.4

Expanding self-awareness (from your internal frame of reference)

You are advised not to rush through this exercise, for a greater understanding of your own frame of reference will aid your self-awareness and how what is within it may get in the way of entering a client's frame of reference. As this exercise is very individual, no 'answers' will be provided.

1. **Name**   How important is it to you?

2. **Gender**   Are you satisfied with being who you are?

3. **Body**   Are you satisfied with your physical appearance?

4. **Abilities**   What are you particularly good at?

5. **Mind**   Do you feel OK about your intellectual ability?

6. **Age**   Are you comfortable with the age you are now?

7. **Birth**   How do you feel about where you were born?

8. **Culture(s)**   Where were you brought up? If you have moved between different cultures, what influences has this had?

9. **People**   Who influenced you most when growing up?

10. **Mother**   What is your opinion of your mother?

11. **Father**   What is your opinion of your father? If you have no parents, how has that influenced you?

12. **Siblings**   What is your opinion of your brothers/sisters? If you have no siblings what influence has that had?

13. **Education**   What influence did your education have? What would you like to have achieved which you did not?

14. **Employment**   List the various jobs you have had, the people you remember associated with those jobs, and the overall influence of the work and the associated people.

15. **Spouse**   If you are married, how has your spouse influenced you?

16. **Children**   How have your children influenced you? If you wanted children, and were unable to have them, how has that influenced you?

17. **Unmarried**   If you are unmarried, or have no partner, what influence does that have?

18. **Preferences** How do your sexual preferences influence you?

19. **Values**   What values do you have, and what influence do they exert? Have you taken them over from other people without thought?

20. **Beliefs**   What are your fundamental beliefs? How did you acquire them?

21. **Religion**   If you are religious, what influence does that exert? If you have no religion, what influence does that exert?

22. **Experiences**   What life experiences are significant for you, and why?

23. **Health**   How have any illnesses or accidents influenced you?

24. **Memories**   What memories do you treasure, and what memories do you try hard to forget?

25. **Relationships**   What relationships in the past are you glad you had, and what relationships do you wish you had never had?

26. **Circumstances**   What life circumstances, past or present, do you welcome, and which do you regret?

27. **Authority**   Who represents authority for you, in the past and now? What influence do these authority figures exert on you?

28. **Strengths**   What are your major strengths, and how might these influence your listening to clients?

29. **Weaknesses**   What are your major weaknesses, and how might these influence your ability to listen to clients?

30. **Virtues**   What do you consider to be your virtues? How do they influence your behaviour?

31. **Vices**   Do you have any vices, and how do they influence your relationships?

How much insight do you think you gained by working through those thirty-one questions on your frame of reference?

LEARNING TO USE FREE ASSOCIATION

Free association, a psychoanalytical technique created by Sigmund Freud, is designed to facilitate access to unconscious parts of the mind outside direct awareness (silent thoughts and emotions seldom available to awareness, slips of the tongue [Freudian slips] caused by unconscious mental activity). Three assumptions operate:

- that all lines of thought tend to lead to what is significant

- that your unconscious will lead the associations towards what is significant

- that resistance is minimised by relaxation, but concentration increases it.

The basic rule of free association is that you take note of everything that comes into your mind, without any attempt to control or bring reason to bear. 'Everything' means thoughts, feelings, ideas, even if they are disagreeable, even if they seem unimportant or nonsensical. 'Everything' may include views and opinions, past experiences, flashes of fantasy, religion, morals, the quarrel with someone, ambitions; the list is endless, yet everything has a place, and a specific meaning for you. If your psyche is leading you, then ask, 'why has this come up now? What is the meaning?'

Identifying difficulties in free association

It is possible that free association is not for everyone. Some people take to it like the proverbial duck to water; others shy away from anything approaching introspection. Free association is not a miracle-worker, neither is it a panacea. But if it is persevered with, and undertaken with as much dedication as learning any other skill, the majority of people will find it answers many of their questions, and certainly shows the inner workings of the mind.

The following types of people might experience difficulty working with free association, but that does not mean that they should not try:

- people who steer clear of anything to do with self-development

- people who have difficulty with intimate relationships

- people who cannot make judgments for themselves; who are afraid to speak lest what they say does not meet with approval

- people who are so caught up in the trap of their conflicts that their whole life is over-controlled by negative thinking

- people who would be so ashamed by what free association reveals that they would feel safer if they never started.

Exercise 3.5

Starting to use free association

Spend time getting yourself comfortable and relaxed. Imagine you are looking at a cinema screen, upon which a picture will be projected. If you find this difficult, just let your mind wander, until a word, a thought, a feeling comes to you. Another suggestion is that you imagine you are drifting down a stream on a raft. As you pass, you see certain people, places, incidents that have meaning for you. Do not stop and dwell on any one thing, but, as in the example given above, let your mind make associations. You may do this for five minutes or longer. Your psyche will tell you when it is time to end. Trust it!

Do not make notes while you are free-associating, for that would interrupt the stream of consciousness. When you feel the association has ended, then you start making notes, but don't break the recall by analysing them. You may wonder if you will be able to recall all the material. You may consider yourself to have a not very good memory; you might not, but your psyche has the perfect memory. Trust it!

Start with the last word, idea or feeling, and work back to the beginning, jotting down just words or short phrases. Don't fret if you cannot remember every single one. You might recall the missing ones at the next stage. One of the things about memory is that it improves with use. The more you practise accurate recall, the easier it will become.

When you have completed your list (and we suggest that you keep a special notebook for your free associations), then you can start making connections, and exploring themes. What you will probably discover is that not everything comes at once. When you are psychologically ready, and not before, the psyche will reveal more. From time to time read what you have written, and take heart at the progress you have made since you started.

Another way is to have an audio recorder running while you are free-associating. You might feel a bit strange talking aloud, but if you are used to talking to yourself, that should not present too much of a problem.

CASE STUDY

James faces the truth (William speaking)

One of the areas James (a nurse) and I discussed was that he was (in his words) too fond of judging people. This involved him in telling them what he thought they should be doing, and not doing. He felt that his own moral standards were 'right', and that the world would be a better place if people behaved like him.

In order for James to practise free association, he had to make an agreement with his wife, Jenny, so that at a specific time, when the bedroom door was closed, no interruptions, short of a major disaster, would be allowed. He liked the idea of recording his sessions. He tried to set a regular time weekly, as far as his shifts would allow.

In one of his sessions, he achieved what for him was a monumental insight. He had been thinking (and talking) about his ward assessment, where a senior nurse commented on his attitude of 'always blaming other people'. This had led to an argument, then later to James apologising, and promising to look at his attitude.

In his next free association session he started with the word 'blame', and the final theme was just one word, 'victim'. In between the start and finish, James recalled many instances to which the word blame was attached. As he meditated on the victim theme, he recalled his feelings of being a victim at the hands of an abusive teacher at his junior school. His father told him to 'be a man'. James felt helpless. He now realised that he judged other people to put himself in the right; and that he blamed other people to divert attention from himself. He was able to share his insights with me, and then, at a later stage, with the members of his team.

Taken from Stewart, W, (1998). *Self-Counselling* (pp 22–25), and used with permission.

SUMMARY

Counselling is about helping clients develop their self-awareness. To facilitate this process, it is imperative that counsellors work towards increasing their own self-awareness. This chapter has highlighted three well-recognised models for expanding self-awareness: Adolf Meyer's Life Chart, Abraham Maslow's Hierarchy of Human Needs and The Johari Window, created by Joseph Luft and Harry Ingram. To further enhance understanding of the models, websites have been provided. Moreover, exercises based on each model have been included with the specific aim of gaining self-awareness. Using the psychoanalytic technique of free association, and an exercise intended to explore your internal frame of reference, are additional items incorporated to aid the development of self-knowledge.

Our next task is to address what counsellors need to do in readiness for the first meeting with a client. This is the essence of chapter 4.

> *I want, by understanding myself, to understand others. I want*
> *to be all that I am capable of becoming.*
>
> Katherine Mansfield
> (1888–1923 – prominent New Zealand author)

REFERENCES

Burnard, P. (1997). *Know Yourself! Self-awareness Activities for Nurses and other Health Professionals.* London: Whurr.

Gibran, K. (2013). *The Prophet.* Aziloth Books.

Luft J, Ingham H. (1955). *The Johari Window: A Graphic Model for Interpersonal Relations.* University of California. Western Training Lab.

Maslow, A. (1943). *A Theory of Human Motivation. Psychological Review* 50: 370–96.

Maslow, A. (1997). *Motivation and Personality.* Pearson; 3rd edition.

Maslow, A. (2013). *A Theory of Human Motivation*, Wilder Publications.

Stewart, W, (1998). *Self-Counselling: How to develop the skills to positively manage your life.* Oxford: How To Books.

CHAPTER 4

Helping the Client Feel Safe

To be trusted is a greater compliment than to be loved.
George MacDonald (1824–1905) Scottish author and poet

In Chapter 3, we highlighted the importance of developing self-awareness to enhance counsellor practice and provided suggestions and exercises for gaining self-awareness. This chapter covers a variety of topics – setting the scene for the first session with a new client being its main thrust. To bring meaning to the skills presented, we introduce five fictitious clients: Pat, Paul, Hayley, Ellen and Danny, who you will continue to meet in Chapters 5, 6 and 7. Other relevant themes addressed include establishing clear boundaries and boundary issues, counselling contracts, the 'so called' fifty-minute therapeutic hour, note-taking and record keeping, referral issues and recording sessions.

THE FIRST MEETING

'Baring your soul' to a complete stranger can be a daunting prospect – it takes courage and trust; and an aspect of counselling that cannot be emphasised strongly enough is helping clients to feel safe, at ease and accepted, when they cross the threshold of the counselling room for the first time. Thorough preparation for the first meeting and creating a welcoming, warm and safe environment are paramount to enable clients to start voicing their concerns, and to alleviate their nervousness or anxiety about venturing into unknown territory. It's worth bearing in mind too that counsellors are also entering uncharted territory when they meet a new client and may feel apprehensive. Being well prepared can greatly reduce a sense of uneasiness, thus, it can pay dividends for both client and counsellor.

Paying attention to meeting, greeting and seating

For counselling to be an empowering experience for the client, the counsellor needs to work hard at building a relationship of trust, safety and equality, which is not always easy, particularly in the beginning when the client is likely to feel vulnerable and uncomfortable. Counselling rarely happens on neutral territory – it usually takes place at a counselling centre, or a counsellor's premises – which in itself can hinder the development of a trusting and safe relationship as it places the client and counsellor on unequal footing. Giving careful thought to how the counselling room is set up can set the scene for reducing the equality gap. Practical steps the counsellor can take to create an atmosphere of trust, safety and neutrality include:

- Making certain that the room is non-clinical and inviting – warm, but not too warm, light, but not overly bright.

- Ensuring the room is uncluttered and free of personal belongings such as family photographs, books, DVDs and the like. On the other hand, these can provide a feeling of warmth and openness.

- Adding some personal touches such as a vase of fresh flowers, a bottle of water and glass and a discreet box of tissues.

- Positioning chairs at a comfortable distance apart and slightly at an angle. This helps clients who have difficulty making direct eye contact feel less intimidated. To prevent an air of one-upmanship, identical and comfortable chairs (but not too comfortable) should be used. Where you place the chairs in relation to the door is also important to consider, especially when working with childhood trauma survivors, many of whom feel unsafe, panicky or fearful sitting with their back to a door.

- Keeping potential barriers such as desks or large tables out of the therapeutic space.

- Guaranteeing privacy by unplugging the telephone, switching mobiles off, shutting the computer down, putting a notice on the door to prevent intrusions.

- Positioning a small clock in a place where you can glance at it surreptitiously to avoid running over time or so you can remind the client when a session is nearing the end. Looking at your watch can be distracting to clients: some might see it as a sign of disinterest, disrespect, or that you are getting bored and are wishing the session would come to an end.

- William speaking; I have conducted successful counselling in the most unlikely surroundings: a crowded canteen; sitting in the park; in a home with children playing on the floor. What is important is that we learn to engage the client wherever the client feels most comfortable.

Counsellor safety

In addition to striving to create an atmosphere of comfort, safety and neutrality for the client, it is vital to recognise that safety is a two-way street and to consider your personal safety. Ensure that someone else is close to hand while you are counselling, let someone else know where you are and what time you anticipate finishing, and have a panic button nearby (and regularly check that it is working). This raises the issue of client safety as well as counsellor safety. William says: in all my years as a therapist and a psychiatric social worker I have never felt compromised or threatened by a client. That is not to say it cannot happen. So be careful. Some clients ask if they can bring a friend with them. Sally did this and although it felt awkward at first, the end result was productive. It showed Sally and her girlfriend that I was adaptable. More than that, it afforded Sally a degree of safety. It also gave Sally and her friend something to talk over when they left. The next time, Sally came on her own.

Greeting the client

First impressions count. Greeting the client in the waiting room (if there is one) with a warm smile, comfortable eye contact, firm handshake – if it feels appropriate – and a brief introduction, communicates an amenable attitude. Saying something informal along the lines of, Hello, my name is William, and yours is? Or, Hi, my name is Jan, how would you like me to address you? and listening to how the client responds can provide useful information; for example, if the client says 'I am Mr . . .', or 'my name is Mrs . . .' it suggests the client is more at ease with a formal, rather than informal, approach. Clients' physical appearance and mode of dress (i.e. casual or smart; well groomed, poorly groomed) can also speak volumes about their disposition without a word being spoken.

Once greeted, lead the client to the counselling room avoiding any form of touch, and invite her to choose a chair.

Issuing an open invitation to talk with our five fictitious clients

Your opening sentence should be empathic and your tone of voice and posture should demonstrate to the client that you are ready to give your full attention:

1. Pat, perhaps you would like to tell me in your own time what has prompted you to seek counselling?

2. Paul, we have fifty minutes to talk together today. Where would it help to start?

3. *To Hayley, an anxious client, who sits in silence on the edge of the chair with her feet pointing towards the door:* Hayley, I sense that you are feeling on edge and are struggling to find the words to begin? Would it help to start by telling me a little bit about yourself . . .

4. *To Ellen, who is staring out of the window and looks miles away:* Ellen, you seem to be somewhat preoccupied, or perhaps have a lot on your mind . . . would it help to say a little about what's going on with you . . .

5. *To Danny, a resistant client, sent by a third party – e.g. the Magistrates Court – who has pushed his chair further away from the counsellor, and is sitting with his arms and legs tightly crossed:* Danny, I get the impression that this is the last place you want to be right now . . . perhaps it might help if I explain a bit about the counselling . . .

Building trust

The quality of the therapeutic relationship, also referred to as the therapeutic alliance, hinges on the counsellor's ability to cultivate the client's capacity to trust over time. Establishing trust can be particularly challenging with clients whose faith has been shattered by traumatic early experiences such as abandonment, betrayal, abuse, rape, neglect or violence. Developing trust is a key aspect of a counsellor's work that requires constant consideration. The client's trust can be earned by offering the skills of active listening; accurate, sensitive responding; reflecting feelings; empathy; genuineness; and by actively modelling trust through being honest, open, reliable, loyal and consistent. Investing time wisely to build the client's trust can result in an enriching harvest of personal growth for the client.

Planting the seeds of trust with our five fictitious clients

Pat, I can see that you are very distressed because of what has happened.

Paul, I appreciate that talking about your job being made redundant is painful for you.

Hayley, I understand that it is not easy for you to talk about your concerns, and I feel very humbled by your trust in me . . .

Ellen, I've noticed that you seem a little less tense than when you first arrived; your shoulders have lowered, and your breathing has slowed down. Could it be that you are feeling a bit more relaxed . . .

Danny, I respect your honesty in telling me that you are reluctant to be here . . .

Knowing what to avoid

- Avoid restricting the client by placing emphasis on such topics as 'difficulties', 'problems', 'help'; for example, saying, 'Please go ahead and tell me the problem', 'What difficulties are you having?', 'How can I help you?' Be careful about statements such as 'I hope I can help you'. We may not be able to help at all, at least not in the sense of doing something. What we can do is to listen and help the clients explore their feelings.

- Avoid minimising counselling with expressions such as: 'Let's have a chat', or 'Shall we have a little talk?' Counselling is not a chat. We talk, yes, but 'chat' carries with it inferences of a social meeting, which is not the purpose of counselling. To think of it as chat demeans the process.

BOUNDARIES IN COUNSELLING

Constructing clear boundaries with the client provides the scaffolding for building a therapeutic relationship, along with creating rapport (being 'attuned' to the client's needs – getting on the client's wavelength). However, before discussing boundary-setting in counselling in more detail, it is useful to understand the concept of boundaries, as clients often present with boundary issues.

What is rapport?

Generally, rapport is a comfortable, relaxed, unconstrained, mutually accepting interaction between people. More specifically, when applied to counselling it is the feeling of accord, harmony or quality that is the foundation for any therapeutic relationship, without which healing and growth may not take place. Rapport develops in the presence of:

- Active listening

- Accurate, sensitive responding

- Reflecting feelings

- Clear demonstration of the core conditions of empathy, warmth, genuineness and unconditional positive regard

- A sincere desire to understand

- An ability to be fully present with the client, wherever that might be

- Compassion for the client's suffering and distress.

Rapport has three essential ingredients:

1. *Harmony*, something for which we strive, sometimes achieve and so easily lose. It is an elusive shadow that somehow we must turn into substance.

2. *Compatibility*, which is influenced by such factors as:
   - Personality
   - Appearance
   - Intelligence
   - Emotional stability
   - Understanding
   - Kindness/tenderness
   - Common interest.

3. *Affinity*, which is the quality of the relationship. Counselling forms a significant bond between counsellor and client, who have become bonded together for a specific purpose. When that purpose has been fulfilled, the relationship, the bond of affinity, will be severed. The more one invests in a relationship, the stronger the bond grows; and the breaking of it may bring pain.

Rapport is not something a person gains, like a certificate of competence. It is a transient state, more easily lost than achieved, always under threat from misinterpretation, lack of awareness of the interaction with the client and ineffective listening. The more one is able to engage the client's frame of reference, the deeper will be the rapport.

Rigid boundaries

People with rigid boundaries tend to be self-sufficient. They 'erect an impenetrable wall' to prevent others entering their space. They keep others at a distance, shut others out, or reveal little or nothing about themselves, their thoughts or feelings. Rigid boundaries prevent emotional connection and intimacy. Inflexible boundaries may stem from being hurt, rejected or let down in the past, and a need to protect oneself from further pain. The firmly held conviction that 'If I don't let anyone get close, I won't be hurt or abandoned again' operates an internal marker that sends a non-verbal warning signal to others not to get too close.

Enmeshed boundaries

Whereas rigid boundaries are usually formed to prevent the risk of being hurt, people with enmeshed boundaries (although they may not be aware of it) can leave themselves wide open to being hurt, which is equally as harmful as setting rigid boundaries.

People with enmeshed boundaries have little sense of themselves as being separate in relationships. For example, a mother might encourage an overly close relationship with her child to compensate for her own inner emptiness, or inappropriately turn her daughter into an intimate friend and confidante at too young an age.

Children who are raised in an environment where boundaries are fragile, ignored or non-existent may unwittingly, in later life, expose themselves to flagrant boundary infringements. For example, a child who has been emotionally, physically or sexually abused might easily be led into prostitution, or become promiscuous, the victim of domestic violence, bullied, raped, sexually assaulted by a stranger, or ensnared into dangerous situations or relationships.

If inappropriate boundaries have been the norm, or people are not aware when their boundaries are being violated, saying 'no' to unwanted sex, touch or other forms of abuse, or recognising when they are being manipulated by another to feed that person's own needs, may not even enter the equation. Such is their desperate need for love and affection that they are blind or naive to the exploitation by others aimed at satisfying the instigators' own needs. Lax boundaries can also indicate an ambivalent or unhealthy attachment to the original perpetrator of the abuse. Individuals with enmeshed boundaries often have difficulty knowing where to draw the line.

Healthy boundaries

In relationships, the word 'boundary' can be defined as an invisible line or perimeter that enables each person to maintain a separate sense of their own identity. People with healthy boundaries choose who they allow to enter their space, and honour other people's boundaries. Healthy boundaries promote safety, independence, self-respect and respect from others and foster emotional connection and intimacy. People with healthy boundaries know exactly where to draw the line, and if their boundaries are desecrated by others, they are likely to get upset, angry, indignant or irritated.

Developing healthy boundaries

Developing healthy boundaries involves becoming aware of when others are overstepping the mark, not tolerating others intruding into your personal space, setting clear limits about what is acceptable and not acceptable, and learning to take responsibility for your own safety (physically, emotionally and sexually). Creating healthy boundaries demonstrates self-respect, and encourages respect from others.

For an interesting article on developing healthy boundaries, see http://www.counsellingonstirling.com.au/boundaries.html

CASE STUDY

Mary with male counsellor

As Mary is leaving after her first session, she says, 'I would really like a hug.' John feels uncomfortable because he had the feeling throughout that Mary was flirting with him. He says, 'I make it a rule never to hug my clients, because this would change our relationship and it would be inappropriate and it might interfere with your therapy. Shall we make another appointment?'

Discussion

Some therapists are not averse to appropriate physical contact. If Mary had not given off signals that she was flirting with John, or if she had been distressed, he might have responded differently. John's training was psychodynamic, where no physical contact is permitted, so he was acting within his own boundary. What is important in this brief case is that some dynamic was taking place that set up warning signs of danger.

Boundary-setting in counselling

Establishing clear boundaries in counselling is designed to keep the client and counsellor's realms seperate. Boundaries may include agreement over such things as the duration of counselling, length of counselling sessions, limits of confidentiality, appropriate touching, number and duration of phone calls, sending and responding to emails, or strategies for managing episodes of self-harm or suicidal thoughts.

The terms on which counselling is being offered should be made clear to clients before counselling commences. These may be agreed verbally, or they may be set out in a formal written contract between counsellor and client, and signed by both parties. Subsequent revision of these terms should be agreed in advance of any change. Clear contracting enhances, and shows respect for, the client's autonomy. A contract helps to ensure the professional nature of the relationship and may, in addition to the ground rules already mentioned, include:

- venue

- fees, if appropriate

- frequency of sessions

- how counselling will be evaluated

- process of referral, if and when necessary

- broad details of the counselling relationship

- duties and responsibilities of each party

- details of counsellor's supervision

- goals of counselling

- means by which the goals will be achieved

- the provision and completion of 'homework'

- the setting of boundaries and expectations

- the terms of the therapeutic relationship

- provision of renegotiation of contract.

Example of a written counselling contract

This contract is made between:

Counsellor: _____   **Client:** _____

on the _____   **year** _____

1. CONFIDENTIALITY

Although our sessions are confidential, I reserve the right to breach confidentiality in exceptional circumstances – possible examples include:

  i. If you disclose any information during the course of counselling that indicates that you are at risk of seriously harming yourself, or injuring someone else.

  ii. If it becomes evident during counselling that you have committed a crime such as murder/and or attempted murder, arson, armed robbery, child abuse, child or drug trafficking, downloading and/or using children in pornography, kidnapping or child abduction, rape and/or sexual assault, or you express intent to commit a crime such as an act of terrorism.

  iii If I am ordered by a court to disclose information about you.

As part of my ongoing training, professional development as a counsellor, and to ensure efficacy of my client work, I attend sessions every four weeks with an experienced and qualified supervisor, at which I present my case work. Should I discuss your case, in order to safeguard confidentiality and protect your anonymity, I will not disclose your name or any possible identifying details.

Before considering breaching confidentiality, I will consult with my counselling supervisor. Additionally, I will discuss the situation with you if this is feasible.

2. NUMBER OF SESSIONS

We have provisionally agreed that you will commit to attending fifteen counselling sessions. The sessions will last for fifty minutes and will take place at:

_____

To ensure continuity, sessions will take place at the same time each week, commencing on _____ at _____. Should additional sessions be identified as necessary during the fifteen sessions contracted for, we will negotiate a new contract.

3. FEES

We have agreed that you will pay my standard fee of £ _____ per fifty minute session. Moreover, we have agreed that should your financial situation change during the course of counselling, we will negotiate a reduced fee until your financial situation improves. As agreed in the assessment interview, you will receive a fee invoice every four weeks via your email address. Payment of fees can be made by cheque, or electronically by credit/debit card, and should be paid within two weeks of receipt. My fees are reviewed on a yearly basis every March, and you will be notified of any forthcoming increase four weeks before the new charges take effect.

4. MISSED OR CANCELLED APPOINTMENTS

The fifteen time-slots allocated to you for counselling, is your time, and will not be assigned to another client, even if you are on holiday, or cannot attend because of illness or other unavoidable circumstances. Whereas scheduled breaks such as holidays will not be charged for, my normal fee will be charged for non-attendance or cancelled sessions.

5. ARRIVING LATE FOR SESSIONS, OR LEAVING EARLY

Should you arrive late for a session, or decide to end a session before the scheduled time, my standard fee remains applicable. If you arrive late for a session, I will not be able to extend the session beyond the allocated time.

6. MY HOLIDAYS AND BANK HOLIDAYS

I take seven weeks' holidays per year – two weeks at Christmas, two weeks at Easter, and three weeks during the summer period (between July and September). I will provide you with as much notice as possible of my holiday breaks, and you will not be charged for sessions when I am on holiday. Should I need to cancel a session through illness, or for other extenuating circumstances, I will endeavour to give you as much notice as possible, and wherever possible I will offer you an alternative appointment in the same week as the cancelled appointment. If, however, a mutually convenient time and day cannot be agreed within the timescale, you will not be charged. Should a session fall on a bank holiday, we will discuss this in advance and, if possible, arrange an appointment on a different day within the same week. Should an alternative day prove impossible for you, no fee will be charged.

7. NOTE KEEPING AND RECORDS

As an aide memoir, I will keep brief confidential notes of our counselling sessions. Additional notes and records kept in your file will include liaison with other professionals concerned with your case; supervision notes relevant to your case; correspondence received, requested or sent in relation to your case, and any correspondence received from you. To ensure privacy and maximum security, your notes will be locked in a filing cabinet at my premises, to which only I have a key. In accordance with the timescale for storage of records as recommended by my professional body, The British Association for Counselling and Psychotherapy (BACP) notes and records pertaining to your case will be retained for seven years.

See *Ethical Framework for the Counselling Professions* (http://www. bacp.co.uk) for further information. When the seven years expires all notes and records retained concerning your case will be destroyed by shredding or incineration.

Access to your notes and records

In line with the Data Protection Act (1998) (see http://www.ico.gov.uk/ what_we_cover/data_protection/your_rights.aspx)

I believe in your right to access information held about you, including all pertinent notes, letters, and computerised correspondence. If you wish to read any notes personally made by me throughout our counselling contract, or other information/correspondence kept in your file concerning your case, you can either:

a. ask me informally to see your notes and records, or:

b. make a formal request to view them under the Data Protection Act.

Before seeing your notes, any references to third parties will be blurred or disguised, to protect their confidentiality.

8. TERMINATION OF COUNSELLING

Ending counselling, particularly long-term counselling, can be a difficult time for both client and counsellor, thus at regular intervals throughout our sessions together, you will be encouraged to share your thoughts and feelings, and any concerns you may have, about counselling drawing to a close. While it is your right to terminate counselling with me if it is not meeting your needs and expectations, I would encourage you to consider the implications of ending prematurely or abruptly without allowing yourself the time or opportunity of saying a proper goodbye. Should you wish to terminate counselling before the contracted number of sessions, please provide me with at least two weeks' notice.

Should any damage be caused by you to my premises, counselling room, furniture, fixtures and fittings, or physical harm committed to me during the course of our sessions, I reserve the right to terminate counselling immediately.

9. ACCREDITATION

I am a British Association for Counselling and Psychotherapy (BACP) accredited counsellor, and adhere to the BACP *Ethical Framework for the Counselling Professions*. (See http://www.bacp.co.uk for further information).

Should you, at any time, be dissatisfied with my work, and this matter cannot be resolved between us, you have the right to register a formal complaint to the BACP.

Please read the foregoing carefully and if you are satisfied everything is correct, please sign below.

Client's Signature   Date

Counsellor's Signature   Date

For a more detailed counselling contract, see http://dundeecounselling.com/counselling/sample-contract.pdf

Boundary issues

It is the counsellor's duty to act in the best interests of the client and establishing and maintaining firm boundaries is of paramount importance. Some clients who seek counselling are very needy – they may have come from backgrounds where they have felt 'invisible', unlovable, or unworthy of receiving care and attention. In an attempt to be liked and accepted, or to gain extra attention or time from the counsellor, they may try to stretch the boundaries. Here are a few hypothetical examples:

- Miranda sends texts in between sessions to her counsellor without seeking the counsellor's permission.

- Reece turns up at the counsellor's premises without an appointment.

- Kristen gives the counsellor a hug at the end of the session without asking.

- Sonia invites her counsellor to her twenty-first birthday party.

- Bryan lavishes the counsellor with expensive gifts.

CASE STUDY

Gifts explored (William speaking)

Receiving gifts from clients is a well-debated topic; some views are that they are never appropriate. I take the view that it depends on the circumstances. When would a gift be appropriate? Take, for example, a client who arrives at the first session with a gift; what might that be saying? When we visit a friend, we often take a gift; but therapy is a professional relationship. And while the therapist is no doubt friendly, therapist and client are not friends. So, it is possible that the client might want to establish a friendly relationship. How should the gift be received? To reject a gift with brusque 'I'm sorry, I have a policy not to accept gifts from clients' would seem harsh and the client would probably feel rejected. 'Thank you. I will accept your gift this time, but I feel uncomfortable about accepting gifts from clients. I hope you understand' is generous and accepting.

Sandra has been working with Tom for several weeks and the focus has been on his difficulty in establishing and maintaining relationships with women. He arrives with a large bouquet of red roses.

Sandra: Tom, those are beautiful roses and I'll find a vase for them later. However, I wonder why you brought them?

Tom: I was passing the florist and I thought of you and just bought them.

Sandra: Almost as if you were buying them for your girlfriend?

Tom: Something like that. But you're not my girlfriend. Oh my! I've goofed.

Sandra: That was insightful, Tom. It's what we refer to as transference, feelings towards the therapist which rightly belong to another person.

Discussion

The relationship that Sandra and Tom had established was firm enough for her to challenge Tom and to explain the basic principle of transference. She was then able to use this example of how Tom might make an approach to a woman, where roses would be appropriate when the relationship had moved beyond the first stage.

For more on gifts in therapy, see http://nationalpsychologist.com/2012/09/gifts-in-therapy-some-are-appropriate/101741.html

Counsellor boundary issues

Counsellors too can blur the boundaries, which can cause bewilderment to clients over roles and expectations, create an unhealthy dependence, intensify their problems, or emotionally and psychologically harm the client. Here are some examples:

- Engaging in sexual activity with a client.
- Touching the client without being given permission.
- Allowing sessions to run way beyond the agreed time.
- Meeting outside the counselling environment (having lunch; meeting the client's family; accepting a lift from a client; greeting the client in the supermarket; telephoning, emailing or texting the client, except in the case of an emergency such as the need to cancel, or change an appointment).
- Taking the client to conferences.
- Accepting monetary/expensive gifts from the client.

- Giving gifts – although different counselling orientations hold divergent views on this. For example, some counsellors might give the client an object of small value such as a stone, or poem, when going on a long holiday break, as a way of acknowledging the relationship, or a card to mark a milestone in the client's life.

- Accepting a client's offer to do a job because the client has a particular skill.

- Inappropriate counsellor self-disclosure (incongruously shifting the focus of attention from client to counsellor).

- Not referring a client when it is clear that the counsellor is not qualified or sufficiently experienced to serve the client's needs.

Whose needs?

When counsellors find themselves acting out of character with a client, they need to examine their motivation. These are some useful questions to consider:

- How might my actions affect the counselling relationship?

- How might my behaviour be interpreted by my colleagues? Would I feel comfortable telling them or my supervisor what I've done?

- Why am I treating this client in an exclusive way?

- Am I exploiting the client in any way?

- Am I trying to buy the client's trust, affection, to get in his good books?

- Who does my action benefit – me or the client?

Understanding the therapeutic hour

Most counsellors work to what is called the 'therapeutic hour' or 'fifty-minute hour'. This allows the counsellor time to make any notes before seeing the next client; beyond this time, efficiency begins to drop off rapidly. However, not all counsellors adhere to this practice. Sometimes extra time is desirable, and much will depend on the complexity of the case. But the time should not be extended by accident or by either the client or the counsellor wishing to have more of the other's time; it should be planned. If you find yourself consistently running over the agreed time, then you would profit from exploring this with your supervisor.

Counselling can be emotionally demanding and exhausting. The knowledge that there is a time limit can be a positive safeguard for both client and counsellor.

What if the client thinks of something important just as the session is ending?

This is a difficult one, and it is certainly something you might want to discuss with your client before it happens. In counselling circles, this phenomenon is known as the 'hand on the door' – the client, just leaving, halts and discloses something quite dramatic. This immediately thrusts the counsellor on the horns of a dilemma – to extend the time or leave the disclosure hanging around for another week.

You have to make a decision – continue with the session or close it. You may say something like, 'I heard what you said, however, our time has gone, we will explore it next time if you wish.' This leaves the client knowing that you did hear, and the matter is clearly in the client's control.

CASE STUDY

Meg heads for the door

Meg, a trainee counsellor, was coming to me (William) for personal therapy as part of her training. In the fourth session, we had been discussing a particular issue. As we were closing the session, I said to Meg, 'What will you take away with you from today?' She said, 'My supervisor suggested I talk to you about my feelings with the training group.' We both laughed; she and I knew that that was a beautiful demonstration of the 'hand on the door phenomenon'. The following week we did discuss it, and the reason for waiting until the last minute. Meg freely admitted that the feelings she needed to discuss were too raw and she needed time to sort them out.

(Taken from Stewart, W. & Martin, A. (1999). *Going for Counselling*, p.116.)

Ending sessions on time

It is important to end sessions on time. This helps the client feel safe, and to understand the boundaries. When a session is nearing an end, it can be helpful to say something like, 'We have about ten minutes left of this session. Perhaps it would be helpful to summarise what we have talked about today?' It can often prove beneficial to let your client summarise what has been discussed during the session. Something like, 'What will you take away with you from today?' helps the client to summarise. Your closing sentences need to be clear, and should indicate that it's time to end the session.

Things to avoid

- Don't introduce **new topics** into the concluding period. If you do this, it may confuse your client. He or she will think that they can still go on for a while. If your client introduces a new subject in the last few minutes of the session, you could say, 'I can see that this is very important to you, and I think it is an area we could look at in more depth in our next session together. How would you feel about that?'

- Some clients wait until they are leaving before disclosing an important piece of information, for example, 'Oh, by the way . . .' This may reflect the client's feeling of shame or embarrassment, or the realisation that this is their last opportunity to 'let the cat out of the bag'. Don't be manipulated into giving **extra time**. Again, show the client respect by saying something like: 'I appreciate your courage in telling me that. I can see that it wasn't easy for you, and it sounds as if you have been holding on to that secret for a long time. Would it help if we allocated the next session to giving the situation the attention it deserves?' Often, just verbalising a painful secret, and being heard, can bring a tremendous sense of relief.

- Don't get hooked into **the presenting problem**. The problem that the client chooses to talk about, or the 'presenting problem' as it is sometimes called, is of considerable significance. It is what clients complain of, their 'admission ticket' to counselling, a 'trial balloon'. Sometimes it is something that is not of primary importance in order to test out the counsellor, but more often, it represents that aspect of the client's problem which, at this present time, is giving him the most anxiety. Perhaps it would be too emotionally demanding to talk about the significant problem before the counselling relationship had been firmly established. Whatever the reasons, it is always wise to sit back and wait for the client to develop the theme. At the same time, it is essential to acknowledge the presenting problem, but being aware that there are probably other issues to be considered.

NOTE TAKING AND RECORD KEEPING

In certain situations, some notes are essential, if only to keep the key issues before one's eyes. Such notes need only be single words, enough to act as refreshers later in the session. Single words or short sentences can usually be written without taking one's eyes off the client for too long. Referring to the notes from time to time may give the client confidence that what has been noted is there to be used.

Note taking may also be used effectively to slow a very talkative client. The client should be made aware of the purpose of the notes and of their confidentiality.

Counselling records serve four main purposes:

- To aid good counselling practice
- Help administration
- Training
- Research.

A good record should be readable. A good recording style is plain, clear and as brief as treatment will permit. We cannot record accurately if we have not heard and observed accurately. Clarity and brevity indicate analytical thinking. The record will be a thoughtful reflection of what took place in the interview.

Suggested items to include:

- How and why the client came to you: was it a referral or self-referred?

- The presenting problem.

- The facts.

- The relationship between the client and any significant others.

- Personal history.

- Any significant comments made either by you or the client that bring out important feelings, attitudes and opinions or refer to the 'larger problem'.

- Your own activity within the session; thoughts, feelings, behaviours, interventions.

- As counselling progresses, the record should reflect development and include your periodic evaluations and statements of aims.

- Future dates for sessions.

- Referrals if any.

A final point should be made about computer-kept records. The whole issue of record keeping presents difficulties of confidentiality; counsellors certainly must consider the implications of keeping client records on computer. Such questions as storing (on hard disk, file hosting service or external storage device); security of material (where is it kept?); access (password; who has access?); how long the records are kept and for what purposes; and, if you are part of a computer network, how you protect the material all have to be considered. Computer-kept records can save an enormous amount of time and space but client confidentiality must always be uppermost in our minds.

Legal and ethical issues

One of the major recent developments in legal requirements concerning record keeping occurred when data protection principles were extended to include written records by the Data Protection Act 1998. This legislation creates two levels of duty. Therapeutic records fall within the category that has stricter requirements concerning the protection of 'sensitive personal data'.

Some counsellors find it better to write brief notes after the session, noting down key words and themes that emerged during the session as an aide memoir. It is important to consult these notes prior to the next session to refresh one's memory of the previous session. Such notes can also be useful as a starting point for summarising what took place in the previous session; they can then be used to ask clients what they most remember about the previous session (which can sometimes be very different from the things the counsellor remembers). It was discussed under Confidentiality in Chapter 1 that counsellors may be required by a court to disclose secret information, and this would probably include having to produce their records.

For an article on privacy and confidentiality by BACP, see http://www.bacp. co.uk/ethical_framework/ETHICAL%20FRAMEWORK%20(BSL%20 VERSION)/Respectingprivacyandconfidentiality%20.php

Under the Freedom of Information Act UK (2000), it is conceivable that clients could ask to see their records, even though the Act refers to records held by public authorities. So the Act could apply to counsellors engaged by the NHS and other public authorities, such as school/college counsellors. Though the situation regarding private counsellors is uncertain, the authors of this book would never deny a request from clients to examine their records. This raises the important issue of never committing anything to paper that would cause embarrassment or distress to a client if your records ever became public, either because the client requested to read them or because they were part of a court case.

(Adapted from Stewart, William. (2005). *An A–Z of Counselling Theory and Practice*. 4th edition, pp: 419–421) and used with permission.)

RECORDING SESSIONS

Some counsellors find it useful to use recorded sessions as a way of monitoring their performance, evaluating their interventions, and for the purpose or receiving constructive feedback in supervision. However, clients should be given a choice as to whether recording sessions is acceptable, and recording should never take place without the client's agreement, or without the client signing a consent form. Moreover, issues concerning confidentiality over who hears the tapes, and what happens when they are finished with, need to be clearly communicated to the client.

The presence of a tape recorder in sessions can be off-putting to some clients. If the client expresses discomfort during a session that is being recorded, the counsellor should respect the client's wishes and abandon the idea.

REFERRING A CLIENT

Not every counsellor is the best person for all clients, so from time to time it may become necessary for the client's development that he is referred to another counsellor or counselling agency.

It may become necessary, therefore, to refer a client for one or a combination of the following reasons:

- medical
- social
- pastoral
- psychiatric
- psychological
- emotional
- spiritual
- legal.

It is helpful, therefore, to know the resources available in your own locality, agencies as well as people.

Referral maybe delayed because of:

- The counsellor's hurt pride at not being able to continue with the client until completion.
- Not creating an awareness in the mind of the client from the start that referral is a possibility.

- Not admitting limitations.

- Not working through and helping the client understand why referral is indicated.

- Not being able to separate from the client.

The client might see referral as rejection or abandonment rather than developmental. Sometimes there is the tendency to refer too quickly. Perhaps the counsellor may see a need for referral but this is totally rejected by the client. The limitations should then be brought into the open and discussed. The counsellor then may need to seek expert help if work with the client is to be productive. Working with a client who is reluctant to be referred is both demanding and challenging but the counsellor will need a great deal of support.

Referral is particularly difficult for clients who feel they have already been pushed from one counsellor to another; this could lead to a feeling that they are beyond help. It is certainly true that the longer the relationship the more difficult referral might be, even though the need is recognised by the counsellor and accepted by the client. But just as it is possible to work toward separation at the end of counselling, so it is equally possible to achieve this in referral.

You should do all you can to make the transition easy – talk about the other counsellor or agency, arrange a visit, let the client make contact, work with the client to prepare a summary of what has been achieved so far. Clients who feel involved in the referral are likely to get the most out of the new relationship.

(Taken from Stewart, W. (2013). *An A–Z of Counselling Theory and Practice* p.392)

See also, Bayne, R., Horton, I., Merry, T., & Noyes, E. (1994). *The Counsellor's Handbook: A practical A–Z guide to professional and clinical practice*, London: Chapman and Hall.

CASE STUDY 4.2

Natasha (William speaking)

Natasha, a medical student, asks to see me, the college counsellor. She appears nervous and reticent, and it takes several sessions before she has enough trust in me to let me anywhere near her feelings.

Her presenting problem is that she says she has difficulty relating to other people in her year and this is affecting the grades she is getting.

Her background, the details of which have only slowly taken shape, is of a deprived, highly intelligent child from a broken home. Her mother appears to be a dominant woman with bizarre behaviour, such as leaving Natasha alone in the house for days without food. Natasha developed the habit of fantasising, so that her dolls and other playthings were real to her, and became a part of her world. This was so intense that she was more at home with her imaginary friends than with people.

This fantasy world waned a little while she was at secondary school, but now, in her first year at medical school, she was finding the pressure of contact with other people too stressful, and she was retreating more into her fantasy world.

In the fourth session, she starts talking about feeling controlled by various 'people' who live within her. These people make her act in strange ways, such as being very hyperactive. Another makes her spend, spend, spend, so much so that she is many hundreds of pounds in debt, usually for clothes she doesn't need.

She gives names to these four people, who are all famous in the pop world. Natasha never knows which of the four she will wake with, or which will emerge during the course of a day.

In this, her fourth session, she finally discloses the details of her 'four companions,' as she puts it, and says, 'You don't think I'm going mad, do you?'

William's response

Natasha, let me recap: you came because you feel uncomfortable with your fellow students, and you find it difficult relating to them. It took a long time for you to trust me with the intimate details of your life, which has been fairly traumatic and stressful. As a child, you drew comfort from imaginary people and you enjoyed a rich fantasy world. This didn't stop you doing well academically, but now you are here, it seems that the additional stress has made you withdraw into your inner world again, and now you're pressured by four people who seem to take over against your will. You've reached a stage when you feel you can't cope with what's happening, and this has raised doubts about your sanity. How does that sound, Natasha?

Natasha:	Very accurate, but it still doesn't answer my question: am I going mad?
William:	I don't want to hedge that question, yet I don't feel competent to give you an answer, either. Yes, I could say, 'Of course not, Natasha.' But somehow that might seem just like empty reassurance. I say that, because I'm in no way competent to make that judgment.
Natasha:	Why not, you seem fairly confident and competent to me?
William:	I work with people who have many sorts of problems, true, but what you seem to be asking me is the sort of question you need to be asking a doctor who is qualified . . .
Natasha [Interrupting]:	A psychiatrist, you mean?
William:	Yes, if that is what's required. And, although I have lots of relevant experience, I am not a psychiatrist; neither do I have the facilities and resources that would be available to a psychiatrist.
Natasha:	So that means you do think I'm mad.
William:	I hear your tremendous anxiety, Natasha, that if you do see a psychiatrist, he will confirm that you are mad.
Natasha:	Well, won't he?
William:	As I say, I'm not a psychiatrist, but I don't think they label people like that today. From my experience, they're more concerned with helping people to function at their optimum level. What would you say your optimum level would be, Natasha?
Natasha:	That's a good question. It's been so long since I've functioned at all, I've forgotten what it would be like to be free.
William:	At the moment then, you're feeling pretty low, not able to raise your head above water, as it were, and if somehow you could be freed from the various constraints, you would be able to find a new level to function at.

Natasha:	Yes, I can see your drift. You want to help me, but you're not qualified to, and the only people who can help are psychiatrists, and that means a mental hospital.
William:	It might, though again I'm not at all certain about that, either. The first step would be for us, and I mean us, to talk to the college doctor, and ask him to advise. What do you think about that?
Natasha:	Deep down I know you're right, but I'm terrified. You will come with me?
William:	Your terror comes through very strongly. Right now, you're all hunched up in the chair, just like a small child who is being frightened by some horror film on the TV. I'm also conscious that you feel very much alone and vulnerable. I feel quite protective toward you, so I guess that's a reflection of something happening between us. For me, it would feel wrong if I didn't do all I could to help in the transition from me to someone else. I would feel as if I was abandoning you, and I don't want to do that.
Natasha [almost crying]	Thank you. What do I do now?
William:	I'm going to suggest that I make a phone call to the doctor and request an urgent appointment. No, Natasha, stay, please, don't leave. Remember, we're doing this together.
William [on telephone]:	Hello, Doctor, this is William from the student counselling service. I have a female student with me who needs an urgent appointment to see you. She is here with me at present and I would like to come along with her. Can you see her soon? You can see her right away. That's great. Thanks, her name is Natasha.
William [to Natasha]:	You heard that, Natasha. The doctor will see us straight away. When we get there, how do you want to play this?
Natasha:	I don't know. I think I might dry up, I'm so nervous. Will you tell him?
William:	Yes, if that's what you want, certainly, but I don't want to take over, you know. Let's see how it goes and play it by ear.

Epilogue

The college doctor was sympathetic and understanding, though, like me, he didn't feel qualified to offer an opinion. Natasha let me do most of the talking, although I was able to draw her out a bit, without going into too much detail. The doctor, while Natasha and I were there, rang the psychiatric consultant to the college, who arranged to see Natasha with me and the doctor later that day.

Subsequent to that consultation, Natasha was admitted to a psychiatric unit for observation, medication and psychotherapy. She was there for three months, and then returned to the medical school, with provision for regular sessions of psychotherapy. She continued with her medication for several months.

I met Natasha on occasions in the canteen, though we never again entered into a counselling relationship. Natasha eventually completed her course of study.

Discussion

My own background in psychiatry suggested that Natasha was suffering from what was once called 'multiple personality disorder' (MPD), and is now called 'dissociative identity disorder' (DID). I considered it would be unprofessional of me to make a clinical diagnosis, as I am not a psychiatrist. Although I felt able to act as counsellor to Natasha, I lacked the medical backup necessary. It was difficult for me not to give in to Natasha's pleas of why couldn't she stay with me. It had been extremely difficult for her even to come for counselling, and equally difficult to start to build a relationship. This was one case I took to my supervisor, who was a psychiatrist, and it took some time before I worked through the feeling that I had betrayed Natasha.

SUMMARY

In this chapter, we have provided insight into setting the scene for the first session with a new client, together with examples of appropriate questions to ask to help put the client at ease and build trust. The importance of establishing clear boundaries has been emphasised; an example of a written counselling contract presented, and case studies designed to draw attention to specific topics being discussed included. The background to the 'fifty-minute therapeutic hour' has been explained, and note-taking and record keeping, referral issues and recording sessions, examined. In Chapter 5, we explore the next important stage – developing the skills to enable clients to explore their problems.

When love and skill work together,
Expect a masterpiece.

John Ruskin

REFERENCES

Stewart, W. & Martin, A. (1999). *Going for Counselling.* Oxford: How To Books.

Stewart, W. (2013). *An A–Z of Counselling Theory and Practice* (5th edition) Cengage Learning.

Helping the Client Explore the Problem (Part 1)

So when you are listening to somebody, completely, attentively,
then you are listening not only to the words, but also to the feeling
of what is being conveyed, to the whole of it, not part of it.

Jiddu Krishnamurti (Author),
You are the World: Authentic Report of
Talks and Discussions in American Universities

Having examined, in the previous chapter, various topics related to establishing a climate of safety and trust designed to enable counselling to start off on a good footing in the previous chapter, the next two chapters concentrate on the fundamentals of counselling – what the counsellor does to facilitate the counselling process. In this chapter, the spotlight is placed on basic skills used by counsellors to facilitate exploration of the client's problem: primary level empathy, active listening, attending, appropriate use of silences, paraphrasing, reflecting feelings, and open and closed questions. Examples of the skills in action are presented to augment learning, and pitfalls that can hinder client–counsellor communication are also given prominence.

Essentially, the core skills for a blossoming client experience are characterised by good listening skills on the part of the counsellor.

The principal listening skills used by the counsellor to facilitate exploration of the problem are:

- primary empathy
- active listening and attending

- paraphrasing content and reflecting feelings

- using open questions

- summarising (Chapter 6)

- focusing (Chapter 6)

- concreteness (Chapter 6)

PRIMARY LEVEL EMPATHY

To introduce you to the basic skills counsellors need to acquire to facilitate exploration of the client's issues, we start by examining primary empathy (the capacity to step into the client's shoes and step out again; to accurately perceive the client's internal world through the client's eyes). Empathy hinges on the quality of active listening. Empathy will not thrive in an atmosphere of imperfect listening. The client will intuitively know if we are listening by the quality of our responses and by how precisely we respond.

Empathic responding

Communicating empathy is central to active listening – hearing what the client says from their internal frame of reference and responding in such a way that the client knows and feels that the counsellor is striving to accurately understand their difficulties. Crucial to remember is that empathy is about distinguishing and acknowledging the client's frame of reference, not conveying our own.

Exercise 5.1

Self-test empathy exercise

Try to picture yourself in a situation when you felt:

1. Anger
2. Sadness
3. Joy
4. Fear
5. Embarrassment
6. Guilt
7. Hate
8. Confused
9. Bored
10. Inferior
11. Lonely
12. Rejected

- In each situation, try to become aware of what is happening in your mind, your body and your emotions. When you are aware of something happening, try to stay with it and not shrug it off.

- The more we allow our feelings to speak to us, the more self-understanding we shall gain and the more accurate will be our understanding of other people's feelings.

Exercise 5.2

Empathy exercise

This exercise follows on from the previous one.

- Take one of the words you worked with, perhaps the one that caused you the most pain.

- Write an imaginary letter to a close friend. Make it a factual one, without any feelings in it.

- Rewrite your letter, and for every fact you identify, include one or more feelings you associate with the fact.

- What is the difference between the two letters?

Primary level empathy in action

Client and counsellor talking.

Client 1:   I keep telling myself not to move too quickly with Jenny. She's so quiet, and when she does say anything, it's usually how nervous she is. It's obvious to me that when I say anything to her she gets fidgety and anxious, and then I wish I hadn't opened my mouth. It's like a checkmate. If I move I push her away, and if I don't move, nothing will happen between us, and I'll lose her anyway.

(Facts and feelings identified by counsellor: Anxious, catch-22, cautious, frustrated, protective, regret.)

Counsellor: George, you feel both protective of Jenny because you want to respect her pace, yet you also feel on edge because you're afraid that the relationship is not going anywhere.

Client 2:   I'm enjoying the work, and get on really well with my colleagues, but I am struggling to keep up with the long hours. I can't sleep – keep waking up at 4:30am, have lost my appetite, and am getting headaches.

(Facts and feelings identified by counsellor: Enthusiastic, stressed, exhausted, falling apart).

Counsellor: While on the one hand you like your job, and have a good relationship with your co-workers; on the other you are feeling the pressure from having to put in such long hours, which is making it difficult for you keep afloat and is taking a considerable toll on your overall well-being.

Knowing if empathy has been achieved

Client responses such as 'You've got it in one', 'that's it exactly', 'you've hit the nail right on the head', or 'that's it in a nutshell' generally indicate that the counsellor has accurately perceived the situation from the client's frame of reference.

ACTIVE LISTENING

Active listening is a powerful tool for improving understanding. It enhances mutual trust and respect; it demonstrates interest in the client and illustrates that you are keen to hear about, and grasp, the client's situation. The tools of active listening include, but are not limited to, attending, listening with an open mind, listening for meaning, listening beyond the words to hear the client's feelings, listening to the whole person, and observing the client's verbal and non-verbal signals for signs of possible conflict. Active listening is an art that requires much more than simply listening – it entails energetic use of our senses: our ears to hear, our eyes to see and our sense of smell, touch and taste to perceive the full picture. Perfecting the art of active listening implies constantly sharpening your tools.

The ultimate proof of active listening is effective responding

Sensitive, active listening is an important way to bring about personality changes in attitudes and the way we behave toward ourselves and others. When we listen, people tend to become:

- more emotionally mature
- more open to experiences

- less defensive
- more democratic
- less authoritarian.

When we are listened to, we listen to ourselves with more care and are able to express thoughts and feelings more clearly.

Self-esteem is enhanced through active listening, because the threat of having one's ideas and feelings criticised is greatly reduced. Because we do not have to defend, we are able to see ourselves for what we truly are, and are then in a better position to change.

Listening, and responding to what we hear, is influenced by our own frame of reference. Therapeutic listening is also influenced by one's theoretical model.

Examples of poor listening

Good listening can be affected by numerous factors – here are ten examples of poor listening that could affect client–counsellor interaction:

1. Not paying attention – wandering off at a tangent, daydreaming, clock-watching, preoccupation with other things/other client concerns.

2. Listening only for the facts and not hearing the client's feelings.

3. Pretend-listening – faking listening, acting interested while planning what to say next.

4. Selective listening – tuning in to elements of the client's story that interest you and filtering out the rest.

5. Listening but not hearing the meaning – missing the point, losing the gist.

6. Mental rehearsal – calculating how to respond before the client has finished talking.

7. Interrupting the client in mid-sentence – breaking the client's train of thought.

8. Second-guessing what the client is going to say next – predicting the client's next statement.

9. Appeasing the client to maintain harmony by agreeing with what she has said rather than sensitively drawing attention to identified cognitive distortions or negative thought patterns that could be preventing the client from moving forward.

10. Sidestepping difficult material – avoiding emotionally laden experiences, memories or words.

Internal and external obstacles to listening

Examples of internal listening blocks include:

- The listener wishes to 'do well' and constantly watches himself for a glowing performance.

- The listener is irritated by something the client says, and is caught up with her own emotions.

- The listener is afraid to listen, because of the responsibility involved, e.g. coping with the client's distress.

- The listener's attitude. For example, disapproves of the client's tattoos, body piercings, clothes or accent.

- The listener listens to his own expectations of what the client's problem is.

- Prejudice. Any 'ism's', e.g. racism, sexism. Listener stereotypes the client and fails to listen for differences.

- The listener's own thoughts are triggered by something the client has said.

- The listener concentrates too much on the problem rather than listening to the client's feelings about the problem.

- The listener is tired, especially if the client talks in a monotonous tone.

- The listener wants to rearrange the client's life to her own expectations.

Examples of external listening blocks include:

- Telephone ringing.
- Noise outside the room.
- Listener fidgeting.
- Listener looking at watch.
- Someone knocking on the door.
- Listener sighing, yawning.
- Room too hot or cold.
- Distractions – books, papers.

- Listener not concentrating on what the speaker is saying.
- Insufficient organised time to listen.

Listening with the third ear

Theodor Reik (1888–1969), a prominent psychoanalyst, and author of *Listening with the Third Ear: The Inner Experience of a Psychoanalyst* (1972) Arena Books, coined the term 'listening with the third ear' to emphasise the quality of psychotherapy, where active listening goes beyond the five senses. The 'third ear' hears what is said, as well as hearing what is not being expressed (the emotions behind the words – the sensations – the silent language expressed by the body, the client's internal experience).

Principles for third ear listening

- Have a reason or purpose for listening.
- Suspend judgment.
- Resist distractions.
- Wait before responding.
- Repeat verbatim.
- Rephrase the message accurately.
- Identify important themes.
- Reflect content and search for meaning.
- Be ready to respond.

An illustration can be drawn from music. Music is written on five lines and four spaces. A tune could be written only on the lines, but it would be dull and lifeless; it needs the spaces to give it life. So in listening, we need to be able to hear what is not being said, what is implied. In other words, we need to read what is in the spaces.

Contrasting good and poor listening

With effective listening, we communicate interest in the client, show respect for the client's thoughts, feelings and actions (i.e. unconditionally accept the client even though we may not concur with their beliefs, values or behaviour), and validate the client as a person of worth.

Listening demonstrates, it does not tell. Listening catches on. Just as non-constructive anger is typically greeted with antagonism, good listening cultivates enhanced listening.

Listening is a beneficial activity and the person who consistently listens with understanding is the person who is most likely to be listened to.

Amenable listening can bring about changes in attitudes and the way we behave toward others and ourselves. When we genuinely feel heard, we tend to respond in a more emotionally mature way, become more trusting, more open, more accepting, more independent. We listen to ourselves with more care, and can express our thoughts and feelings more clearly, free from fear of being judged or criticised, or erecting barriers to protect ourselves. We can shed our masks of pretence, discover our real selves and allow ourselves to become at one with who we truly are. Good listening feeds on itself – what we give out invariably flows back.

In contrast, poor listening has many unpleasant by-products. It can keep us stuck in a state of limbo, embarrassed to speak out, afraid to come out of our shell, ashamed to show who we really are, battened down emotionally, firmly anchored in the victim position, hurting inside, fearful of criticism, or shackled to painful unresolved issues or long-held hidden and toxic secrets. Poor listening is pervasive – it keeps us emotionally impoverished, vulnerable, and fearful of trusting, reaching out, rejection and intimacy.

Responding as a part of listening

Passive listening, without responding, is deadening and demeaning. We should never assume that we have really understood until we can communicate that understanding to the full satisfaction of the client. Effective listening hinges on constant clarification to establish true understanding.

Effective listeners:

1. Put the talker at ease.

2. Limit their own talking.

3. Are attentive.

4. Remove distractions.

5. Get inside the talker's frame of reference.

6. Are patient and don't interrupt.

7. Watch for feeling words.

8. Listen to the paralinguistics (utterances, manner of speaking, pitch, volume, intonation).

9. Are aware of their own biases.

10. Are aware of body language.

Knowing what to avoid

- When we try to get people to see themselves as we see them, or would like to see them, this is control and direction, and is more for our needs than for theirs. The less we need to evaluate, influence, control and direct, the more we enable ourselves to listen with understanding.

- When we respond to the demand for decisions, actions, judgments and evaluations, or agree with someone against someone else, we are in danger of losing our objectivity. The surface question is usually the vehicle that has a deeper need as its passenger.

- When we shoulder responsibility for other people, we remove from them the right to be active participants in the problem-solving process. Active involvement releases energy, it does not drain it from the other person. Active participation is a process of thinking with people, instead of thinking for or about them.

- Judgment – critical or favourable – is generally patronising.

- Platitudes and clichés demonstrate either disinterest or a verbal poverty.

- Verbal reassurances are insulting, for they demean the problem.

Conveying non-acceptance

Demonstrating unconditional acceptance of the client is crucial to the client's personal growth. Non-acceptance is characterised by:

- Advising, giving solutions – 'Why don't you . . .'

- Evaluating, blaming – 'You are definitely wrong . . .'

- Interpreting, analysing – 'What you need is . . .'

- Lecturing, informing – 'Here are the facts . . .'

- Name-calling, shaming – 'You are stupid . . .'

- Ordering, directing – 'You have to . . .'

- Praising, agreeing – 'You are definitely right . . .'

- Preaching, moralising – 'You ought to . . .'

- Questioning, probing – 'Why did you . . . ?'

- Sympathising, supporting – 'You'll be OK . . .'

- Warning, threatening – 'You had better not . . .'

- Withdrawing, avoiding – 'Let's forget it . . .'

Staying in tune with the client

Remaining on the same wavelength as clients involves entering the client's frame of reference (the client's internal world) and listening for total meaning of content and feelings, both of which require hearing and responding to. In some instances, the content is far less important than the feeling, for the words are but vehicles. We must try to remain sensitive to the total meaning the message has for the client:

- What is the client trying to convey?
- What does this mean to the client?
- How does the client see this situation?

Note all cues: not all communication is verbal. Truly sensitive listening notes:

- body posture
- breathing changes
- eye movements
- facial expression
- hand movements
- hesitancies
- inflection
- mumbled words
- stressed words.

Thinking and feeling

Trainee counsellors learn quickly that beginning sentences with 'I think' is bad form, so they preface their remarks with 'I feel' and go on to report thoughts. This use of 'I feel' often results in muddled communication. Thinking (head talk) seeks to explain interaction – the prose of communication. Feeling (heart talk) seeks to understand interaction – the poetry of communication.

Thinking:

- 'Think' statements refer to what the environment means to us.

- They attempt to define, assert, offer an opinion, rationalise or make cause-and-effect connections between different events.

- 'Think' statements are bound by the rules of logic and scientific inquiry; they may be true or untrue.

- A 'think' statement can generally be proved or disproved.

- 'Think' statements require words to be communicated.

- Most of us have been trained to make 'think' statements exclusively.

- We are constantly engaged in cognitive work: observing, inferring, categorising, generalising and summarising.

- Occasionally we report to others what goes on in our head.

- Frequently we are asked for:

    Facts: 'Where did you put the car keys?'

    Opinions: 'Which tastes better, French or Spanish wine?'

    Speculation: 'What happens when we achieve population saturation?', 'What are you thinking about?'

Humans like to think and our ability to do it is usually on the short list of characteristics that distinguish us from other species.

Feeling:

- 'Feel' statements refer to what is implied, internal affective, immediate, non-rational, emotional – a 'gut' response to something personal and distinctive happening within.

- Like dreams, 'feel' statements are neither true nor false, good nor bad; they can only be honestly or dishonestly communicated.

- Many of us have conditioned ourselves to screen out our internal reactions: we allow ourselves to say we feel 'interested', 'uncomfortable' but are scared to disclose our more intense feelings.

- By getting in touch with what is happening within us, we enrich our own lives and those with whom we communicate.

- Internal changes provide direct cues to the feelings we are experiencing: a change in bodily functioning – muscle tightness, restlessness, frowning, smiling, inability to stay with a conversation – tell us how we are reacting to what is happening.

Watch yourself when you say 'I feel that . . .' The 'that' is a tip-off that you are making a 'think' statement with a feel prefix.

Examples of thinking and feeling statements:

Example: 'I feel like having a drink.' **Rephrased:** 'I'm thirsty, so I think I'll have a drink.'

Example: 'I feel your brashness is a cover for your insecurity.' **Rephrased:** 'It's my opinion that you cover up your insecurity with brashness.'

Example: 'I feel that all men are created equal.' **Rephrased:** 'I believe that all men are created equal.'

Thinking and feeling – applying the principle

When responding to what a client says it is helpful to look at it in three parts: facts (these may be expressed or implied), expressed and implied feelings.

Paraphrasing deals mainly with the facts, so it might seem artificial to try to separate facts and feelings. However, the rationale for this is that the format suggested by Gerard Egan in *The Skilled Helper* makes use of the facts. 'You feel (an emotion) because (a fact).' This simplified version of what Egan says is a helpful way of working through various exercises.

If you read a statement or listen to something on radio or TV, and then break it down into facts and feelings, you will find that your listening skills are enhanced. The next stage would be to create, maybe, six or so short sentences: You feel—because—.

When you have worked through the statement, start to put it all together so that your response flows.

CASE STUDY

Listening to feelings – Mr and Mrs Shuttler face separation

This case study is included because it offers a simple four-part format for counsellors to analyse their own sessions.

Mrs Edith Shuttler, husband, Bernie, both eighty years of age. They are visited by a member of a pastoral team attached to the local churches.

Mrs Shuttler: Bernie's not very well; it's his arthritis, mostly in his legs and back. He was an engine driver on the railway you know.

Mr Shuttler: And she worked in the Post Office for nigh on thirty years. We've lived in this little terraced house, our own, you know, and in this village for sixty years, and staunch members of the Chapel. I brought you here as my bride, didn't I, Edith? Money-wise we're comfortable, with two work pensions plus the old age pension. Aye, it's not money. [pause] It's Edith, they told us six months ago that Edith only has a few months to live, lung cancer – rapid – they said, but now she can't do it all any more.

Mrs Shuttler: We've never bothered anybody until now, perhaps we've been too independent, but I'm worried about Bernie, how he'll manage this place. I've looked after the garden the last three years, because he couldn't. And then there's our dog, Patch, he's twelve, and Sam, the cat, he's three. We only have one son, Brian, he's fifty now, he's not married, lives in Australia. He never writes. He borrowed money from Bernie and has never paid it back. I don't think he cares about us any more. I don't know how Bernie will manage on his own, when I've gone. He's never been one much for housework, have you love? We've been married sixty years, next month, you know.

Mr Shuttler: Aye, we were just out o' the cradle, you might say, weren't we, Edith?

Mrs Shuttler: So you see dear, we've been together a long time, got to know each other's funny little ways. Who'd understand Bernie like me? We've never been parted, now I suppose somebody else will have to look after him, but who? You'd die if you had to go in one of those places, wouldn't you dear?

Mr Shuttler: And what about Patch and Sam?

Mrs Shuttler: If only Brian . . .

Mr Shuttler: Now dear, don't upset yourself. He'll not come back. I know you've prayed for that, but he's stubborn, and Australia's a long way.

Analysis

1. Mr and Mrs Shuttler are faced with having to cope with the trauma of a terminal illness.

2. They are suffering from alienation from their son Brian who could offer support.

3. They are both unwell.

4. They have each other for company.

5. They are reasonably well off.

6. They have had a lifetime of married memories.

7. They are anticipating separation.

8. They can share their sorrow of the parting.

9. Mr and Mrs Shuttler's ages are likely to work against the enforced change associated with terminal illness.

10. They have a firm faith in God.

Summary of working with Mr and Mrs Shuttler

1. Thoughtfulness in details

- Mobility.

- Possible reconciliation.

- Support during period of disengagement.

- Preparation for dying.

- Appropriate help without eroding their independence.

- Practical help with pets and garden.

2. **Privacy of the counselling session**

- The counsellor would have to decide whether to carry out counselling in the home. If so, and if the couple want to have separate sessions, privacy may become an issue.

3. **Engaging the client in specific goals**

- To help Mrs Shuttler to die with dignity.
- To help Mr Shuttler toward acceptance.

4. **Develop a flexible approach**

- Support Mr Shuttler during and afterward.
- Rally support from the community.
- Offer to mediate in a reconciliation with Brian, *if* they wish this.

Question: what have you learned from this case study and how could you use it in your own counselling?

(Adapted from Stewart, W. *An A–Z of Counselling Theory and Practice* (5th edition) Cengage Learning pp 296–398, and used with permission.)

SUMMARY

Listening is far from the passive state that some people think it to be. Active listening – as presented here – is a skill of great sophistication, which is available to all who would attempt to acquire and practise it. Words are vehicles for feelings, and feelings are the cement that holds together the bricks of a relationship. So it is essential to respond to both words (content) and feelings.

Responding is giving feedback, but not feedback that merely repeats what the person says – that is parroting, which is unconstructive.

Constructive, positive feedback is two-pronged; sincerely given, it can be a priceless gift to building the client's self-esteem and acknowledging the client's achievements and progress. Alternatively, while negative feedback may feel uncomfortable to give, if imparted sensitively and caringly, it has potential to facilitate the client's personal growth.

ATTENDING

The greatest gift you can give another is the purity
of your attention.

Richard Moss (Teacher and author)

Attending demonstrates that we are physically and emotionally available to the client. It involves giving the client our undivided attention – listening to the facts, and feelings, and paying attention to the client's body language.

Attending means concentrating and involves:

- Our body

  The way we sit: distance, angle of chairs

  A naturally open posture

  Demonstrating involvement and interest, by moving forward from time to time

  Maintaining comfortable eye contact

  Being aware of one's own facial expressions and body language

  Being relaxed, without slouching

- Our mind

  Thoughts uncluttered and focused

  Open attitude

- Our feelings

  To give full attention we must be secure, calm and confident. A disturbed spirit conflicts with attending. At some of the more dramatic moments of life, just having another person with us helps to prevent psychological collapse. Our face shows where our heart is.

When (though not necessarily during) counselling, counsellors should ask themselves:

- Was I effectively present and in emotional contact with this client?

- Did I give my whole attention or was part of it diverted?

- Did my non-verbal behaviour reinforce my internal attitudes?

- In what ways was I distracted from giving my full attention to this client?

- What can I do to handle these distractions?

Minimal encouragers

Minimal encouragers are single words, brief phrases or sounds that demonstrate to the client that you are fully attending. They are designed to encourage the client to say more, and to reveal to the client you are listening, interested and open to hearing additional information. Here are some examples of attending responses:

- Oh . . .
- And?
- Go on . . .
- Uh-huh
- Umm-hmmm
- I'm listening . . .
- And after that . . .
- Tell me more . . .
- But . . . ?
- Then?

Attending means total concentration. We can look as if we are attending, but our thoughts can be a thousand miles away. We may fool ourselves, but the other person will be intuitively aware that we have left to go on another journey. At some of the more dramatic moments of our life, just having another person with us helps us to feel in control, when otherwise we might collapse.

Silences

Silence is referred to in psychotherapeutic literature as:

- An indicator of resistance

- A necessary and productive part of the therapeutic process

- An intervention by the therapist

- An integrating process.

Silences enable the client to make associations and connections and engage in problem solving. Breaking the silence may interfere with what is happening within the client. The positive value of silences is stressed in the person-centred and humanistic approaches, as a means of adding depth to the relationship. Silence enables clients to hear what they and the counsellor have said, and releases the counsellor's attention to observe non-verbal behaviour.

Silence happens between people, rather than within one of them, and is an essential characteristic of the relationship. Silences may arise from resentment, by not having been listened to, being argued with, put down, or being given incorrect, mistimed or unacceptable interpretations.

In family therapy, 'dysfunctional silence' is used by one member of the family in order to sabotage change. Silence, on the other hand, is essential in techniques such as meditation, relaxation and imagery.

Therapists may have to work hard on their ability to tolerate silence. What could be a constructive silence is easily ruined by too quick an intervention.

One way of maintaining momentum, although it may seem a paradox, is the constructive use of silence. The silence that comes from blockage has already been mentioned. In that sort of silence, the counsellor may be able to help by suggesting something to the client, but the client should be given time to think and also to feel. So often, what could be a constructive silence is ruined by an over-anxious counsellor, unable to tolerate the silence, or possibly feeling that the client cannot tolerate it.

Silences may also arise as a result of the interaction between the counsellor and the client. Perhaps the counsellor has pushed the client too far, too quickly, thus causing alarm. In this instance, silence is a retreat. The client may feel resentful that they are not really being listened to. Perhaps they keep making a point that the counsellor keeps missing. Something the counsellor says may set up emotional vibrations that the client finds difficult to handle. Once again, they may retreat into silence. They may feel like saying something critical but do not want to hurt the counsellor, so they keep silent.

Broadly speaking, silences are of two kinds: positive and negative. In the first, the atmosphere is comfortable, like sitting with a friend by a nice log fire, sharing a meal. The other is full of tension and uncomfortable. In the former, movement forward usually presents no problem. A comment such as 'That feels really comfortable. I wonder what was passing through your mind just then?' may well open doors that hitherto have been barred.

With negative silences, it may be less easy to get things going again. It depends on what has created the silence. If we feel that we have wittingly or unwittingly caused the silence, we should say so. A moment's reflection may show us the reason. If not, a simple comment, 'We've gone quiet and I feel uncomfortable. I've a feeling that something I said has caused it. Am I right?' may prove to be just the thing to get things moving. If the client responds positively, this can provide a useful focus for movement. Even if the counsellor is unable to think what has caused the silence, taking the 'blame', as it were, may be a productive way of breaking the silence without too much trauma. Silences that are allowed to go on may demoralise both counsellor and client.

If we feel that the negative silence arises more from within the client than as a result of our intervention, again we may help to break out of this by a comment such as, 'This silence makes me feel—. Perhaps you're finding it difficult to put something into words?' This open approach then leaves clients free to choose how they will respond. It is possible that they may not have felt the silence as uncomfortable, and may seem surprised that the counsellor did. None the less, this too could lead to a fruitful discussion on feelings.

Silence as a minimal encourager

Just as each client's life experiences, feelings and beliefs are unique, so it is with counsellors – we each bring our lived experiences, training and casework experiences into the counselling arena. Diversity of experiences and divergent standpoints are healthy – they bring fresh perspectives, voices of experience that can be shared, and varied points of view to consider. While collaborative book-writing on a subject close to the authors' hearts can prove both interesting and stimulating it can inevitably raise a disparity of opinion. The real-life views that follow illustrate perfectly the authors' differing beliefs on the value of silence in counselling.

Use of silences (Jan's view)

In some instances, remaining quiet can be a valuable minimal encourager as it provides time and space for the client to think, feel and express. However, while some clients are comfortable with silences, others can feel threatened or intimidated by them. Thus, counsellors need to be extremely cautious about allowing long silences, particularly in the early stages of counselling when the client may be feeling fragile, vulnerable and exposed.

Tense silences can be very distressing, particularly for many trauma survivors, who could have spent years locked in a world of silence, and who may view the silent counsellor as threatening, authoritarian, all-powerful, remote – even abusive.

Reading the silence

Read the client's silence with your eyes and instincts – listen to its intensity – is it a golden silence? Does the client appear relaxed, calm and contemplative? Or is it a vociferous silence (sends shivers up and down your spine)? Does the client appear to be anxious, fidgety or looking as if she can't wait to leave? Trust your gut reaction. If you sense that the client is struggling with the silence, consider actively intervening to end the silence and put the client at ease or to prevent the client from 'suffering in silence'.

While the positive value of tolerating silences may be emphasised in some counselling traditions as sacrosanct to allow time for the 'penny to drop', it needs to be borne in mind that silences are only effective if the client feels comfortable with them. Leaving a client 'stuck in a threatening silence' is not only dispassionate, it may well drive the client to abandon counselling holding the belief that counselling is more harmful than helpful.

Use of silences (William's view)

On the one hand, we have to be careful that we don't interpret silences wrongly; for example as resistance, for they may be a necessary process to help the client integrate what has been said and perhaps gain some insight or deal with some deep emotion. Don't give the impression of being caught up by an express train. On the other hand, take note of the client who must always rush in and say something. Counsellors who are never silent deprive themselves and their clients of the opportunity to listen to the deeper meanings that lie beyond words. When silence is thought to be resistance or blocking, the counsellor may use a prompt, by repeating something previously said or by drawing attention to the nature of the silence. Some silences are as deep as communing with another spirit.

In closing this section on silence, it is worth repeating what was said earlier: do not be in too much of a hurry to break silences; do not feel that every gap in conversation has to be filled immediately with words. Some of the most constructive work is done in silence.

Attending responses in action with our five fictitious clients

1. *Pat:*   'It's really embarrassing to talk about what he did.'

   Jan: 'Embarrassing?'

Pat:	'Yes, you see, I think it was partly my fault . . .'
Jan:	'Please go on.'

2. *Paul:*   'I've tried getting another job and have sent off six application forms . . .'

William:	'And?'
Paul:	'And I've heard absolutely nothing, it's so . . .'
William:	'So?'
Paul:	'Disheartening. I almost feel like giving up.'

3. *Hayley:*   'I keep cutting and burning myself.'

Jan:	'Go on.'
Hayley:	'I feel so ashamed and disgusted with myself . . .'
Jan:	[Leans forward towards Hayley and remains silent.]
Hayley:	[Bursts into tears and says] 'I really hate myself, and I can't take much more.'
Jan:	'Can't take much more?'

4. *Ellen:*   'I felt so low when my Charlie died, but now . . .'

William:	'But now?'
Ellen:	'Well now I have met a kind and caring man who wants me to move in with him, but . . .'
William:	'But?'
Ellen:	'But I know my Charlie wouldn't approve – don't get me wrong – he wouldn't want me to be unhappy.'
William:	'Tell me a bit more.'

5. *Danny:*   'I keep losing my temper – that's the problem.'

Jan:	'Uh-huh.'
Danny:	'It's got me into trouble – I nearly got sent to prison.'
Jan:	'Sent to prison.'

PARAPHRASING

Paraphrasing refers to reflecting back the client's communication in your own words.

Paraphrasing can bring clarification. It means reflecting the content, mirroring the literal meaning of the communication.

Sometimes paraphrasing is necessary; at others, reflecting feelings is more appropriate. In every communication, words are vehicles for feelings, so it is essential to hear and respond to both content and feeling.

When listening, we focus initially upon the content. In doing so, we want to be sure that we have all the details of the client's experiences. Otherwise, we will not be able to help the client to understand them. *A paraphrased response will capture the main points communicated.*

Focusing on content

WHO? WHAT? WHY? WHEN? WHERE? HOW?
I keep six honest serving-men
(They taught me all I knew);
Their names are What and Why and When
And How and Where and Who.
Just So Stories, 'The Elephant's Child', Rudyard Kipling, (1902)

If we can supply answers to the above questions, we can be sure that we have the basic ingredients of the client's experience.

Useful formats for responding to content are:

'You're saying _____ '

or

'In other words _____ '

or

'It sounds as if _____ '

However, if not careful, such responses can sound stilted and stereotyped. Try to retain freshness.

Paraphrasing is not parroting

A paraphrase is a brief response, in the hearer's own words, that captures the main points of the content of what the other person has said. It may condense or expand what has been said. In general conversation, many assumptions are made about what has been said. Counselling is not an 'ordinary' conversation. *Effective paraphrasing is part of effective listening which ensures understanding.*

Words carry feelings, so not only is it necessary to understand the client's words, we must also try to understand why particular words, in preference to others, are used.

If clients have been expressing their thoughts with difficulty, then is a good time to paraphrase. Letting clients hear the meaning as understood by someone else may help them to clarify, more precisely, what they do mean. Paraphrasing may echo feeling words without responding to them. Here are some examples of paraphrasing responses:

- What I seem to be hearing is . . .

- So what you are saying is . . .

- So it's as though . . .

- In other words, what you're saying is . . .

- What appears to be coming across is . . .

- From what you have told me it seems as if . . .

- So, to paraphrase then . . .

- From listening to you, would it be correct to say that . . .

- So, in effect, what you are saying is . . .

Paraphrasing in action

Client and counsellor talking.

1. *Client:*   I used to . . . enjoy going out and having . . . fun. Now I have to really force myself, and I, I . . . don't enjoy myself any more. All the time I just have a, a . . . feeling of [longer pause] sadness. I'm not really part of the group any more.

(The key words and phrases here are going out; fun; force; sadness; not part of.)

Counsellor: In the past, Andrew, you had a great time socialising. Right now, however, you've lost your drive, and don't get much pleasure from going out and meeting people. For a lot of the time you feel down and flat and not really part of what's going on around you.

2. *Client:* I don't expect Sam to help with *all* the household chores, but he knows very well I need time to study for my nursing finals. I can't spend all my spare time cooking and cleaning and waiting on him hand and foot.

(The key words and phrases here are expect; chores; time; exams; hand and foot.)

Counsellor: Susan, you would like Sam to support you more, and take his share of the work around the house, so that you can find more time to study instead of running after him. You would like a bit more sharing.

To conclude our discussion on paraphrasing we continue our dialogue with our five fictitious clients, with the counsellor speaking to each of them:

Pat: 'So what you are saying is that you think you might be partly to blame for what happened . . .'

Paul: 'It sounds as if not getting any replies to your job applications so far is making you wonder whether it's worth bothering applying for any more . . .'

Hayley: 'From what you have told me it seems as though you are having a difficult time right now, and things are getting too much for you . . .'

Ellen: 'What you seem to be saying is that you think you would be letting Charlie down in some way if you accepted this man's offer . . .'

Danny: 'From my understanding, your anger is landing you in trouble, and the Magistrates' Court is concerned that if you don't learn to manage it constructively you'll end up in serious trouble . . .'

REFLECTING FEELINGS

Being in touch with, and connected to, our feelings and emotions is crucial to physical and psychological well-being, and many clients seek counselling to help them identify and work through distressing and difficult emotions – indeed, helping clients to recognise and process painful emotions is a key task for most counsellors.

Reflecting concentrates on the feelings within a statement. Paraphrasing and reflecting are invariably linked. In practice, it may be artificial to try to separate them. Reflecting feelings accurately depends on empathic understanding.

In listening to someone who is talking about a problem, neither pity nor sympathy is constructive. Both are highly subjective. Reflecting involves both listening and understanding and communicating that understanding. If our understanding remains locked up within us, we contribute little to the communication.

The ability to accurately reflect feelings involves viewing the world from the other person's frame of reference; thoughts, feelings and behaviours. Effective responding indicates a basic acceptance of people.

Reflecting does not act as a communication 'stopper' on the flow of talk, on emotions, or make people feel inadequate, inferior, defensive, or as though they are being patronised. Effective responses are made in language that is easily understood. They have a clarity and freshness of expression. Effective responses are accompanied by good vocal and bodily communication. Here are some examples of reflecting feeling responses:

- You feel . . . because . . .
- I sense that you feel . . .
- So you feel as though . . .
- The situation has left you feeling . . .
- I seem to be picking up a feeling of . . .
- Could it be that you are feeling . . .
- It seems as if you are feeling . . .
- You come across as feeling . . .
- You appear to be feeling . . .
- Perhaps you feel . . .

Keeping within the parameters of the client's comfort zone

Reflecting feelings essentially holds a mirror up to clients to help them clarify how they might be feeling, gives them space to sort out their feelings and, most importantly, affords the opportunity to gain relief from, or better control over, previously unexpressed emotions or feelings that have been tightly bottled up inside. **But beware** – encouraging clients who have deeply repressed and intense emotions due to early traumatic experiences (e.g. incest, child abuse, abandonment, neglect) to uncover their feelings too early on in the counselling relationship can lead to dire consequences, such as the client becoming overwhelmed with emotions, re-traumatised, or regressing (reverting to childlike behaviour in order to escape from, or cope with, their feelings). **To keep out of the danger feelings zone, stay firmly focused on working with surface feelings until the relationship is securely established, and the client has developed sufficient ego strength to face, and work with, and through, intense emotions.**

Listening for clues

Client comments such as those listed below can alert the counsellor to the client's difficulty with expressing feelings and emotions:

- Feelings weren't allowed in our family . . .

- I'm not sure how I feel about . . .

- I haven't got a clue how I feel . . .

- I don't know how to handle my feelings . . .

- I don't know what my feelings are . . .

- I don't do feelings . . .

- I feel numb . . .

- I've no idea how to express my feelings . . .

- I don't get emotional . . .

- I don't have words to express my feelings . . .

- I find it so difficult to express my feelings . . .

- I never get angry . . .

- It's a sign of weakness to cry . . .

Responding effectively to feelings

Choosing the right time to respond is important. To respond effectively:

- Observe facial and bodily movements.
- Listen to the words and their meanings.
- Tune in to your own emotional reactions to what the client is communicating.
- Sense the meaning of the communication.
- Take into account the degree of the client's self-awareness.
- Respond appropriately and so facilitate communication.
- Use vocal and bodily language that is congruent with each other.
- Check out the accuracy of your understanding.
- Use real, rather than stereotyped, language.

Examples of stereotyped responses:

- 'Thank you for sharing.'
- 'Am I on the right track?'
- 'Am I getting the picture?'
- 'Have a good day.'

Such phrases frequently pepper counselling literature, so much so that the word 'sharing' has lost much of its meaning. 'You have shared many deep feelings today' would be appropriate.

Reflecting feelings in action

Client and counsellor talking.

1. Client: I'm twenty-three, but I'll have to leave home soon. I'm not sure I'll cope though. Mum and Dad smother me, and can't see why I want to lead my own life.

(The key words are have to; cope; smother; own life.)

Counsellor: Alex, you sound confused and very uncertain that you would be doing the right thing, moving away from home. You feel suffocated by your parents, and want your independence, but it seems as if the price of this will be to separate from your parents.

2. Client: I'd just had enough of Dave. You should have heard the way he yelled at Emma. I mean, she's only ten months old. Did I do the right thing leaving? Should we try again?

(The key words are had enough; Emma; right thing; try again.)

Counsellor: Christine, what I hear is that you couldn't put up with Dave's behaviour any longer, but are possibly having some regrets about leaving him and are wondering whether to attempt reconciliation. At the same time, you are concerned for Emma's safety. You would like me to tell you what to do to resolve this conflict.

To conclude this section we demonstrate reflecting feelings responses with our five fictitious clients, with the counsellor speaking to each:

Pat: 'You say you feel ashamed about what happened because you think it might have been partly your fault . . .'

Paul: 'I can appreciate your feelings of despondency and disappointment when you have put so much effort into applying for jobs and haven't been offered an interview yet.'

Hayley: 'You mentioned earlier feeling ashamed, disgusted and hating yourself because you keep cutting or burning yourself. It sounds to me as if you are carrying around very strong feelings that are weighing heavily on you . . .'

Ellen: 'You feel you would be disloyal to Charlie if you accepted this man's offer to move in with him, yet you also state that he wouldn't want you to be unhappy . . .'

Danny: 'I can understand you feeling resentful because the Magistrates' Court has made you come, and because you think you have been given no choice in the matter.'

ASKING APPROPRIATE QUESTIONS

Basically, there are three types of questions: closed, tag and open questions. What is the difference?

Closed questions

Closed questions are useful for seeking factual information, or data gathering. They usually elicit a 'yes', 'no' or brief response. They are typically effortless to answer, and require little thought. They also keep the reins of the communication with the counsellor. For example:

- How old are you?
- What is your date of birth?

- Have you had counselling before?

- Are you married?

- Have you any children?

- Do you drink?

- Are you taking any medication?

- Did you suffer any form of abuse as a child?

- Do you, or have you, self-harmed?

- Do you get on well with your parents?

- Do you think counselling can help you?

While closed questions have their place in counselling, it's best to avoid them where possible, or at least to keep them to a minimum, for example, to check out needed specifics.

Tag questions

Tag questions refer to declarative statements or opinions turned into questions by adding a raised-tone 'question tag'. They aim to seek verification: 'Am I right?' or 'I'm sure you'll agree that . . .' – like closed questions they usually bring forth a 'yes' or 'no' reply or brief phrase, and keep the reins of the communication with the counsellor, thus discouraging open communication. Here are some examples:

- You will continue coming for counselling, won't you?

- You won't forget to complete your homework assignment, will you?

- You must admit that was a foolish thing to do, wasn't it?

- You have made a note of my holidays, haven't you?

- It would be good if you could stop that behaviour, wouldn't it?

- It's all right if I change the time of our next session, isn't it?

- CBT (cognitive behavioural therapy) might be helpful for some clients, but not for all, right?

- You don't mind if I open the window do you?

- You got a lot out of our last session, didn't you?

- I am convinced that long-term counselling is the most appropriate way to deal with your problems, aren't you?

An abundance of closed or tagged questions may cause the client to feel grilled, put on the spot, or uncomfortable.

Open questions

Open questions hand the reins of communication to the client. They are designed to help clients think, reflect, focus, elaborate or be more specific, and express their thoughts and feelings. Further, they are intended to encourage exploration, seek clarification, gauge feelings, establish mutual understanding, build rapport, and discourage a 'yes' or 'no' response. Open questions, which encourage the client to talk, are structured in a manner that enables clients to 'fill in the blanks', or assemble the 'missing pieces of the jigsaw'. Here are some examples:

- Earlier you mentioned . . . I wasn't quite clear what you meant . . . perhaps you could give me a specific example?
- What plans have you made for . . . ?
- What inspired you to . . . ?
- What's uppermost in your mind at the moment?
- What other topics would you like to discuss?
- What happened then?
- How do you feel about the situation?
- What other issues are important to you?
- What is your greatest fear about . . . ?
- What is the best thing about . . . ?
- Where does this fit on your list of priorities?
- What would you like to see change?
- What is the next step you need to take?

Important to be aware of is that open questions can be turned into closed questions when a statement is accompanied with:

- Could it be?

- Do you think/feel?

- Does this mean?

- Have you considered?

- Am I (would I be) right?

- Is that . . . ?

- Don't you think?

Using open questions with our five fictitious clients

Pat: 'What makes you think you were partly responsible for your dreadful ordeal?'

Paul: 'Can you clarify what type of jobs you have been applying for?'

Hayley: 'I appreciate that this might be hard for you, but I am wondering if you could try to put into words what situations or feelings trigger you to hurt yourself so I can attempt to understand . . . please take your time . . .'

Ellen: 'Although I understand how much you loved Charlie, just for the moment I am wondering, without being disrespectful, if it might help if you could leave him out of the equation to enable you to focus on your own thoughts and feelings about moving in with . . .'

Danny: 'I'm trying to grasp what's going on for you when your anger gets the better of you . . . one possibility that springs to mind is that losing your cool might be associated with feeling threatened in some way . . . please tell me if I am barking up the wrong tree . . .'

Other questioning traps to avoid falling into

1. Asking two or more questions at the same time, which creates confusion in the client's mind. Usually the client will answer the last question asked.

2. Wrongly timed questions that interrupt and hinder the helping process.

3. Asking too many questions, which may give the impression that we can provide solutions to other people's problems.

4. Bombarding the client with questions, which may give the impression of an inquisition.

5. Asking **prying questions** – which are asked out of your curiosity about areas not yet opened up by the client. 'Tell me exactly what he did when he abused you?'

6. Asking **limiting questions** – such as, 'Don't you think that . . . ?'; 'Isn't it a fact that . . . ?'

7. Asking **punishing questions** – the purpose of which are to expose the other person without appearing to, and put the person on the spot: 'With your vast experience you can answer the question, surely?'

8. Asking **hypothetical questions** – which are often motivated by criticism: 'If you were making that report, wouldn't you say it differently?' Such questions typically begin with 'If', 'What if', 'How about'.

9. Asking **demand or command questions** – which are designed to impress urgency or importance. 'Have you done anything about . . . ?'

10. Asking **screened questions** – which are designed to get the other person to make a decision that fits with your hidden agenda.

11. Asking **leading questions** – which manoeuvre the other person into a vulnerable position. Leading questions are often used in court to confuse or steer the witness's answer. 'Is it fair to say that you . . . ?' 'Would you agree that . . . ?'

12. Asking **rhetorical questions** – which forestall a response because the questioner fears the reply might not be a favourable one. Such questions attempt to secure a guaranteed agreement. No response is required: 'I'm coming for the weekend, OK?'

13. Asking **'Now I've got you' questions** – where the motive is to dig a trap for the other person to fall into 'Weren't you the one who . . . ?'

14. Making **statements that sound like questions** – 'You argue with your partner a lot, **don't you?**'

Asking appropriate questions can assist in clarifying something that is not quite clear. 'I don't understand. Do you mean . . . ?' will usually help the client by letting her see that the counsellor is still with her.

Questions should normally be based on material already provided by the client, rather than based on the counsellor's inquisitiveness. Facts may be necessary, but not to the extent that they impede the client from talking.

Questions should never intrude into the counselling process. They should always be a natural part of what is going on, and the client should always be able to understand the relevance of the question at the time it is asked. There is a time to ask a question and a time to not. (Stewart, 1983.)

For more on using questions, see http://www.counsellingconnection.com/index.php/2009/07/10/counselling-microskills-questioning/ and for a video on summarising and asking questions see https://www.youtube.com/watch?v=zoMnSHBq77I.

BRICK BY BRICK

Respond to what the person has said, rather than asking questions. Think of the counselling process as building a wall, brick by brick. The client makes a statement (brick one), followed by the counsellor's response (brick two), and so on. In this way, we do not rush ahead and cause anxiety by pushing indelicately into sensitive areas not yet ready to be explored.

CASE STUDY

Peter feels under stress

The situation

Bill works as a counsellor at the local health clinic. He receives a call from one of the GPs. 'Bill can you fit in one of my patients, Peter Allan? It's quite urgent.' Bill was waiting for another client, so he asked Peter to come in, and gave him an appointment after the next client. Bill noticed that Peter was looking tearful and tense. His hands were shaking. At the appointed time, Peter came in and sat down.

Peter's story

Age, thirty-four.

Personnel Manager in the NHS. Graduated from Keele University twelve years before, and has been in his present job for two years, having worked in local government before that. He married Alexis six years ago. They have one child aged four years. Alexis is six months pregnant.

Peter says, 'I don't think I can cope any more, that's the truth. There's my parents, miles away in Harrogate. Mum's not well and starting to lose her memory. Dad keeps ringing me and saying, "You're a bright lad, Peter, tell me what to do with Mum. I can't get her to eat." There's that, and the pregnancy, and Alexis is as moody as a yo-yo. Our sex life has gone down the chute. Then there's the mortgage. Of course, she would decide to live in the most expensive part of the village. And there's the job. That's been getting at me. Not sleeping properly, and I know I'm short-tempered and it's now affecting me at work, snappy with colleagues, and worst of all, interviewing people terrifies me. It all came to a head yesterday when I stormed out of a negotiation with some Union chaps. The GP thought you might be able to help.'

Response, paraphrasing content and reflecting feelings

'Things have been getting on top of you, parents, marriage, finance and job. It sounds as if you're afraid that you've blown things with what happened with the Union. It seems that everybody expects great things of you, but they don't see the stress you're feeling. Everything appears to be under threat, your job, marriage and health. You feel as if the world is collapsing around you, and yet nobody understands and they keep piling the pressure on. You feel torn between looking after yourself and your family, and the constant demands from your father. Maybe you wish you could be left alone. I think I hear some resentment when you say Alexis would want to live in the most expensive part of the village, as if that has been gnawing away at you. You also seem to be saying I've let myself down at work, as if people won't trust you any more, and that maybe you feel you can't trust yourself. You feel at the end of your tether.'

Examples of unhelpful, investigative questions

- What makes you think you can't cope? I mean, you're well qualified, and experienced.

- What exactly is wrong with your mother? How old are your parents? Couldn't they get help from Social Services?

- How did Alexis manage the first pregnancy?

- How much is your mortgage?

- What exactly is wrong with your sex life?

- Why did you decide to live just there?

- Had the doctor prescribed sleeping pills?

- How many people were at the meeting?

(Adapted from Stewart, William *An A–Z of Counselling Theory and Practice* (5th edition) Cengage Learning and used with permission.)

FINAL SUMMARY

This chapter has highlighted the basic skills used by counsellors to facilitate exploration of the client's problem. Predominantly we have focused on primary level empathy, active listening, attending, appropriate use of silences, paraphrasing, reflecting feelings, and open and closed questions. To enhance learning and counsellor competence, examples of the skills in action have been presented. Moreover, we have accentuated some potential pitfalls to avoid that can impede client–counsellor interaction. Our next task is to focus on the skills counsellors use to facilitate clients to be more specific about their difficulties; namely, summarising, focusing and concreteness.

> *The greatest compliment that was ever paid me was when one asked me what I thought, and attended to my answer.*
>
> Henry David Thoreau

Listen and watch on YouTube the audio files and videos from the Institute of Counselling, https://www.youtube.com/channel/UCd5TSm5vM7eWalHwhb-_O6Q

REFERENCES

Egan, G. (2007). *The Skilled Helper*, 8th edition (International Student Edition). CA: Thomson/Brooks Cole. This book is now in its 10th edition.

Reik, T. (1948). *Listening with the Third Ear: The inner experience of a psychoanalyst.* New York: Grove Press.

Stewart, W. (1983). *Counselling in Nursing.* London: Harper & Row.

CHAPTER 6

Helping the Client Explore the Problem (Part 2)

Don't let life discourage you; everyone who got where he is had to start where he was.

Ralph Waldo Emerson (1803–82)

This chapter builds on the basic listening skills covered in Chapter 5. It introduces you to three additional skills that enable clients to explore and clarify their issues effectively, namely, summarising, focusing and being concrete. Additionally, through a series of nine stimulating exercises, you are offered the chance to practise using the skills presented in this and the previous chapter. Seven exercises are designed specifically to develop your skills of primary level empathy, paraphrasing, reflecting feelings, structuring open questions, summarising, focusing and being concrete; the remaining two exercises focus on increasing your feelings vocabulary (to build a better emotional connection with clients) and to gauge your current status in terms of being an effective listener.

SUMMARISING

Summarising is a bit like making a précis of a document. It hinges on active listening, and also being able to pick up the main points and put them succinctly, capturing the essence of the statement. In a way, it is very similar to a combination of paraphrasing and reflecting feelings, yet without concentrating on any one issue.

Summarising is useful because it brings the session up to date, and helps the client to focus on the central issue or issues, as seen through the eyes of the counsellor. Summarising is helpful when either the client or the counsellor feels stuck; thus, it can provide opportunity for assessment and looking for new direction. It is also helpful at the start of a new session, although it is better for the client to do this, with prompts from the counsellor.

Summarising is the process of tying together all that has been talked about during part, or all, of the counselling session. It attempts to draw together the main threads of what has been discussed. It clarifies what has been accomplished and what still needs to be done.

Summarising is used to:

- Focus scattered facts, thoughts, feelings and meanings.

- Prompt the client to further explore a particular theme.

- Close a particular theme.

- Help the client to find direction.

- Help to free a client who is stuck.

- Provide a 'platform' to view the way ahead.

- Help the counsellor when feeling stuck.

- Help clients to view their frame of reference from another perspective.

Summarising enables the counsellor to get a better understanding of the client's view of things, and enables the client to see what progress has been made. When summarising, the counsellor should pull together the most relevant points, state them as simply and clearly as possible, and then check with the client the accuracy of the summary.

Summarising should not be overdone and should not be experienced by the client as an intrusion. Summarising may happen at any time during a session – it can be particularly valuable to highlight recurring themes. A summary at the end of a session is vital for several reasons. It gives the client an opportunity to hear again the main points; it gives the counsellor an opportunity to clarify and consolidate her understanding of what has taken place; it provides an opportunity for both, and particularly the client, to think about the next session.

(Paraphrased from Stewart, W. (1983))

The aim of summarising

- To outline relevant facts, thoughts, feelings and meanings.

- To prompt further exploration of a particular theme.

- To close the discussion on a particular theme.

- To help both counsellor and client find direction.

- To move the interview forward.

Summarising should:

- be simple, clear and jargon-free

- be checked for accuracy

- catch the essential meanings.

CASE STUDY

Jane, aged twenty

Jane says:

> I have strong religious beliefs that sex outside marriage is wrong. Alan has tried to persuade me to have sex because he would like me to have a baby. He has told me if I have a baby, he will be sure that I am truly in love with him. But the whole idea of having a baby outside marriage is too much for me. Alan says he is not ready for marriage and settling down yet, and I would like to carry on with my career in teaching. If I do what he wants I'm not being true to myself, and if I don't I'll probably lose him.

Counsellor:

> Jane, you seem very confused with all that's happening in your life right now *[empathic responding]*. Alan wants you to have a baby, but you're not sure about that. It's important for you to be married before you consider having a family, but Alan doesn't think the same way. For the moment, you would like to continue with your teaching career because that is important to you. You are afraid if you stick to your principles, Alan might end your relationship.

Examples of summarising responses

- Let me see if I can sum up the main points that you have talked about today.

- Perhaps we can take a look at what we have seen so far?

- So, to recap then . . .

- Can we hold things there for a moment and go over what you have just said?

- Perhaps it might help if I encapsulate what I think I am hearing?

- Let me just check that I understand you correctly.

- Let's see if we can pull a few threads together here.

- We've covered a lot of ground in this session and we only have ten minutes left. Perhaps it would help to précis what's been discussed. Maybe you could summarise what you see as the key topics we've covered.

Summarising in action

To conclude this section we use summarising responses with our five fictitious clients.

Pat responds to open question with:

> Well, we both had too much to drink and he offered to escort me home. I asked him in for coffee and well . . . he . . . he . . . raped me.

Counsellor responds with:

> Pat, can I check out that I understand you correctly? What I hear you saying is that both of you were worse the wear from alcohol, and when he took you home you invited him in for coffee, and it ended up with you being raped . . . and you feel in some way that you are to blame for what happened by inviting him into your home.

Paul responds to open question with:

> Well, I've applied for three posts as manager for different engineering companies, and three for the position of supervisor with manufacturing plants. I don't have much experience in anything else.

Counsellor responds with:

> Paul, can we recap on what you have told me so far? You have applied to three engineering firms for the post of manager and to three manufacturing plants

for the post of supervisor. You feel your experience in other fields is somewhat limited, and this may be holding you back?

Hayley responds to open question with:

It's really difficult to explain . . . things build up and up and I get totally overwhelmed with feelings but I can't tell you what the feelings are, or . . . I feel . . . totally numb . . . unreal . . . like it's not me . . . can't feel anything . . . I just know I have to do something to stop the horrible feelings and . . . cutting myself is the only thing . . . the only thing that ends the feelings . . .

Counsellor responds with:

Hayley, can I reiterate what you've said to ensure I've got things clear in my mind, and to check out that I understand you correctly . . . there seems to be two reasons that drive you to injure yourself . . . either you feel completely crushed by unbearable feelings that you can't put a name to, or you feel absolutely nothing . . . as if you are not part of this world . . . not yourself . . . or someone else has taken you over . . . and cutting yourself is the only answer you know of, to relieve these alarming feelings . . .

Ellen responds to open question with:

In many ways, I would like to move in with Peter. I really enjoy his company and he has a great sense of humour – he really makes me laugh. He's ever so kind too; nothing is too much trouble, and he says he loves me a lot. But, I can't stop thinking what my Charlie would think of me – I'm sure he wouldn't like me living with another man.

Counsellor responds with:

Ellen, it sounds like you are torn between the devil and the deep blue sea. To make sure I have the picture straight, let me just restate what I hear you saying . . . A big part of you would like to share your life with Peter because he loves you, is kind and considerate, fun to be with, and has brought a ray of sunshine back into your life, but . . . and it's a big but . . . you are in total dilemma because you think Charlie might not approve of you living with another man.

Danny responds to open question with:

Well, it was a Friday night, and I'd had a few – as you do – and there was a fight at the club, and I lobbed a chair at a guy. It hit him on the head and he was hauled off to hospital to get his wounds stitched up. The Old Bill arrived and I hurled a bit of verbal at them, so they arrested me and banged me up in a cell, telling me to calm down and sleep it off. Next morning I was up before the beaks on a charge of ABH (actual bodily harm).

Counsellor responds with:

Danny, can I briefly recount what you have just said . . . you'd been on a Friday night drinking binge, got involved in a brawl, lost your rag, lashed out, and a chap got injured. The police took you into custody because you attacked them verbally; you were locked up overnight, and charged with actual bodily harm in court the following morning.

FOCUSING

- Focusing helps the client get to grips with a complex situation by teasing out details and exploring specific parts in depth.

- Focusing helps the client look beyond the problem to possible solutions or alternatives.

- Focusing helps both client and counsellor not to get lost.

- Focusing involves a certain degree of direction and control by the counsellor, which has to be carefully used.

Principles of focusing:

- If there is a crisis, first help the client to manage the crisis.

- Focus on issues that the client sees as important.

- Begin with a problem that seems to be causing the client pain.

- Focus on an issue that the client is willing to work on, even if it does not seem important to you.

- Begin with some manageable part of the problem.

- Begin with a problem that can be managed relatively easily.

- When possible, move from less severe to more severe problems.

- Focus on a problem where the benefits will outweigh the costs.

- Make the initial experience of counselling rewarding as an incentive to continue.

- Work for something with quick success.

- Work from the simple to the complex.

Underlying focusing is the client's need to feel some reward and some hope. Focusing implies a certain degree of direction and guidance of the exploration and not everything can be worked out at once.

Focusing uses specific questions to tease out detail and to explore particular topics in depth. There needs to be a focus in the helping process, around which the resources of the client can be mobilised. Focusing helps client and counsellor to find out where to start or, having started, in which direction to continue.

When clients are suffering from high stress levels, or have a 'lot on their mind', it can limit their powers of concentration, and restrict their ability to think and communicate clearly and cohesively. They may speak rapidly or disjointedly, digress, go round in proverbial circles, or jump from subject to subject without coming up for air. Here is an example of not joined up/scattered thinking:

> I just don't know what to do . . . my mum's poorly and . . . the girls won't give me a hand with the housework, my friend's coming to stay for a week . . . I really ought to spend more time with my mum . . . I must remember to take my library books back . . . I don't ask much of the girls . . . I must check what time my friend's flight arrives . . . no idea what we're going to have for dinner tonight . . . maybe it would be better if Mum came to stay with us . . . I must put the washing machine on . . . I wonder what's on TV tonight . . .

When clients speak in a jumbled fashion, or it becomes blatantly clear that their head is 'spinning', applying the skill of focusing can work wonders in slowing the client's thoughts from racing at a hundred miles an hour. Focusing implies a certain degree of counsellor direction and guidance of the exploration. The aim of focusing responses is to help the client keep on track, or get them back on track if they are wandering off on a tangent or losing the thread. Clients often need help to get to grips with complex issues. Focusing uses specific questions to tease out detail, and to facilitate prioritisation of issues.

Examples of focusing responses

- You mentioned . . . then you said . . . also you brought up that . . . These all seem to be important issues. Maybe it would help to pick them apart a bit . . .

- So you have identified that . . . also that . . . it seems as if the most pressing issue is . . . would it help to focus on that first?

- What I am hearing is that . . . and . . . are having a profound effect on you. Maybe it would be useful to focus our attention on each of these concerns separately?

- Was it before . . . or after?

Examples of using the principles of focusing

Examples

1. Carol, in her mid-thirties, was left a widow eighteen months ago. She is experiencing financial difficulties. A male friend has suggested she lives with him. This means moving some distance away. Her children do not want to move.

All of these issues are important; some of them need longer work. Helping Carol get the finances sorted out would be the most practical, and release energy to deal with some of the other issues.

Response

I've heard what you've been saying, and there is a lot there. It seems as if the main strands are . . . Which do you think is the most urgent issue to explore first?

2. George, aged eighty, is dying of cancer. As the pastoral counsellor, Anne, listens to him, she picks up George's concern for his wife. At the same time, she detects underlying fears about his own death, fears he is not admitting to.

Anne's response

George, I hear a number of issues you would probably like to talk about, not necessarily right now. My hunch is that the one you would like to spend time talking over is your concern for your wife, and how she is managing.

Types of response

The 'contrast response'

The term 'contrast response' describes a marked awareness of the differences between two conditions or events, which results from bringing them together. 'If you think about staying in your present job, or moving to another job, what would it be like then?'

Example

The counsellor says, 'Carol, perhaps we can take a look at what we have seen so far. Your husband died eighteen months ago, and since then you have had financial worries. Fred has asked you to go and live with him. However, this means moving away from the area and your children are very reluctant to go. If you think about your life as it is now, and then think about Fred's offer to live with him, what differences do you think it will make?'

The 'choice-point response'

The term 'choice-point' describes any set of circumstances in which a choice from among several alternatives is required. 'From what you've said, it looks as if these are the major issues (itemising them). Which of these would you feel most comfortable working with first?'

Example

The counsellor says, 'Carol, let's pull a few things together here. Sadly, your husband died eighteen months ago, and you are left with the children to cope with on your own. Fred has asked you to move in with him, but your children are opposed to the idea of moving away. You are also very concerned about how you are managing financially. It seems as if there are a lot of separate issues we could talk about, and I'm wondering which one you would like to focus on first?'

The 'figure-ground response'

The term 'figure-ground' describes how a person perceives the relationship between the object of the attention or focus, the figure, and the rest of what is around, the perceptual field, the ground. The figure generally has form or structure and appears to be in front of the ground. The figure is given shape (or form) and the background is left unshaped and lacking in form. 'These are the various points of the problem; it seems to me that the most worthwhile to address first could be the need for you to get a job. How do you feel about that?'

Thus, figure-ground focusing helps to give one part of the problem shape and form and so helps the client to more readily grasp hold of something and work with it.

Example

The counsellor says, 'Carol, can we stop for a minute and look at what you have told me so far. First, there's the issue of managing your finances. Second, there's the issue of whether you should live with Fred. Third, there's the issue of your children not wanting to move away from the area. I noticed when you mentioned your financial situation that you looked extremely anxious, and my feeling is that working on the finances might be beneficial to begin with. How does that sound to you?'

When working on any of the above techniques, the choice is best put last, otherwise it becomes lost. There should be no further exploration after you have invited the client to consider a particular response. The specific response should be the last thing the client hears, and so responds to.

- Step 1: ask the client to use just one word to describe her problem.

- Step 2: ask the client to put the word in a phrase.

- Step 3: put the phrase into a simple sentence that describes the problem.

- Step 4: ask the client to move from a simple sentence to a more detailed description.

This is a simple technique to bring a session into focus, and can be used at any stage or step of the helping process. For instance, clients can be asked to use one word to describe what they want.

Leverage questions that you can help clients ask themselves

- What problem or opportunity should I really be working on?

- Which issue, if faced, would make a substantial difference in my life?

- Which problem or opportunity has the greatest payoff value?

- Which issue do I have both the will and the courage to work on?

- Which problem, if managed, will take care of other problems?

- Which opportunity, if developed, will help me deal with critical problems?

- What is the best place for me to start?

- If I need to start slowly, where should I start?

- If I need a boost or a quick win, which problem or opportunity should I work on?

Helping the client focus is one way of moving the interview forward, and helps to prevent stagnation.

Going over old ground, and old feelings, might mean that the client needs to gain fresh insight; it might also mean that the client lacks awareness, and that is where focusing comes in. Focusing is a way of providing a structure, a way of cutting through the emotional jungle.

Focusing responses with our five fictitious clients

Counsellor responds to Pat with:

You told me you were raped by this man, and that you feel you may have brought it on yourself in some way. There appear to be two issues here, and it seems as if being raped is causing you a great deal of distress. How would you feel about exploring that issue first? *(figure-ground)*

Counsellor responds to Paul with:

You mentioned that you have applied for six different jobs without success, and you feel your lack of experience in areas other than engineering and manufacturing might be a stumbling block. Perhaps it might be helpful to focus on one specific issue. What would be most helpful for you to talk about first? *(choice-point)*

Counsellor responds to Hayley with:

You have shared with me some of the feelings you get before you harm yourself. You have also told me that these feelings won't go away, and that you feel compelled to cut and burn yourself as a way of escaping from these awful feelings. When you spoke about cutting yourself, I noticed you rubbing the scar on your wrist, which looks very painful and raw. I wonder whether it would help to talk about that scar and what it means to you? *(figure-ground)*

Counsellor responds to Ellen with:

You say that a big part of you wants to share your life with Peter, but you feel Charlie would disapprove, and this leaves you feeling that you would be disloyal to him in some way. There seem to be a lot of painful issues we could talk about, Ellen, and I'm wondering which one it would be most helpful for you to talk about first? *(choice-point)*

Counsellor responds to Danny with:

Danny, from where I am sitting there seem to be many issues involved here. First, there's the issue of your anger, which you seem to have difficulty controlling. Second, there's the issue of your drinking, which seems to spark your anger. Third, there's the issue of injuring someone as a result of not being able to control your anger, and fourth there's the issue of having a criminal record and how this might affect your life in the future. If you could look ahead a bit, how different would you like things to look for you in the future? *(contrast)*

BEING CONCRETE TO HELP THE CLIENT BE MORE SPECIFIC

Being concrete means enabling clients to be concrete or specific, which at times can be quite difficult, yet is essential if they are to come to terms fully with whatever is causing them concern. The opposite of being concrete, direct and specific is making 'generalised', indirect and vague statements. So often, in general conversation, as well as in counselling, we confuse the issue by not being concrete, specific and direct. A generalisation does not discriminate; it lumps all parts together.

A generality common in everyday speech is 'you'. Clients who say, 'You never know when people approve of what you're doing', when encouraged to rephrase it to, 'I never know when people approve of what I'm doing', will usually be able to perceive their statement in a different light. The client needs to be able to identify thoughts, feelings, behaviour and experiences in specific ways. Personalising a statement in this way makes it pertinent and real. In one sense, it is owning the problem. Being specific opens the way for a realistic acknowledgement of feelings.

The opposite of being concrete – direct and specific – is making generalised indirect and vague statements. So often, in general conversation, as well as in counselling, we confuse the issue by not being concrete, specific and direct.

Counsellors who themselves speak in generalities would find it difficult to demonstrate being concrete.

Overcoming client resistance

Owning, and not merely reporting, such feelings, opens the door to exploring them. While this may be uncomfortable for the client, it is vital. Sometimes thoughts, feelings and behaviours are expressed before the counselling relationship has been established firmly enough to explore them. If such thoughts, feelings and behaviours are central to the client's problem, the client will return to them at some stage. Concreteness requires clients to be prepared to examine themselves closely, and not to hide behind the facade of generality.

Clients may fiercely resist attempts to encourage them to be specific, particularly about feelings. They may have to be led gently into what, for many, is a new experience. Counsellors can collude with clients by allowing them to talk about feelings second-hand, as if they belonged to other people and not to them. 'Is this how *you* feel?' or 'Is that something like *your* situation?' (even though both of these are closed questions) may be enough to bring the interview back into focus from second-hand reporting, to 'This is what is happening to me, *now.*'

Questions to aid concreteness

Elaboration questions

Elaboration questions give the client the opportunity to expand on what has already been talked about. For example:

- 'Would you care to elaborate?'

- 'What else is there?'

- 'Could you expand on what you've just said?'

- 'Can you think of anything else that might be contributing to the problem?'

Specification questions

Specification questions aim to elicit detail about a problem. For example:

- You've referred to your propensity to . . . can you be more specific?

- In what way, precisely, is the situation causing you concern?

- Can you give me a specific example of what he says that upsets you?

Focusing on feelings questions

Focusing on feelings questions aim to elicit the feelings generated by a problem area. For example:

- How does that leave you feeling?

- Can you describe exactly how you are feeling?

- How do you feel about that?

- Can you name the feeling?

- Could it be that you are feeling . . .

- Your body language suggests that you might possibly be feeling . . . I'm wondering if that's close to the mark or whether I am way off beam . . .

- You seem to be really struggling to try to explain in words how you feel. I could be barking up the wrong tree, but the impression I am getting is that you might possibly be feeling . . .

Personal responsibility questions

Personal responsibility questions imply that the other has a responsibility not only for owning the problem, but also for making the choices that contribute to solving it. For example:

- You say that you have tried . . . is there anything else you can think of that could help you achieve your goal?

- You mentioned that you and your partner are always arguing. Thinking about your most recent quarrel, to what extent do you think you might have contributed to it?

- Have you considered any action you could implement that would improve the situation?

- You say that people walk all over you. What do you think you could do to prevent people treating you like a doormat?

Examples

Mavis, to Marion, the works supervisor

Mavis *[generalised and vague]*: 'I know I haven't been very regular at work recently, I haven't been very well. That's the truth of it.'

Mavis *[concrete and specific]*: 'I know that over the past month I've been off work six times. I've been attending the doctor for about six months with vague abdominal pains. They haven't yet reached a firm diagnosis, but they think it's probably something to do with the gall bladder.'

Robert, to Joy, the school counsellor

Robert *[generalised and vague]*: 'People keep picking on me.'

Robert *[concrete and specific]*: 'My classmates pick on me because I wear glasses.'

Trudy, student teacher, to Liz, her supervisor

Trudy *[generalised and vague]*: 'I know I'm dreadfully inconsistent in my work.'

Trudy *[concrete and specific]:* 'I make all sorts of teaching plans, yet when it comes to the day, I don't stick to them. I think the students run the class, not me.'

Being concrete and specific with our five fictitious clients

Counsellor to Pat: You say you feel you may have brought the rape on yourself in some way. To help me understand, can you be more specific? *(specification question)*

Counsellor to Paul: You say that have applied for six different jobs and haven't had any replies. How has this left you feeling? *(focusing on feelings question)*

Counsellor to Hayley: Can you talk me through what thoughts are going through your mind just before you cut yourself? *(elaboration question)*

Counsellor to Ellen: You have told me that a large part of you wants to share your life with Peter. Can you say precisely what it is that appeals to you about living with him? *(specification question)*

Counsellor to Danny: Danny, you say that you injured a guy, and this happened after you had been on a drinking binge. How much do you think your drinking contributed towards you getting angry and aggressive? *(personal responsibility question)*

Summary

To help the client explore the problem the counsellor uses the skills of:

- primary level empathy
- active listening
- attending
- paraphrasing content
- reflecting feelings
- using open questions
- summarising
- focusing
- concreteness.

Exercises

Presented next are nine exercises designed to enable you to practise the skills discussed. Below is a suggested framework on how to formulate your responses for the case study exercises.

1. Read each sentence in the case study carefully.

2. Identify the facts.

3. Identify the expressed feelings.

4. Identify the implied feelings, those that lie beneath the surface, those that are being hinted at, those that strike a chord within you.

5. Think of as many words as possible to describe the feelings.

6. Put the whole lot together in one response.

Exercise 6.1

Primary level empathy

Case study 1 – Julie

Julie says, 'It's difficult here tonight; I can't seem to get involved with the group. We've been going an hour, and everything has been so painful. I'm not up to it right now. I get the impression that all my friends' relationships are parting at the seams, and when that happens here in the group too [pause] well, I'd like to be understanding and accepting, and all that, but I'd rather run away right now.'

- Identify the feelings, and then outline a response of about four to six lines.

Primary level empathy

Case study 2 – Margaret to Keith

'Keith, you're usually warm and accepting with me, but I'm still not sure of where I stand with you. I guess I want you to be affectionate with me, and that's not you. Maybe what I'm saying is that I need a lot of attention. I know that whenever I say something, I expect you to understand how I'm feeling. I'm wondering now if I've been putting too many demands on you?'

- Identify the feelings, and then outline a response of about four to six lines.

Primary level empathy

Case study 3 – Matthew

Matthew says, 'Six months ago, I wouldn't have dreamed I'd be saying what I'm about to say, to one person, maybe, but not to a group of people. That says a lot for what I feel about this group. I want you to know, I'm gay. Knowing that about me may help you understand the way I react. But more than that, I'm uneasy about my sexuality. It bothers me and makes me uncertain about who I am. That's the uncertain chap you see here. I think I can say this now because I trust you to understand me and not to think of me as a problem person who needs help.'

- Identify the feelings, and then outline a response of about four to six lines.

This concludes the primary level empathy exercises. Turn to Appendix 2 for suggested responses.

Exercise 6.2

Listening

Read each statement carefully and assess whether the client feels listened to or not listened to. Place a tick in the space you think is correct.

	Listened to	Not Listened to
1. You cut me off and start telling me about your experiences.	___	___
2. You accept me as I am – warts and all.	___	___
3. You don't hide behind barriers.	___	___
4. You want to solve my problem for me.	___	___
5. You try to grasp my meaning when I feel confused.	___	___
6. You resist the temptation to give me good advice.	___	___
7. You hand me back the compliment I have given you.	___	___
8. You resist telling me that funny joke you are dying to tell me.	___	___
9. You get embarrassed and avoid what I want to say.	___	___
10. You need to feel successful.	___	___
11. You allow me to express my negative feelings towards you without becoming defensive.	___	___
12. You give me your undivided attention.	___	___
13. You make judgments about me because of my language, grammar or accent.	___	___

14. You do not judge my beliefs even when they conflict with yours. _____ _____

15. You gaze out of the window. _____ _____

16. You trust me to find my own solution to my problem. _____ _____

17. You plan my action for me, instead of letting me find my own action. _____ _____

18. You allow me time to think, feel and express. _____ _____

19. You tap your fingers on the arm of the chair. _____ _____

20. You speak with enthusiasm and at an appropriate volume. _____ _____

21. You choose an appropriate time to respond. _____ _____

22. You do not look at me when I am speaking. _____ _____

23. You enable me to make my experience feel important. _____ _____

24. You keep fidgeting. _____ _____

25. You keep looking at your watch. _____ _____

26. You look down your nose at me. _____ _____

27. You say you understand before you have heard what I have to say. _____ _____

28. You have a solution to my problem before I have had the opportunity to explore my problem fully. _____ _____

29. You interrupt me before I have finished talking. _____ _____

30. You are not aware of the feelings behind my words. _____ _____

31. You look directly at me, and face me. _____ _____

32. You use open and appropriate gestures. _____ _____

33. You quietly enter my internal world and try to grasp how it feels to be me. _____ _____

34. You allow me to express myself even if you don't agree with my language. _____ _____

35. You accept my gift of thanks. _____ _____

36. You don't preach morals or condemn me for
    my behaviour.   _____   _____

37. You are interested in everything I have to say.   _____   _____

38. You spend an hour with me and make that time feel
    very special.   _____   _____

39. You do not laugh at me, or ridicule me.   _____   _____

40. You are kind, gentle and encouraging.   _____   _____

41. You try to understand me because you really care.   _____   _____

42. You try to help me become liberated from the destructive
    barriers I have erected with sensitivity and gentleness. _____   _____

43. You lean towards me and tilt your head.   _____   _____

44. You cross your legs and fold your arms.   _____   _____

45. You talk at me instead of talking with me.   _____   _____

This concludes the listening exercise. Turn to Appendix 2 for the answers.

Exercise 6.3

Paraphrasing

Case study 1 – Alex

Alex says, 'I'm twenty-three, but I'll have to leave home. I'm not sure how I'll cope though. Mum and Dad smother me, and can't see why I want to lead my own life.'

- Outline a paraphrase. First of all, identify the key words or phrases, and then write down your response.

Paraphrasing

Case study 2 – James

James says, 'I want to take up nursing but my mates are giving me a hard time, they say it's only a job for women and gays, not real men. It's the job for me though. What should I do?'

- Outline a paraphrase. First of all, identify the key words or phrases, and then write down your response.

This ends the paraphrasing exercises. Turn to Appendix 2 for suggested responses.

Exercise 6.4

Reflecting feelings

To enable us to reflect feelings it helps to develop a wide vocabulary of feeling words. List four alternative words or phrases for the statements given below.

I feel abandoned   *You feel* _____ _____ _____ _____

I feel afraid   *You feel* _____ _____ _____ _____

I feel aimless   *You feel* _____ _____ _____ _____

I feel angry   *You feel* _____ _____ _____ _____

I feel anguished   *You feel* _____ _____ _____ _____

I feel antagonistic   *You feel* _____ _____ _____ _____

I feel anxious   *You feel* _____ _____ _____ _____

I feel appreciated   *You feel* _____ _____ _____ _____

I feel apprehensive   *You feel* _____ _____ _____ _____

I feel ashamed   *You feel* _____ _____ _____ _____

I feel bitter   *You feel* _____ _____ _____ _____

I feel bored   *You feel* _____ _____ _____ _____

I feel confused   *You feel* _____ _____ _____ _____

I feel delighted   *You feel* _____ _____ _____ _____

I feel depressed   *You feel* _____ _____ _____ _____

I feel devastated   *You feel* _____ _____ _____ _____

I feel doubtful   *You feel* _____ _____ _____ _____

I feel energetic   *You feel* _____ _____ _____ _____

I feel envious   *You feel* _____ _____ _____ _____

I feel embarrassed   *You feel* _____ _____ _____ _____

I feel empty   *You feel* _____ _____ _____ _____

I feel exasperated   *You feel* _____ _____ _____ _____

I feel excited   *You feel* _____ _____ _____ _____

I feel grief   *You feel* _____ _____ _____ _____

I feel guilty   *You feel* _____ _____ _____ _____

I feel helpless   *You feel* _____ _____ _____ _____

I feel hopeless   *You feel* _____ _____ _____ _____

I feel hurt   *You feel* _____ _____ _____ _____

I feel inadequate   *You feel* _____ _____ _____ _____

I feel inferior   *You feel* _____ _____ _____ _____

I feel lonely   *You feel* _____ _____ _____ _____

I feel lost   *You feel* _____ _____ _____ _____

I feel miserable   *You feel* _____ _____ _____ _____

I feel numb   *You feel* _____ _____ _____ _____

I feel overwhelmed   *You feel* _____ _____ _____ _____

I feel rejected   *You feel* _____ _____ _____ _____

I feel sad   *You feel* _____ _____ _____ _____

I feel shocked   *You feel* _____ _____ _____ _____

I feel silly   *You feel* _____ _____ _____ _____

I feel stifled   *You feel* _____ _____ _____ _____

I feel tense   *You feel* _____ _____ _____ _____

I feel tired   *You feel* _____ _____ _____ _____

I feel trapped   *You feel* _____ _____ _____ _____

I feel useless   *You feel* _____ _____ _____ _____

I feel vulnerable   *You feel* _____ _____ _____ _____

When you have completed the exercise turn to Appendix 2 and compare your answers.

Exercise 6.5

Reflecting feelings
Case study 1 – Mary

Mary says, 'I will be a success. I can do it if I work hard. If it takes eighteen hours a day chained to a VDU, I'll do it. If husband and family suffer, too bad. I hope they don't, but it'll be worth it in the end. Success is what matters to me.'

- Identify the key words, and then create a response of about six lines.

Reflecting feelings
Case study 2 – Sam

Sam says, 'I can never find the time to do the things I enjoy. I'm just getting ready to go out for a swim, or go jogging, when Bill reminds me there's some letters to write to customers, or Susan collars me into helping with some household chores. It's getting increasingly difficult to get the fun out of life that I expect to have. It's depressing.'

- Identify the key words, and then create a response of about six lines.

This concludes the reflecting feelings exercises. Turn to Appendix 2 for suggested responses.

Exercise 6.6

Open questions
Case study 1 – Joe

Joe says, 'Honestly, I don't know what to do. It sounds really silly, I'm twenty-eight but I'm afraid of women. I like them, I think, but I never know what to do. Maybe it's because I like them too much. I start to get to know a girl, and it's OK. Then I just fall head over heels for her. It scares me. I always end up getting hurt. That's how it's happened before, and that's how it is with Emma.'

Here are five closed questions:

1. How many times has this happened before?

2. Are you in love with Emma?

3. When was the last time this happened to you?

4. Is she in love with you?

5. Are you afraid of girls hurting you or you hurting them?

- Restructure these five closed questions into open questions.

Open questions
Case study 2 – Amanda

Amanda says, 'I don't know what to do. My husband is going out to America on contract. Charles wants me to go with him, but I'm afraid. I've never been away from this country. If I stay here, I can carry on working and earn some extra money, which we desperately need. But if I don't go, I shan't see him for months on end. What should I do?'

Here are five closed questions:

1. What part of America?

2. How long will he be away for?

3. You're afraid of going, aren't you?

4. How much money will you be able to earn while he's away?

5. What sort of work does Charles do?

- Restructure these five closed questions into open questions.

This completes the open questions exercises. When you have restructured the closed questions, turn to Appendix 2 for suggested responses.

Exercise 6.7

Summarising
Case study 1 – Tom

Tom says, 'Now don't you start Andy. I had enough of that with my old man when he was alive, never forgave me for letting the side down. I can hear him now, going on and on, "All our family have gone to the grammar school and have all done well, we want to be proud of you too." What a load of rubbish! I'd had enough of school. I suppose I'm the black sheep. The only child and what have I got to be proud of?'

- Identify the key words, and then construct a brief summary.

Summarising

Case study 2 – Tom

Tom says, 'A bastard, that's what I am, Andy. All right, in law, I'm not, but that's what I am, a bastard, bastard, bastard. God, what a mess. You know how I found out? When I was fifteen, Mother and the old man were having one of their endless rows one night. I was in the attic doing some experiment, my workshop was up there; I think they'd forgotten me. I heard the old man shout at her. "I suppose you've got another fancy man, and then I'll have to take his child as mine, just like I did Tom." I couldn't hear any more, the door was slammed.'

● Identify the key words, and then construct a brief summary.

This completes the summarising exercises. Turn to Appendix 2 for suggested responses.

Exercise 6.8

Focusing

Case study – Sally

Sally, twenty, a student nurse, is speaking to the college counsellor: 'I'm in a mess. I moved out of the hospital residence six months ago into a house with four other students, several miles from the college, so I had to buy a car. Two of the others have moved on since then, and the two new ones are awful. They leave the kitchen like a pigsty, and we have endless rows. The atmosphere is so unpleasant. Plus the fact that they're so noisy, loud music and banging doors.

A month ago, someone hit my car when it was parked outside in the street. I'm only covered third party, so couldn't claim on the insurance, and it's going to cost a bomb to repair. I'm already badly overdrawn and the bank keeps writing to me. They take off so much when my pay cheque goes in that I barely have enough to live on. In fact, I eat so badly that I'm losing weight like an anorexic. To crown it all, my last assignment at college was awful. They made me resit, and I can't find the energy to even start it. What am I going to do?'

1. Formulate a contrast response to Sally.

2. Formulate a choice-point response to Sally.

3. Formulate a figure-ground response to Sally.

This completes the focusing exercises. Turn to Appendix 2 for suggested responses.

Exercise 6.9

Being concrete

In these exercises, your task is to turn a generalised, vague statement into a concrete one. The aim of these exercises is three-fold:

1. To help you when a client is making a concrete or generalised statement.

2. To help you make more concrete than generalised statements.

3. To enable you, through being more concrete, to help clients explore their situation more effectively.

Case study 1 – Adam, generalised and vague

Adam says, 'I'm not very considerate to my wife.'

- Imagine you are Adam. What sort of things would you say that would tell the listener precisely just how you relate to your wife?

Case study 2 – Judith, generalised and vague

Judith says, 'I find these counselling training groups really difficult.'

- Imagine you are Judith. What sort of things would you say that would tell the listener precisely what your difficulties are?

Case study 3 – Bill, generalised and vague

Bill says, 'I feel uneasy about the relationship with my mother.'

- Imagine you are Bill. What sort of things would you say that would tell the listener precisely your feelings about your mother?

This concludes the being concrete exercises. Turn to Appendix 2 for suggested responses.

FINAL SUMMARY

In this chapter, supported by examples, appropriate responses and case studies, we have drawn your attention to three skills that further encourage client exploration and clarification: namely summarising, focusing and being concrete. Diverse scenarios have been integrated to demonstrate the skills in practice.

Moreover, exercises have been incorporated, specifically designed to facilitate development of the counselling skills presented in this sixth chapter, as well as in Chapter 5.

The basic listening and responding skills presented in Chapter 5, and in the current chapter, are crucial in paving the way for clients to explore their difficulties. More sophisticated counselling skills may be required, such as challenging and confronting the client, advanced level empathy, immediacy, counsellor self-disclosure and focusing on 'unfinished business', in order to facilitate a deeper understanding of the root causes of the client's difficulties (both from the client's and counsellor's perspective). Advanced counselling skills are thus the primary focus of Chapter 7.

> *In helping others, we shall help ourselves, for whatever good we give out completes the circle and comes back to us.*
>
> Flora Edwards (South-African born industrialist)

REFERENCES

Egan, G. (2007). *The Skilled Helper*, 8th edition (International Student Edition). CA: Thomson/Brooks Cole. This book is now in its 10th edition.

Stewart, W. (1983). *Counselling in Nursing.* London: Harper & Row.

CHAPTER 7

Helping the Client Understand the Problem

There is no challenge more challenging than the challenge to improve yourself.

Michael F. Staley (Author)

Using the basic active listening skills may take the client some way along the path of self-awareness, yet more may be needed to help the client gain a deeper understanding of the problem and its root cause. In this chapter, we provide insight into the skills the counsellor uses to facilitate understanding. These skills, termed 'challenging and confronting', invite clients to examine their behaviour and its consequences. In other words, by encouraging the client to come face-to-face with herself, she develops the skill of self-challenge and the potential to change. However, it needs to be borne in mind that in the context of counselling, challenges and confrontations are always offered with the client's best interests at heart – as a gift, not an attack. The skills need to be used with great sensitivity, care and respect. They need to come out of a deep empathy with the client, and should not be used until trust has been well established. We also explore advanced level empathy and include several exercises and examples of using advanced empathy, possibly one of the most difficult of all the counselling skills to acquire and use effectively. Immediacy is another skill that requires practice, reflecting how you, yourself, feel about the interaction. The pros and cons of self-disclosure are discussed and show it can be productive.

CHALLENGING AND CONFRONTING

In counselling, the aim of a challenge (also referred to as confrontation) is to help the client face reality, as it is seen through the eyes of the counsellor. The force of the challenge depends on the type of therapy. In some instances it is offered as an observation, in others it is very strong and confronting.

There are times when it is wiser to ignore than to comment. There are times, however, when it could be valuable for the client to know how the counsellor feels about something. The client may benefit from being confronted with the possible outcome of her behaviour or some contemplated course of action.

The aim of challenging is to provide accurate information and to offer our perspective. We challenge the strengths of the client rather than the weaknesses – we point out the strengths, assets and resources that the client may fail to fully use. Challenging and confronting helps clients develop new perspectives.

CONFRONTING A CLIENT

Many people get the misguided image of counsellors as a bunch of head nodders or do-gooders, who are paid a lot of money for just sitting and listening. Confronting a client with something she might prefer not to see, might not want to hear, or might not want to know, is not easy. It can be a painful learning process for the client, as well a risky business for the counsellor. It takes guts to challenge a client, and the counsellor may well be left wondering whether she has said the right thing. It can also be an exhausting experience for both.

What confrontation is and is not

- Confrontation is not verbal fisticuffs or a head-on clash!
- Confrontation should be a tentative suggestion, not a declaration.
- Confrontation is an observation, not an accusation.
- Confrontation should be made only after careful deliberation.
- Confrontation should never be used as retaliation, or as a put-down.
- Confrontation is safest when the relationship is well established.

The main areas of confrontation are:

1. Discrepancies, distortions and manipulations.
2. Negative thought patterns and behaviours.
3. Games, tricks and smoke screens.
4. Excuses: manipulation, complacency, rationalisations, procrastinations, passing the buck.

Forms of confronting:

1. 'Your perspective is . . . mine is . . .'

2. 'When you say/do . . . I think/feel . . .'

3. 'On the one hand, you are saying . . . on the other, you are saying . . .'

4. 'You have said (or done) . . . my reaction is . . .'

Examples of confrontations

Discrepancy

- 'You say that being rejected has really upset you, yet you smile as you talk about it.'

- 'When you arrived, I observed a smiling and happy-go-lucky person sitting opposite me, and yet this doesn't seem to fit with the words I am hearing.'

- 'On the one hand you say you love your wife, but on the other you say you have a mistress.'

- 'You have mentioned to me several times that you hate arriving late for appointments, yet I've noticed that you have been late for the last two sessions, and I'm wondering what that's about?'

- 'You speak of your many losses, yet you smile continuously.'

- 'You say you are fine, yet you seem to be very close to tears.'

Distortion of feelings

- 'You say you feel really depressed, yet you laugh whenever you say that, as if it was nothing at all.'

- 'You say you are not worried about your exams, yet you are spending all your evenings in the students' bar drowning your sorrows.'

- 'You say you feel lonely, yet you shrug it off as though it's not important.'

Manipulation

- 'You say your parents have never really understood you. However, the way you said that makes me wonder if you are trying to play on my sympathy in some way?'

- 'You know you have the ability to pass your first year finals, yet you say you haven't bothered to write up your assignments. You are hoping that I can bail you out of this tricky situation by having a word with your tutor.'

Negative thought patterns

- 'You say that you don't think you are up to handling this change in your life. Yet you are clearly a resourceful person. You're intelligent and motivated and have coped well with changes in the past.'

- 'You say you are finding it difficult to decide whether you should accept this new job. Yet from other things you have told me, you strike me as a person who normally finds it easy to make decisions.'

Excuses

- 'You say you believe in taking responsibility for what you do, yet I hear you blaming your wife and daughter for everything that is wrong in your relationship with them.'

- 'You say you want to go back to college, and yet it feels as though you are putting obstacles in the way when I hear you keep saying: "Yes but . . . "'

- 'You say you are keen to apply for a new job, yet you seem reluctant to update your CV.'

Complacency

- 'You say you've been out of work for six months, and it really gets you down. Yet in all that time you haven't applied for any jobs, and you're quite happy to collect your money every week; "That's what I've paid in for all these years!" you said.'

- 'You say you would like a better relationship with your wife. Yet for the past six months you have been going out almost every evening with the lads.'

Procrastination

- 'A month ago you moaned because you hadn't worked for six months. You made a contract then to start looking for work, now you're telling me you haven't even tried. You haven't kept your contract, and didn't realise how the time was flying.'

- 'In our fifth session, you told me how desperate you were to give up smoking, and you had joined a "smoke stop" group. Yet now you are telling me that you haven't attended for the past three weeks.'

Rationalisation

- 'Last time you admitted that you kept putting off looking for a job, now you're saying you couldn't go because the weather was wet.'

- 'In the last group session you told us all you wanted to settle down with your partner, now you're saying you want to sow a few wild oats.'

Effective confrontation

A confrontation should be preceded by careful consideration:

1. What is the purpose of the confrontation?

2. Can I handle the consequences?

3. Does the confrontation relate to the here and now?

4. Whose needs are being met by the confrontation?

Effective confrontation usually contains elements of some or all of the following:

1. A reflection or summary of what the client has said so that the client feels heard and understood.

2. A statement of the counsellor's present feelings.

3. A concrete statement of what the counsellor has noticed or observed, given without interpretation.

Examples of confronting

1. *Client:*

Jane says, 'I don't know what's wrong with me; I can never seem to get to work on time. Not only am I late, but often I'm so tired I can't get up. Evenings are all right, though. I go to church every evening, and most nights I'm with the team around the down-and-outs of the city. I really enjoy that, and somehow I don't feel tired.'

Counsellor:

'Jane, you obviously have an absorbing passion for the down-and-outs and this takes you out pretty late, yet you often have trouble getting to work on time. I wonder if there a discrepancy somewhere there, between responsibility to your employer and your charitable works.'

2. *Group Member:*

Albert says, 'What's the matter with me? I sit here in this training group, week after week and wonder what I'm getting out of it, or if I've anything to give. It's so frustrating. I have plenty to say, but nobody seems to want to listen.'

Group Leader:

'Albert, I hear your frustration, you want to say something in the group, you feel you have plenty to say, yet, you merge into the background like the wallpaper, as if you wanted to make yourself invisible. When you've taken your courage in both hands and spoken out, I've appreciated what you've said, usually to the point of the discussion, as if you've given it a lot of thought. Yet there are many other times when you have tried to speak, and your voice has been so soft, as if you were apologising for speaking.'

3. *Clive [looking tearful]:*

'I've failed my finals, but I don't really care. My good social life makes up for all that, and I can try again in three months' time. Maybe if I don't make it I could try something else. What do you think?'

Counsellor:

'Clive, on the one hand you are saying you don't care that you've failed your finals, but you look very downhearted. You think you could try something else, yet you want to have another crack at the finals in three months. What do you think about these discrepancies?'

Confrontation responses with our five fictitious clients

Counsellor to Pat: Pat, when I hear you talking about being raped, you appear very calm. However, this doesn't seem to fit with your body language, which seems to be saying how desperate you really feel.

Counsellor to Paul: Paul, you say that you desperately want to get a job, however, you then tell me that you have given up trying. There seems to be a contradiction here.

Counsellor to Hayley: Hayley, you say that you feel absolutely useless and this is what makes you hurt yourself, yet just now you told me that you had got a place at university, which seems to contradict your view of yourself.

Counsellor to Ellen: Ellen, on the one hand you say that the idea of sharing your life with Peter appeals to you, and on the other that you would feel guilty because you think you would be letting Charlie down. There seems to be a discrepancy between your wanting to remain loyal to Charlie and wanting to have a new life with Peter.

Counsellor to Danny: Danny, you say that you don't think it's alcohol that makes you aggressive, and yet you have told me that you are a different person when you haven't been drinking.

WILLIAM SPEAKING ABOUT CONFRONTING

Jess was a member of one of my groups, and it was soon apparent that her attitude towards me as leader was almost one of reverence. She hung on my every word, and consistently jumped to my defence when other members disagreed with me. Andy, another member, challenged her. 'Every time William speaks you support him, as if he can't do anything wrong.' Jess looked shocked. 'But he's the leader! He's so experienced. Of course he's right.' It took many months before Jess could begin to think about challenging what I said. Gradually her attitude changed, and she became more assertive within the group.

Discussion

Jess had been brought up in a vicarage, an only child, with elderly parents. She had attended boarding school, and then went into nursing. She had been surrounded by authority figures for her whole life. For her, changing that one attitude, just a bit, raised the level of her self-esteem several points.

USING ADVANCED LEVEL EMPATHY

Advanced level empathy works more (but not exclusively) with implied feelings – those that lie below the surface – and hunches. The aim is to help clients see their problems and concerns more clearly and in a context that will enable them to move forward. Hunches can be communicated as follows:

To get a larger picture

'It seems that the problem is not only in the relationship between you and the charge nurse; it looks as if the war between you has spread to the rest of the team.'

'I've noticed recently that when you talk about your feelings you seem to somehow cushion them. For example, today you said that you got a *"teeny bit"* annoyed with . . ., you were *"quite"* upset with . . ., you feel *"pretty"* anxious about . . . I've got a hunch that maybe cushioning your feelings serves a very important purpose for you . . .'

To challenge indirect expression or implication

'What I think I'm hearing is that it's more than disappointment about the end of the friendship, perhaps it's also about pain and anger.'

To draw logical conclusions

'From what you say about the charge nurse, although you haven't actually used the word, I wonder if you're feeling bitter towards him.'

To challenge hints

'Several times over about the last three sessions, you've brought up relationships with men, though you haven't pursued them, although the door was left open for you. My hunch is that sexual relationships is an important subject, yet you find it difficult to address it.'

To challenge blind spots

'I wonder if the way you laugh at serious things gives some people the impression of an attitude of not caring and of being cynical.'

'I'm wondering if you realise that when you talk about your grandfather your face radiates warmth and you become animated, yet when you mention your father your face goes pale, your voice goes quiet, and you almost seem to shrink in size . . .'

To identify themes

'Several times you've mentioned certain things about women. I wonder if underlying that points to an attitude that puts women down. For example, you said, "I don't think women drivers are as reliable as men". Then you said, "What do you think about that?"'

To own thoughts

'My hunch is that you've already decided to pack that job in, though you haven't said so in so many words.'

The ability to identify implied feelings is closely linked to intuition and imagination. For many of us, however, the imagination and intuition we were born with have been overlaid by thinking and sensing activities. Careful nurturing and use will help them to resurface.

Example 1 – advanced level empathy – Susan to her friend Mandy

'Just listen to us. We're both talking, but we're not really listening, I mean. Are we all so self-centred that we can't take time to listen to each other?'

Identified feelings: Angry, disappointed, furious, ready to explode, ready to pull out, ready to wash your hands of the whole group.

Mandy says, 'Susan, I hear your anger coming from a long way down, as if you've been keeping it in check for some time, and even now you don't really want to let it out in case someone gets hurt. I also sense that tied up with the anger is an intense disappointment, which is almost pushing you out of the group, because we are not listening to your needs.'

Example 2 – advanced level empathy – John talking with Dave, his teenage son

John says, 'Dave, we've been fighting each other for years, not listening to each other, pushing our own views and competing with each other. Today, it's like we've really talked. And you know, Dave, it's been great talking with you rather than at you. Maybe I've been afraid of that.'

Identified feelings: Achieved something, at peace, fulfilled, load taken off, moving closer, new ground, relief, satisfied.

Dave says, 'Dad, it seems as if you and I have been talking at each other from different planets, or from different sides of the earth. Now we're talking face-to-face, man-to-man, and that feels good. It's as if we've both won a tremendous victory, and now you feel we can work hard at establishing peace between us.'

Example 3 – advanced level empathy – George

This example uses the situation in Example 1 of primary level empathy where George is talking to his counsellor about his girlfriend, Jenny, and says, 'I keep telling myself not to move too quickly with Jenny. She's so quiet, and when she does say anything, it's usually how nervous she is. It's obvious to me that when I say anything to her she gets fidgety and anxious, and then I wish I hadn't opened my mouth. It's like a checkmate. If I move I push her away, and if I don't move, nothing will happen between us, and I'll lose her anyway.'

Identified feelings: Anxious, catch-22, cautious, frustrated, protective, regret.

Counsellor says, 'George, it seems that you feel quite frustrated that things are not developing with Jenny as quickly as you would like, and that there's something in the relationship that makes you both back off. Yet I also sense that you feel there's something about you that puts her off, and that maybe you feel things will never come to anything, and yet you feel trapped somehow and not able to let go.'

Forms of advanced empathic responding:

- 'I can sense that you feel . . .'
- 'I have this hunch that . . .'
- 'The picture I am getting . . .'
- 'I have a fantasy that . . .'
- 'The image I am getting is one of . . .'
- 'I imagine you . . .'
- 'I guess it's as if . . .'
- 'My gut feeling is . . .'

When formulating advanced empathic responses it must be remembered that implied facts and feelings are never stated as absolutes; they are hunches, and as such, they must be tentative.

Advanced empathy responses with our five fictitious clients

Counsellor to Pat: Pat, I can sense that you feel very distraught about what has happened, and you seem to be holding on to a lot of pain. *[Pat bursts into tears.]*

Counsellor to Paul: Paul, I have a hunch I would like to share with you. I somehow get a picture of someone who is struggling to keep his head above water, but the setbacks he keeps getting leave him feeling as if he's beginning to drown in a sea of despair.

Counsellor to Hayley: Hayley, the image I am getting is of someone who has lost all hope of ever being able to stop harming herself. It's as if she feels so useless that she deserves to be punished in some way.

Counsellor to Ellen: Ellen, the picture I am getting is like a photograph that has been torn in two. In one part of the photograph, I see a woman who is filled with hope because she has found a man she would like to share her life with. However, the other part shows a very different story. In this part, I see a woman who is filled with confusion and . . . perhaps . . . guilt . . . because she feels as if she is being unfaithful to her beloved Charlie by even considering the idea of sharing her life with another man. It feels to me as if she's in a no win situation; like there is no way she can see how the two torn pieces can ever be repaired.

Counsellor to Danny: Danny, the image I am getting is of a young man who perhaps lacks self-confidence, and who uses drink to give himself Dutch courage to join in, and perhaps to be accepted by his mates? But when he drinks, it seems to completely change his character from a person who is usually quiet and inoffensive, to a person who is loud, punchy and aggressive – a bit like Jekyll and Hyde. I somehow sense that the quiet Danny feels embarrassed and ashamed by the behaviour of the loud and aggressive Danny, and quiet Danny would like to be able to control loud Danny's unacceptable behaviour.

USING IMMEDIACY AS A WAY OF DISCUSSING YOUR RELATIONSHIP WITH THE CLIENT

Immediacy is about open and honest communication. It's about being aware of what is happening in the counselling relationship at any given moment, and reflecting this back to the client tentatively and sensitively. Immediacy can be defined as the skill of discussing your relationship with your clients, and is also referred to as 'here and now', or 'you–me talk'. The aim of immediacy is to address lack of direction that might be having a bearing on the relationship, any tension experienced between client and counsellor, lack of trust, attraction and dependency or counter-dependency. Immediacy makes it possible for both client and counsellor to see more clearly that which is going on between them. Immediacy includes perceiving what is happening and putting it into words, putting yourself on the spot about your own and the client's feelings, and pointing out distortions, games and discrepancies that are going on in the counselling room – in the relationship – in the 'here and now'. It helps the client look at the interaction within the relationship, as it is happening.

Clients often talk about feelings in the past (the then and there), rather than in the 'now'. They also have a tendency to act (or 'act out') the very behaviours and feelings with which they have expressed having difficulty. They may try to set the counsellor up with the kinds of relationships that are causing them difficulties in their everyday lives. Immediacy enables the counsellor to highlight these interactions.

People who rarely talk in the present often dilute the interactions by the use of 'you' instead of 'I'. Clients may be helped to feel the immediacy of the statement when 'I' is used.

Examples of immediacy

- 'Eddie, I want to tell you that right now I'm near to tears. Something you said touched a raw spot about my father and this is something I need to discuss with my supervisor. I just wanted you to know this, in case you noticed my feelings, I don't want them to get in the way.' (For more on immediacy, see http://www.talking-therapy.org.uk/counselling/immediacy/)

- 'You say that you have never been able to talk to your mother, and I wonder if you realise that whenever we start to discuss painful concerns, you give me warning signals to back off?'

- 'I would like us to stop for a moment and see what is happening between us. We have talked freely so far, but now we seem to have reached a kind of "stuckness", which is leaving me feeling quite tense. I wonder if you share my feeling?'

- 'I find it difficult, listening to you, to know how you really feel right now. You talk about everything as if you were talking about somebody else. How do you feel about what I've just said?'

- 'When you talk about your employees, you sound as if you're talking about little children. Just now, you used the same tone with me. I felt really very small and put down. How do you feel about me saying that?'

- 'When you were telling me about being burgled, you looked so calm yet I felt a great surge of anger within me. I wonder, was that my anger, or was I picking up your hidden anger?'

- 'I just want to tell you that right now I'm feeling irritated. Whenever we start to talk about your relationship with your wife you clam up, cross your legs and fold your arms, which tells me to "keep out", and I'm finding that frustrating. I'm wondering if that is how your wife feels when she tries to talk to you?'

Counsellors cannot change clients. What counsellors can do is help clients to change themselves, and this can influence the relationship with third persons in a way that is most constructive. The relationship between counsellor and client therefore becomes a model, and an environment for testing out new behaviours.

As with confronting a client, and advanced empathy, immediacy is more appropriate when the counselling relationship is firmly established. As concreteness contrasts with generality, so here-and-now immediacy contrasts with 'then and there'. The principal difference is that in the one, clients are encouraged to own their feelings and not to generalise; in the other, they are encouraged to own their feelings, as they exist *at that moment*.

Immediacy responses with our five fictitious clients

Counsellor to Pat: Pat, I see you smiling when you talk about being raped, and yet I feel enraged. I'm not too sure where that rage is coming from, but I wonder if I could be picking up the real feeling behind your smile?

Counsellor to Paul: Paul, when you talk about not being successful with getting a job, you sound pretty angry and as if you want to blame someone. It feels right now as if I am the target of your anger, like you want to blame me in some way.

Counsellor to Hayley: Hayley, when you were telling me about how you cut and burn yourself, I felt quite helpless and inadequate. It felt almost like you expected me to provide an instant cure, and because I can't come up with one, I've disappointed you. How do you feel about me saying this?

Counsellor to Ellen: Ellen, when you talked about the habits Charlie had that irritated you, I felt really uncomfortable, and I'm not sure what this is all about. I wonder if I am picking up this feeling from you – like it somehow feels wrong to speak ill of the dead?

Counsellor to Danny: Danny, when you talk about your relationship with your father, I wonder if you realise that your voice gets louder, you clench your fists and your knuckles go white. I'm feeling a bit threatened by it, and I wonder if that's how your father feels when he tries to have a discussion with you?

What immediacy involves:

1. Being open with the client about how you feel about something in the relationship.

2. Disclosing a hunch about the client's behaviour towards you by drawing attention to discrepancies, distortions, avoidances, games.

3. Inviting the client to explore what is happening, with a view to developing a more productive working relationship.

Summary of immediacy

- Immediacy is a difficult skill, because we need to be aware of what is happening in the relationship without becoming preoccupied with it.

- It is demanding because it calls on strength of character, as well as social intelligence and social courage, to bring up relationship issues.

- Immediacy can help both counsellor and client move beyond a variety of relationship obstacles.

- It is also a learning opportunity for clients. If we use immediacy well, clients can see its value and learn how to apply it to their own sticky relationships.

DISCLOSING SELF TO FACILITATE COMMUNICATION

Immediacy and disclosing self often go hand in hand. Frequently it is the disclosure of a behaviour or feeling by the counsellor which starts this way of communicating. A strategy for disclosing self is to use 'I' statements: 'I sense that . . .' or 'I feel that . . .', rather than 'you said . . .' or 'you did . . .'. By using 'I' statements the client is not attacked, and can respond appropriately, either denying or accepting that she feels the same way. It can also encourage the client to use 'I' statements and thus take responsibility for their own thoughts, feelings and behaviour.

Disclosing self is the process by which we let ourselves be known to others, and, in the process, we enhance our self-awareness. Disclosing self means that the counsellor makes a conscious decision to reveal something to the client. Essentially, it means we share with the client a similar experience to the one that is causing her present difficulties, and use the common denominator to work with.

Clear verbal and non-verbal disclosures increase the chance of our message being received without the need for explanation. Appropriate disclosure is critical in relationships. It enhances them, keeps them alive and helps to avoid alienation. One person's low level of disclosure is likely to block another person's willingness to disclose. When we are genuine, in touch with our own inner empathy, we are also in touch with what we are experiencing and send authentic messages, rather than messages which conflict and confuse.

Disclosure involves both negative and positive aspects of self. Not everyone finds it easy to disclose positive aspects of themselves, possibly due to low self-esteem.

One of the risks of disclosure is that it might backfire. We need to ask, 'Why am I doing it?' While disclosing something about yourself certainly might help to deepen the relationship, if the motive is suspect then it could harm the relationship. Some people disclose something to another person too soon in the relationship, and this has the effect of frightening off the other person. The reason for this is there is an implicit understanding that the person receiving the disclosure feels it necessary also to disclose, and if the received disclosure is premature, then this could cause the other person to retreat.

CASE STUDY

Bert

Bert, in his early twenties, met Bill at the tennis club. They got along well and were soon arranging to go out for a drink. As they sat on the lawn of the pub, Bert told Bill that he was gay. Bill clammed up and was clearly uneasy. He made an excuse to leave.

Bert related this in a therapy session, as he talked about what went wrong with his relationships. As we explored this latest incident, he realised that he had told Bill about his sexuality hoping that Bill would tell him he, too, was gay. His answer to the question 'Why am I doing it?' revealed a desire not to be open but to push Bill into a relationship. Bill reacted by being scared off. While there was nothing for Bert to feel ashamed of in his sexuality, the disclosure was premature and wrongly motivated. His disclosure was bordering on manipulation.

Discussion

Disclosure is neither good nor bad; it has gains and risks, and these have to be weighed against each other, though of course we will never know in advance how a disclosure will be received – whether it will be a gain or otherwise. If Bert had considered some of these pointers to gains and risks of disclosure, he might have developed a satisfying relationship with Bill.

Possible gains of disclosing self	Possible risks of disclosing self
Lessened loneliness	Rejection
Greater intimacy	Not liking self
More friendships	Feelings of shame
Self-responsibility	Being misunderstood
More assertive	Wary of confidentiality
Encourages disclosure	Feeling tense/vulnerable
Discovering others' self-acceptance	Too much intimacy, too soon
Control of own life	Too many close relationships
	Too much self-knowledge
	Breaking taboos about disclosures
	Balance of relationship disturbed

Disclosing self is only useful if it encourages the client to self-disclose and open herself up to the counselling process. Accurately used, disclosing self can be helpful and positive, but inappropriate and mistimed disclosures may increase the client's anxiety, particularly if it shifts the emphasis from the client to the counsellor. The client comes with her own set of problems, and it doesn't help her to know what problems the counsellor has. Another danger of disclosing self is the impression that it may give of 'If I have overcome it . . .' or 'This is the way I overcame it . . .', the implication being that the client can do the same. *Disclosing self must be used with caution and discretion.*

Recognising appropriate disclosures

Appropriate disclosures involve sharing of:

- attitudes
- beliefs
- feelings
- reactions to the client
- views.

Disclosures should be:

- direct
- sensitive
- relevant
- non-possessive
- brief
- selective.

Reasons for disclosing self

1. Using self as a model.

2. Showing genuineness in helping.

3. Sharing experiences.

4. Sharing feelings.

5. Sharing opinions.

5. Modelling assertiveness.

Not all counsellors agree with disclosing self. It is embraced in humanistic therapies, but seldom in psychodynamic theories, where it is believed that to disclose self can get in the way of constructive counselling.

Examples of disclosing self:

1. Peter was talking to Roy about his father's recent death. Peter was having difficulty expressing himself until Roy said, 'My father died four years after my mother. When he died, I felt I'd been orphaned. Maybe that is something like how you feel.' Peter sat for several minutes in deep silence before saying, 'You've put into words exactly how I feel. May I talk about my childhood and how Dad and I got on together?'

2. Janet, a nurse, was working with Sheila, one of her patients, when Sheila said, 'Janet, you're very quiet today, and seem on edge, have I upset you in some way?' Janet said, 'Sorry, Sheila, it's not you. Simon and I had an argument before we left for work, and it's still on my mind. Thank you for drawing my attention to it. My feelings could easily have got in the way with you and others. Let's think about you, now.' Having made this disclosure, Janet moves on and returns the focus to the client.

Disclosing self – important points to remember

- Although counsellors should be willing to make disclosures about themselves that might help clients understand some part of their problem more clearly, they should do so only if such disclosures do not disturb or distract the clients in their own work.

- Disclosing self is more appropriate in well-established relationships, and should reflect the needs of the client, not the needs of the counsellor.

Self-disclosure responses to our five fictitious clients

Counsellor to Pat: Pat, I would like to share something with you if you don't mind? I was raped when I was fifteen, and I can remember feeling dirty and contaminated. I also blamed myself because I felt I should have tried harder to stop him. I wonder if that's anywhere close to how you are feeling right now?

Counsellor to Paul: Paul, when you talked about all the application forms you have sent off, it took me back to when my job was made redundant. I can remember sending off loads of application forms, and feeling very rejected when I didn't get any replies. It nearly destroyed my self-confidence. I wonder if you can identify with any of those feelings I experienced?

Counsellor to Hayley: Hayley, would you mind if I shared something with you? When I was a teenager I was fat, and I used to be called horrible names at school. I'll never forget them because they hurt so much – names like 'ugly', 'grotesque', 'fatso', 'freak'. I heard these names so often that I ended up believing that I was some sort of worthless monster, who should be annihilated. I wanted to murder the kids who said it, and then I felt guilty for having such evil thoughts. I hated myself so much I just wanted to die. I wonder whether you can relate to any of those feelings I experienced?

Counsellor to Ellen: Ellen, I can remember feeling incredibly guilty when I formed a new relationship two years after my husband had died. It felt almost as if I was having an affair behind his back and that left me feeling as if I had betrayed his trust in me. I wonder if you are carrying around any feelings similar to those I had?

Counsellor to Danny: Danny, when I was about your age I had a scrape or two with the law. Each time it was when I'd had one over the eight, which made me boisterous and rowdy. I remember thumping my mate once because he'd been chatting my girlfriend up, and then feeling terribly guilty, remorseful and ashamed of myself, when I sobered up and realised what I'd done. I wonder if any of those feelings I experienced are ringing bells with you?

Counsellor self-disclosure is only helpful if it:

- keeps the client on target
- serves the needs of the client
- moves the client forward to self-understanding.

It should be used with tact and sensitivity and only when a relationship of trust has been established between client and counsellor.

Exercises

Your task is to create a confrontation response to each of the following case studies.

Exercise 7.1

Confronting a client

Case study 1 – Vanessa

Vanessa says, 'I do wish I could do something about my weight. Look at me, fifteen stones. But, I'm my own worst enemy. Stuart and I went out last night for a slap-up meal. That's the way of it. One of these days I'll win, though.'

- How would you confront Vanessa?

Case study 2 – Dan

Dan says, 'I don't have any problems with my children, we have a wonderful relationship, that's because Alice and I give them responsibility. They know who's boss, though. Bill wanted a front door key. I told him, "When you're working, my lad, then you can have a key to my house. You're only seventeen yet." He stormed out, muttering something like, "Come into this century, old man." Cheeky young (cough).'

- How would you confront Dan?

We can also use confrontations to bring out strengths of which the client seems unaware, or is discounting. This is, of course, a discrepancy, but of a different kind.

Case study 3 – Keith

Keith was about to be demobbed from the Army, in which he had served for twenty-two years. He was a Sergeant with an exemplary record. He had served in Northern Ireland on two tours, and had been decorated for bravery. One of his duties, for four years, had been in charge of the Sergeants' Mess accounts, a job that carried a lot of financial responsibility. He and Mavis married nineteen years ago. She had been in the WRAC. They have two boys, Adrian, aged eighteen, and John, aged seventeen, both in the Army. They have a stable family life, with both sets of parents still alive.

On his pre-release interview he said to the interviewing officer, 'I'm scared stiff, Sir, of going back into Civvy Street. I've been in the Army since I was eighteen, and boys' service before that, so I've never known anything else since sixteen. I married an Army girl, and we've lived in Army quarters all our married life. Our two boys are in the services. I don't know anything else. When I think about it, I get cold sweats. I'm not sleeping well either, just thinking about it.'

- How would you confront Keith?

This is the end of the confronting exercises. Turn to Appendix 2 for suggested responses.

Exercise 7.2

Identifying your own strengths

Have a dialogue with yourself. Talk about your strengths. Be realistic, not coy. Many people have difficulty even saying they have strengths. Part of your self-development as a counsellor is discovering how you feel about drawing attention to your strong points. Many people are happier talking about their weaknesses and hardly ever realise that they have strengths. Counselling is often concerned with identifying strengths and building on them. The client can no more build on weaknesses than a builder can build a house on a foundation of sand. When you have considered your strengths, write them down in your notebook. Try to list at least five.

Exercise 7.3

Advanced empathy

Suggested framework on how to formulate responses for the advanced empathy case study exercises.

Read the case studies and identify the expressed facts and feelings and the implied facts and feelings. When you have done this, think of what those facts and feelings might imply. When you have done that, think of as many adjectives as you can to describe the implied feelings. Then formulate your response.

Case Study 1 – Nigel to Brenda, a counsellor

'You know me, Brenda, the life and soul of the party. Give me a pint in my hand and I'll keep them amused for hours. It's not like that in the house, though. "Oh, shut up Dad," is all I get. "Don't put on that act here. Be your age." It hurts. Sometimes they get quite angry at my jokes. Why don't they appreciate me?'

• Create a response of about six to eight lines.

Case Study 2 – Kate, a senior nurse teacher, talking to Simon, a colleague

'It's no secret, and you know better than anybody else, I'm a workaholic. I can't remember when I allowed myself to have a day off to do just nothing. It sounds awful when it's put like that. I've been that way for twelve years now. I ought to do something about it, shouldn't I? I'm a free agent. Nobody's making me do it, or holding a gun to my head. I feel caught on a treadmill.'

- Create a response of about six to eight lines.

Case Study 3 – Karen, talking to Joan, one of the counsellors in attendance at the church coffee morning

'I love Jack and my children very much, and I like doing most things around the house. Of course, they get boring at times, but on the whole, I suppose it can be very rewarding at times. I don't really miss working, going to the office every day. Most women complain of being just a homemaker and just a mother. But then, again, I wonder if there's more for me. Others say there has to be. I really don't know.'

- Create a response of about eight to ten lines.

In the above exercise and the next one, you will not be given an analysis. When you compare your response with the one given, see if you can identify why Joan responds the way she does.

Case study 4 – Andrea's fourth counselling session with Martin

Andrea says, 'I'm really disappointed in you, Martin. I thought we could get along together and you could help me. But we're not getting anywhere. You don't understand me. I might as well not be here. I don't even think you care for me, and you don't hear me when I talk. You seem to be somewhere else. What you say has nothing to do with what I've been talking about. I don't know where to turn. I'm just so – oh damn it – I don't know what I'm going to do, but I know you can't help me. There's no hope.'

- Create a response of about eight to ten lines.

This is the end of the advanced empathy exercises. Turn to Appendix 2 for suggested responses.

Exercise 7.4

Immediacy

In these case study exercises, use the following formula:

- disclose specifically how the issue affects you

- create a specific empathic challenge

- as with a challenge, immediacy should be tentative – an invitation to consider.

Case study 1 – Alan

You are a facilitator of a counselling training group of twelve people. One of the group, Alan, is very vocal, and always seems to have an answer to any point that you or anyone else raises. In the third session, you start to feel irritated. The source of your irritation is that whenever silences occur, Alan invariably jumps in with a comment that does not always facilitate what has gone before. You also notice that other members of the group start to fidget and cast knowing glances at one another when Alan starts speaking. The immediate issue is that Alan cuts across what one of the women in the group is saying. What do you say to Alan?

• Create a response to Alan.

Cases study 2 – Jenny

You are a member of a counselling group. There has been a lot of disclosure and some tears. Cathy is talking about the pain of her recent divorce. Many people in the group are looking damp-eyed. Jenny gets up and walks right through the middle of the group to the door, saying, 'I need a smoke'. The group members look very uncomfortable. After a few minutes, Jenny re-crosses the group and sits down. As a member of the group you feel angry at what you feel is an intrusion. What do you say to Jenny?

• Create a response to Jenny.

Case study 3 – Steve

Steve is your client, and this is the sixth session. When he started with you, he said, 'Oh, I'm fairly well off, so the fee isn't a problem.' You, personally, have difficulty talking about charging a fee, you would much rather leave that to someone else to handle, but there is no one else. At least three times during your time together, Steve has said things like, 'I hadn't realised just how expensive this business would be.' You find that this issue is unresolved. You also wonder if Steve thinks that the length of the counselling relationship is more to do with your needs than with his.

• Create a response to Steve.

Case study 4 – Sally

Sally, aged nineteen, is a student at the college where you are the counsellor. She came to you six months ago, referred by her lecturer, for problems with relationships in the group. She came regularly, every week, for six weeks, then started missing sessions altogether. Your policy is to drop a line after one missed appointment expressing concern and hoping that illness or an emergency did not prevent her from attending.

You also remind her of the next agreed appointment. Usually she would attend the next appointment, with apologies that sounded like excuses, rather than reasons. Several times, you have challenged her on this unreliability, and on every occasion she says, 'I really, really promise to do better'. She had a break from counselling for two months, and one month ago started again. She came for two sessions, missed one and is now sitting with you. She says, in a pleading little-girl voice, 'I'm really, really sorry. Can you forgive me?'

● Create a response to Sally.

This is the end of the immediacy case study exercises. Turn to Appendix 2 for suggested responses.

Exercise 7.5

Unfinished business

Unfinished business is a term that originated in gestalt therapy, and it refers to something that has emerged from the background and which is not completed, so the person is left with unfinished business; the *Gestalten* is not completed, and like a complex in psychoanalysis will draw energy to itself, something like a black hole in the universe.

Unfinished business makes itself known through preoccupations, compulsive behaviour, being wary of others and self-defeating behaviour, and may be experienced through physical symptoms, or difficulty in establishing or maintaining satisfactory relationships.

Clients may complain of feeling stuck, or having reached an *impasse*. When clients fully experience the feeling of being stuck, they are then able to get in contact with their frustrations and are then able to do something to change.

Unfinished business must be concentrated on and re-experienced, not just talked about, in order to be resolved in the here and now. Unfinished business is something that acts as a block or interruption to the flow of energy, the task of which is to form a *Gestalten*. When there is completion, we can move on because we are able to build only on what is completed. As each piece of unfinished business is resolved, a *Gestalten* is completed and the way is thus prepared for the client to move on to the next piece of unfinished business.

When a prior need was left unsatisfied, that particular *Gestalten* could not be completed. Part of the counselling task is to help the client to close off and complete what was previously unfinished – similar to finishing a chapter of a book.

Think of someone you have 'unfinished business' with that you would like to resolve.

1. Describe the current situation.

2. What are your thoughts about this person? Try to identify both positive and negative thoughts.

3. What are your feelings about this person? Try to identify both positive and negative feelings.

4. Endeavour to put yourself in this person's shoes, and explore why you think the person is treating you the way he/she is.

5. What could you say to this person to encourage her or him to discuss the unresolved issue?

6. Look carefully at your response to number 5, and consider whether you could pluck up the courage to say this to the person concerned.

Exercise 7.6

Disclosing self: 1

Disclosure of self is different from previous exercises, and is clearly linked to the development of self-awareness. It would be difficult to present an exercise on disclosing self to which every student could respond appropriately, for disclosing self is so uniquely personal. The object of this exercise is that you think about some aspect of living which you feel you have handled reasonably well, or are learning to manage. Remember, the aim of disclosing self is to help the client to move forward, not to pass problems on to the client. To help you, here are some ideas. What could you disclose and to whom? You may choose any other subject or subjects.

There are no suggested responses to this exercise.

What are your views, feelings and thoughts about:

- Religious groups other than your own?

- Your experience of drinking, smoking, drugs?

- Your sexual preferences?

- Your childhood experiences?

- Your feelings about the client you are counselling?

- How much you are worth financially?

- The aspects of your personality you are not happy with?

- Things in the past you are ashamed of?

- The sort of things that can hurt you?

- The parts of your body you don't like?

- Whether or not you feel sexually adequate?

Disclosing self: 2

For this exercise, enlist the help of a friend. Role-play being a counsellor, with your friend taking the part of the client. Ask your friend to talk about something important to him or her for fifteen minutes. During this time, make several personal disclosures and talk about your experiences.

At the end of the fifteen minutes, ask your partner for feedback on the impact of your personal disclosures, e.g.:

- Did your personal disclosures help or hinder your friend? In what way?

- Did your personal disclosures distract your friend?

Self-disclosure and intimacy

Self-disclosure seems to be essential in the development of an intimate relationship; however, too little or too much disclosure tends to hamper the development of a relationship. We also convey feelings related to intimacy by body language, such as distance, through facial expressions, eye contact and non-vocal cues.

The therapeutic relationship is one of depth and intimacy, and is unlike any other relationship. For within the security of this unique relationship clients have the freedom to express their feelings, knowing that the relationship exists primarily for them. The counsellor makes no demands for self, and clients can be exactly themselves. This freedom to be themselves within a warm and trusting – and at times challenging – relationship can be scary for some clients. As clients experience intimacy, so they are able to redraw the boundaries and gradually begin to feel safe with intimacy.

There is no doubt that having an opportunity to talk with someone, to express one's feelings, is a safeguard not only against loneliness and isolation but also against weaving, out of one's defensive mechanisms, a blanket to suffocate feelings. Counselling offers the sort of support that avoids smothering feelings.

SUMMARY

It might be helpful at this point in the book to summarise our journey so far. We have:

- defined counselling and examined various aspects of counselling
- explored counsellor qualities deemed necessary to work effectively with others, and provided opportunities for increasing self-awareness
- given consideration to boundary issues and provided information on what counsellors can do to help their clients feel safe
- explored self-awareness, primary and advanced empathy
- presented a range of basic listening skills and advanced skills, with exercises designed to develop the skills.

We are heading towards the home straight, but there are still a few more important topics we need to pay attention to, the next being, what can counsellors do to help their clients resolve their problems?

> *The possibility of encountering one's reality – learning about one's self – can be frightening and frustrating. Many people expect to discover the worst. A hidden fear lies in the fact that they may also discover the best.*
>
> Muriel James and Dorothy Jongeward,
> *Born to Win: Transactional Analysis with Gestalt Experiments*

CHAPTER 8

Helping the Client Resolve the Problem

There comes a moment when you have to stop revving up the car and shove it into gear.

David Mahoney

We have stressed throughout this book that counselling is about change. However, it's important to recognise that some things cannot be changed. Just as we cannot alter the colour of our eyes or our height, we cannot reverse incurable illness or a physical disability. We cannot give a one-legged man two limbs, or a blind person sight. What counsellors can do in these circumstances is to offer help and support in coming to terms with what cannot be changed, and encouragement to explore strategies for coping with the situation.

Up until now, emphasis has been placed on the value of good communication in the counselling relationship. Yet there comes a time when talking may not be enough and the client needs to take the bull by the horns and *do* something. Put another way, he or she needs to take action to resolve the problem. To this end, the counsellor can play an important role by teaching clients to use a problem-solving and goal setting approach to their difficulties. This method, which is essentially a self-help technique, can be highly effective, especially if the counsellor stays alongside clients as they work through the stages. It enables clients to explore choices perhaps not previously considered, helps them to replace stumbling blocks with stepping stones, and provides the confidence and courage to take risks and implement decisions. And, as an added bonus, once learned, the client has a very useful self-help tool for solving problems that might arise after the counselling relationship ends.

After explaining the process and presenting some examples of goal setting in action, and introducing a model called 'force-field analysis', we have provided an exercise for you to practise the techniques for yourself, so make sure you have your pen and notepad at the ready. We also include a discussion and exercises on assertiveness.

CASE STUDIES

How Scott and Andrew handle change

Introduction

We can modify most things about our personality, albeit only a little, but that small change can make a world of difference to our well-being and self-esteem. Self-doubt can be replaced with self-confidence; low self-esteem can be replaced with high regard. An analogy may point home the message. The Wimbledon star did not arrive there on talent alone; a great deal of dedication and hard slog were also necessary to be a winner.

Self-knowledge plays an important part in changing behaviour. Part of that awareness is being able to accept not only that we need to change, but that there are benefits from changing. Sadly, many of us are quite satisfied with the status quo, and we go all out to maintain that state, at the expense of growth. The opportunity for change rapidly passes by, and often in the passing, we leave behind a trail of damaged relationships.

The Clients

Scott was a successful doctor, but suffered from an overwhelming sense of unworthiness, something that affected his relationships. He freely admitted that it was this that led him into a multitude of unsatisfactory sexual relationships. In one session, when he was talking about himself, I had a mental image of him as a small boy sitting on a dustbin. I told him, and he was moved to tears. That was exactly how he felt about himself – so much garbage, yet he gave all the appearance of a self-possessed and confident man.

Part of our work was to identify the factors that brought him to the dustbin, then work towards changing the feelings. The facts of his life could not be changed, but his interpretation of them could.

Andrew was blinded by an accident. He went through a period of grief, during which time he drank too much. Life had lost its meaning. His self-esteem hit rock bottom. Gradually he accepted his blindness, and became a campaigner for other blind people. He is still blind. The facts cannot be changed, but his feelings towards his 'fate' underwent a change. He could not move forward until he accepted the fact that he was blind, and always would be.

Discussion

Scott accepted that he could change some things; Andrew accepted that something could not be changed. Had Scott continued to kick against his past, he would have remained on the garbage bin. Had Andrew not accepted his blindness, he could have wallowed in self-pity, and his self-esteem would have suffered. His change in lifestyle brought him new experiences, and his example inspired thousands of other blind people.

God, give us the serenity to accept what cannot be changed;
Give us courage to change what should be changed; Give us the
wisdom to distinguish one from the other.
Prayer of Reinhold Niebuhr (1892–1971)

WHAT IS PROBLEM SOLVING?

Problem solving resolves a discrepancy. It changes something that is actual, nearer to what is desired. A goal is a result that will reduce that discrepancy. Problem solving is, in many ways, simply a process of managing information. Indeed, it is probably true to say that in the majority of instances, the only reason we fail to solve problems is that we fail to recognise that we already have sufficient information to do so. Problem solving has two parts:

Decision-making, which consists of choosing courses of action to reach the desired goal.

Problem analysis, which involves identifying various factors and forces that interfere with or facilitate goal achievement. Planning can only take place when decision-making and problem analysis have been thoroughly carried out.

Identifying the premises of problem solving

The premises of problem solving are:

1. To become thoroughly aware of the problem.

2. Problems with one root cause are as rare as two moons in the sky.

3. Effective problem solving means balancing disturbed forces.

4. Valid decisions depend on accurate, clear and complete information.

5. Working with other people can shorten the process time.

6. People given the responsibility of action must be committed to it.

7. There must be a supportive climate.

Not all counselling is concerned with problem solving but a great deal of it is. Some people want to increase their self-awareness, to have more understanding of how they interact with others, or to develop more insight of the helping relationship by first-hand experience. Very often, the client presents the 'problem' to the counsellor in a jumbled and unclear way. In the early stages, therefore, it is useful to have a plan that counsellor and client can work on together to bring order out of chaos. The model presented here may help. As client and counsellor work through this together, step by step, it will let the client see that there is a logical way of tackling the problem. It will also help the counsellor by relieving some of the anxiety of not knowing where to start.

Identifying the problem

A problem clearly stated is a problem half solved.

Dorothea Brande (Writer)

1. Establish the problem

   - Identify the origins.

   - Help the client define and describe the problem by using the six key words – Who? What? Why? When? Where? How?

2. Encourage the client to be precise and avoid generalisations.

   - Explore the problem.

   - Listen with understanding.

   - Keep an open mind and your questions will be open.

   - Respond with empathy.

   - Concentrate on observable and specific behaviours.

3. Eliminate the problem

   - What is not right about the present scene?

   - What goal does the client want to set?

   - What sub-goals can be set to reach the goal?

- How can the first goal – then subsequent goals – be reached?

- Goals must be in specific terms – avoid vague and generalised language.

4. Evaluate

- Whether the goal has been achieved/partly achieved.

- Whether the problem has changed.

Summary

The four stages of problem-solving counselling involve:

- *establishing* the problem

- *exploring* the problem

- *eliminating* the problem

- *evaluation* of the problem-solving process.

GOAL SETTING

One important part of problem solving that can sometimes be difficult is goal setting – working out a satisfactory solution. Many people become counselling clients because they feel stuck in situations from which they can see no way out. Counselling can help them to develop a sense of direction, which often accompanies hope. One important part of problem solving that can sometimes be difficult is goal setting – working out a satisfactory solution.

Goal setting is a highly cognitive approach which many people have difficulty working with. Goal setting must take into account the affective and behavioural factors as well as the creative potential of the client.

Figure 8.1 highlights eight important tasks involved in the process of problem-solving and goal setting.

1. **Assessment – helps clients identify:**

   - What they feel is OK about their life.

   - What they feel is not OK about their life.

   - The resources they have to draw on.

Assessment continues throughout the counselling relationship.

2. **Identifying the initial problem:**

   Help the client to focus on the initial problem by using Rudyard Kipling's 'six honest serving-men and true':

   What? Why? How? Where? When? Who?

3. **Develop new ways of looking at the problem:**

   Looking beyond the now, to what could be.

4. **Goal setting:**

   A goal is what a person would like to attain so that the problem can be more managed more easily and constructively.

5. **Opening up possibilities:**

   There are often several ways in which a problem may be tackled using resources the client may not have recognised.

6. **Making an informed choice:**

   Achieving the best 'fit' between resources, personality and abilities in order to achieve the desired outcome.

7. **Implementing the choice.**

8. **Evaluation.**

Fig. 8.1: Eight important tasks involved in the process of problem solving and goal setting.

Understanding the process of goal setting

To move from:

- **point A**, where the client is, to

- **point B**, where the client would like to be, counsellor and client need to explore feelings, thoughts and behaviours in order to develop a new perspective and work through hindrances. Counsellor and client need to work out strategies in order to reach:

- **point C**, *getting* to where the client wants to be.

Example

Point A: Where the client is:

Harry is dissatisfied with his job.

Point B: Where the client would like to be:

Harry would like a more satisfying job.

Perspective

Why should Harry stay in a job that does not satisfy?

Hindrances

1. Self-defeating beliefs and attitudes. Harry believes that he could never get through an interview.

2. Misplaced loyalty. Harry has been with the company for ten years, and they have given him time off to take a degree course.

3. The comfort zone is preferred. Changing jobs would probably mean that Harry had to travel further to work, and learning a new job requires effort.

Point C: Getting to where the client wants to be:

One of the strategies Harry decided on was to learn to drive a car, as this would make him more mobile. Harry role-played several interviews in which the counsellor put him under progressive pressure, until Harry felt confident about applying for a new post.

Advantages of goal setting

- Focuses attention and action.
- Mobilises energy and effort.
- Increases patience.
- Strategy oriented.

At point A

The counsellor helps clients to:

- understand themselves
- understand the problem(s)
- set goals
- take action.

The client's goal is **self-exploration**.

The counsellor's goal is **responding**.

The counsellor helps clients to:

- tell their story
- focus
- develop new insight and new perspectives.

At point B

The counsellor helps clients to:

- examine their problems
- think how they could be handled differently
- develop their powers of imagination
- think through: 'How will I know when I have got there?'

The client's goal is **self-understanding**.

The counsellor's goal is to **integrate understanding**.

The counsellor helps clients to:

- create a plan
- evaluate the plan
- develop choices and commitment to change.

At point C

The client's goal is **action**.

The counsellor's goal is to **facilitate action**.

The counsellor helps clients to:

- identify and assess action strategies
- formulate plans
- implement plans.

Requirements for effective goal setting

Visions, ideas and possibilities all create enthusiasm; behaviour is driven by creating an achievable plan, which should have the following criteria:

- a clearly defined, and achievable, goal
- how the goal will be evaluated
- a realistic timetable for achieving the goal.

Working for commitment

1. Ownership of the plan is essential for it to work.
2. A plan that has appeal encourages commitment.
3. A detailed plan has a logic to it.
4. An effective plan has an emotional content.
5. Flexibility increases the chance of commitment.
6. Clients need to see that the plan is within their capabilities and that they have the personal and external resources.
7. Client commitment is often influenced by counsellor enthusiasm.
8. Getting started by using problem-solving skills.

BRAINSTORMING

Clients can generate a free flow of ideas that might resolve the problem, by brainstorming their thoughts on a sheet of paper. Encourage them to be adventurous by jotting down whatever comes into their heads, no matter how silly it seems.

CASE STUDY

Jane

Jane was having problems at work. Her boss criticised her work constantly, and generally made life very difficult for her. With the help of her counsellor, she worked through her feelings about the problem (point A), and then brainstormed ideas of how she might solve the problem.

- I could let this barrage of criticism go over my head.

- I could request a meeting with him to discuss what exactly he thinks I am doing wrong.

- I could request a transfer to another section.

- I could discuss the situation with my senior manager.

- I could ask my colleagues if they know why he keeps picking on me.

- I could look for another job.

- I could work for myself.

The next stage for Jane was to make her mind up which alternative felt right for her, and to plan a realistic goal (point C). She decided that there were two goals she wanted to achieve:

1. To resolve the problems she was having with her boss.

2. To become self-employed.

We return to Jane later to see how she planned her action for reaching her goals.

FORCE-FIELD ANALYSIS

Force-field analysis, a decision-making technique developed from psychologist Kurt Lewin's (1890–1947) Field Theory, is designed to help people understand the various internal and external forces that influence the way they make decisions. It is a way of helping people plan how to move forward toward the desired outcome. For most of the time, these forces are in relative balance; but when something disturbs the balance, decisions are more difficult to make. When the forces are identified, counsellor and client work on strategies to help the client reach the desired goal.

Stages in force-field analysis

1. What is the **goal** to be achieved?

2. Identifying **restraining forces** that act as obstacles to outcomes.

3. Identifying **facilitating forces** that act as **aids** to outcomes.

4. Working out how to **weaken** some of the restraining forces, or how to **strengthen** some of the facilitating forces, or both.

5. Using **imagery** to picture moving toward the desired goal and achieving it.

Forces may be **internal** or **external**

Examples of internal forces:

- type of personality
- age
- health
- previous experiences
- motivation
- attitudes
- beliefs.

Examples of external forces

- family and friends
- locality
- job and career
- finance
- mobility
- commitments
- hobbies.

The underlying principle is that, by strengthening the facilitating forces and diminishing the restraining forces, a decision will be easier to make because energy, trapped by the restraining forces, has been released.

The plan of action is born out of using the facilitating forces to reach the defined goal. The plan needs to be simple and easily understood. A useful website is http://accel-team.com/techniques/force_field_analysis.html

Restraining forces

The restraining forces are the obstacles that are, or seem to be, hindering the client from implementing her action plan. Once the restraining forces have been identified, ways of coping with them are discussed. The counsellor must ensure that the client does not dwell on these forces and become demoralised.

Facilitating forces

These are the positive forces to be used by the client. They may be other people, places or things. Any factors that facilitate or assist the client to attain her goal are utilised. This part of the process of searching for facilitating forces actually pushes the client to look at her positive attributes.

Everything in force-field analysis should be specific. Imagine you were telling someone how to get from London to Glasgow; you would be as specific as possible. Force-field analysis is a bit like that. You would know you were in Glasgow when you arrived there. Force-field analysis helps the client be specific.

Plan of action

The plan of action is born out of utilising the facilitating forces to reach the defined goal. The plan should be simple and easily understood by the client.

CASE STUDY

Jane's force-field analysis in action

Let us return to Jane now to see how she used force-field analysis to identify her restraining and facilitating forces, and to plan her action.

Goal 1. Jane's identified goal: to resolve the problems with her boss.

Jane's restraining forces:	Anxiety about confronting the situation.
	Fear of making the situation worse.
	Fear of bursting into tears or getting angry.
	Fear of hearing something she would rather not hear.
Jane's facilitating forces:	Determination.
	Dislike of disharmony.
	Desire to get to the bottom of the problem.

Jane's plan of action:

1. Prepare a 'script' of what she wants to say to her boss.

2. Ask for a meeting with her boss.

3. Practise her relaxation techniques prior to the meeting.

4. Communicate to her boss how much his criticism is upsetting her, and ask him what exactly she is doing that seems to be causing him concern.

5. Be prepared to compromise to reach a solution.

Goal 2. Jane's identified goal: to become self-employed.

Jane's restraining forces: Anxiety about how she will manage for money until her business is established.

Self-doubts about her skills and abilities.

Concern about taking the risk.

Jane's facilitating forces: Self-motivated and works well on her own.

Good organisational and time management skills.

Enjoys new challenges.

Gets on well with people.

Good communication skills.

Jane's plan of action:

- Prepare a skills audit.
- Prepare a business plan.
- Make appointment with bank manager.
- Investigate advertising costs.
- Prepare a marketing strategy.
- Plan publicity campaign.
- Inform tax office and DSS.
- Research for potential clients.
- Plan a start date and go for it!

CASE STUDY

Force-field analysis in action – Marjory

Marjory's doctor has told her she is about 34 lbs overweight and that her blood pressure is too high. The doctor recommends that Marjory lose some weight.

Goal

To lose 15 lbs within 3 months. This goal is both realistic and specific.

Restraining forces

- Marjory likes cooking.
- Marjory's husband, Peter, likes 'three good meals a day and none of this nonsense about dieting for me, thank you'.
- Marjory doesn't like doing exercise.
- Marjory is not convinced that her blood pressure is related to her weight.
- Marjory's grown-up children say, 'We like you as you are, Mum'.

Facilitating forces

- Marjory is a very determined lady.
- Marjory wants to wear dresses a size smaller.
- Marjory has a friend who is enthusiastic that she, too, wants to lose weight.
- Marjory wants to look presentable again in a swimsuit.

Action plan

- Get a well-balanced diet plan from the dietician at the health centre.
- Buy a new pair of reliable bathroom scales.
- Borrow from the library a book on healthy eating.
- Buy a dress one size smaller and keep it visible.

Coping with complex problems

Complex problems may need the creation of sub-goals, steps towards a larger goal. Each sub-goal has the same requirements as a goal.

Workable plans may founder on the rocks of:

1. too much detail
2. not taking into account the difficulties some people experience with a cognitive exercise if it does not take feeling, intuition and initiative into account.

There is more to helping than talking and planning. If clients are to live more effectively, they *must act*. When they refuse to act, they fail to cope with problems in living or do not exploit opportunities. The attainment of goals cannot be left to chance.

Only when the client speaks of the problem in the past tense has the goal been reached. Many programmes may have to be devised before the final outcome is reached. Clients cannot know whether or not they are making progress if they do not know from where they started or the milestones they should have reached.

Goals should be set neither too low nor too high. Goals set inappropriately high can cause the client to feel inadequate. Goals set too low do not generate enthusiasm.

Goals must be tailored to the uniqueness of the individual client.

Goals that are to be accomplished 'sometime or other' are rarely achieved.

Evaluation

Evaluation should identify:

- the different problems and how these were tackled
- the goals and how they have been achieved
- areas of growth and insight.

Evaluation encourages the growth of both client and counsellor. If counsellor and client are active partners in the evaluation process, they learn from each other. Ongoing evaluation gives both partners an opportunity to explore their feelings about what is happening and also to appraise constructively what should be done next.

Summary

- Help the client look beyond the problem and failure, toward success.
- Help the client construct alternative scenarios.

- Encourage the client to be specific.

- Get clients to state goals in terms of definite outcomes.

- Goals should be specific enough to drive action.

- Goals must be verifiable and measurable.

- Goals must be realistic in terms of personal and environmental resources.

- Goals must be chosen and owned by the client.

- Goals must be stated in a realistic time frame.

- Make sure, whenever possible, that the client chooses a preferred scenario from among options.

- Make sure that the chosen option is spelled out in sufficient detail.

- Help clients discover incentives or commitment in order to make the new scenario more attractive.

- Challenge the client to stretch beyond the comfort zone.

- Help clients identify the resources needed to make the preferred scenario work, including supportive and challenging relationships.

- The use of contracts enhances commitment.

Exercise 8.1

Goal setting

Step 1: My goal is

Write down a specific goal you would like to achieve within the next few months.

Step 2: Restraining forces

Identify any obstacles that are getting in the way of you reaching your goal. Include external and internal forces.

Step 3: Facilitating forces

Identify positive forces that can assist you in reaching your goal.

Step 4: Restraining forces

Identify ways you can think of to reduce these forces.

Step 5: Facilitating forces

Identify ways you can think of to increase these forces.

Plan of action

You may find that you do not need all ten steps to complete your plan.

My goal is: _____

The steps I need to take to achieve my goal.

1. _____

   Sub-goal

2. _____

   Sub-goal

3. _____

   Sub-goal

4. _____

   Sub-goal

5. _____

   Sub-goal

6. _____

   Sub-goal

7. _____

   Sub-goal

8. _____

   Sub-goal

9. _____

   Sub-goal

10. _____

   Sub-goal

Evaluation

Step	Goal – action taken	Date achieved
1.	_____	_____
2.	_____	_____
3.	_____	_____
4.	_____	_____
5.	_____	_____
6.	_____	_____
7.	_____	_____
8.	_____	_____
9.	_____	_____
10.	_____	_____

HELPING THE CLIENT BECOME MORE ASSERTIVE

Non-assertive behaviour can impede clients in achieving their goals. Thus, modelling assertiveness and encouraging clients to develop their assertiveness skills can be a valuable tool to help them attain their goals. The ability to be assertive can be empowering – it raises self-esteem, increases self-confidence and restores self-belief. According to Sutton (2000):

> *Assertive people express their needs clearly and honestly. They stand up for their rights and show respect for other people's needs and rights. They are genuine in their communication. They do not blame others. They work towards achieving equal communication and win-win situations, where both parties feel respected, valued and important.* (pp. 122–3)

Due to space limitation, we are restricted to 'scratching the surface' of assertiveness and its advantages, but recommend you take a closer look at the topic. It can be a precious stress, tension and anxiety-reducing technique that can benefit both clients and counsellors.

Assertiveness training

Assertiveness training seeks to help people become aware of:

- **Aggressive behaviour:** Aggressive behaviour is a **fight** response. The goal is conflict. Aggressive people violate the rights of others, humiliate others, put other people down – their goal is win–lose.

- **Indirect aggressive behaviour:** Indirect aggressive behaviour is more difficult to detect than directly aggressive behaviour (manipulation, sarcasm, emotional blackmail are examples). If you ever get the feeling that you've been hit by a sniper's bullet but there is no trace of an attacker, or that 'ouch that hurt' feeling, then chances are you may have been on the receiving end of indirect aggressive behaviour.

- **Passive behaviour:** Passive behaviour is a **flight** response. The goal is to ignore conflict and maintain harmony at all costs. Passive people allow themselves to be trampled on by others, and their rights to be violated. They generally have an overriding need to please.

- **Assertive behaviour:** The goal is direct, honest, open and appropriate verbal and non-verbal behaviour.

The power of self-belief

Our ability to be assertive is influenced by our life experiences. Clients whose upbringing has led to the beliefs that '*I am unworthy*', '*I don't deserve*' can, albeit perhaps unwittingly, set themselves up to behave in such a way that these beliefs become a self-fulfilling prophecy: for example, the client who repeatedly goes back to living with an abusive partner, believing they deserve no better. It is the right of every individual to feel they have a right to exist. Developing assertiveness skills enables non-assertive clients to:

- Manage difficult people and situations more effectively.

- Communicate their thoughts, feelings and needs more openly and genuinely.

- Set clear boundaries – what is personally acceptable/not acceptable.

- Take responsibility for their thoughts, feelings and actions without blaming others.

- Make clear 'I' statements – this is what 'I' think, feel . . .

- Validate their achievements.

- Change their mind without feeling guilty.

- Say 'no' without feeling guilty.

- Ask directly for what they need/want, rather than expecting others to second-guess what they need or want.

- Recognise that they have a responsibility **towards others**, as opposed to having a responsibility **for others**.

- Accept that making mistakes is inevitable for self and others.

- Stand up for their rights without violating the rights of others.

- Work towards achieving a compromise where conflicts exist.

- Respect other people's rights to be assertive.

Using an assertive approach to expressing feelings

As previously mentioned, encouraging clients to own their feelings by using 'I' statements fosters open communication. The following assertive approach is a productive way to express feelings:

- 'I feel . . . *[describe emotion]* with you because . . . *[give reason]*.'

- 'I feel . . . *[describe emotion]* about . . . *[give reason]*.'

Adopting this approach enables clients to express their feelings and the reason for their feelings. It is honest and clear communication. By using 'I' statements, clients are taking responsibility. They are not blaming the other person. To get out of the blaming trap they need to eliminate unassertive statements from their vocabulary.

Examples of blaming non-assertive statements

- 'You have made me . . . *[describe emotion]*.' For example, *'You've made me very upset.'* Reworked: 'I am upset.'

- 'You have . . . *[describe emotion]*.' For example, *'You've hurt me.'* Reworked: 'I feel hurt.'

Examples of assertive statements

- 'I *love* being with you.'

- 'I *really appreciate* it when you help me with the housework.'

- 'I am feeling *very apprehensive* about this interview.'

- 'I feel *annoyed* because you have broken your promise.'

Assertive speech

Many of us fail to be assertive because of the negative labels we carry or because we feel constrained by conforming to stereotypes.

An important technique in assertiveness training is getting people to make positive self-statements instead of negative ones. Participants are encouraged to create assertive hierarchies, starting with an encounter that would be relatively easy to handle and progressing to the most difficult, then to rehearse them in the group. One of the aims in assertive behaviour is to change from being indirect to being direct and from using generalisations to being specific.

Examples:

Generalised: You don't love me.

Specific: When you come home from work, I would like you to kiss me.

Generalised: You never think about anyone but yourself.

Specific: If you know that you're going to be late phone me. I worry about you.

Generalised: You're a male chauvinist pig.

Specific: I want you to listen to me while I'm stating my opinions, even if you don't agree.

Generalised: All you ever do is work.

Specific: I would like us to go to the beach next week.

Generalised: You never talk to me any more.

Specific: I'd like us to sit down together – with no TV – and talk for a few minutes each night.

Assertive speech means:

- Saying no when we mean no, and yes when we mean yes.

- Not being afraid to ask a favour. However, asking favours is not necessarily being assertive; many fiercely independent people find it difficult to ask favours.

- Not being afraid to say how you feel in an open and direct way. However, wisdom has to prevail; there is an appropriate time and place to communicate feelings and being assertive does not mean having to blurt everything out.

- Handling put-downs in a positive way. A simple, 'That remark really hurt me' is far more effective and healthy than ranting and raving or going off in a sulk.

Assertive behaviour is based on being:

- Open rather than obscure.

- Direct rather than indirect.

- Authentic rather than false.

- Appropriate rather than inappropriate.

Understanding assertiveness is not the same thing as being able to practise it; that is where counsellors can help clients, by engaging in role-play. Get clients to adopt an exaggerated non-assertive posture – head down, not looking the counsellor in the eye and speaking in a soft voice. Then get them to reverse that and move on to the next phase.

People who are non-assertive often think negative thoughts about themselves and other people, and compare themselves unfavourably with others. This is where cognitive behavioural therapy is such a boon, for it challenges every faulty thought and helps the client to substitute negative thoughts with positive ones. (See Chapter 11.)

It has to be pointed out that when a person has lived most of their life in the non-assertive mode, change will take time; but change is possible and rewarding. However, therein also lies a snag; other people have become so accustomed to how the client has behaved (and possibly have taken advantage) that their behaviour will have to change accordingly and they might find that so uncomfortable that they resist. So when one person changes, it causes a chain reaction and the client and the counsellor must be prepared for this. And one final word – people often mistake assertion for aggression, but when an assertive message is delivered with caring, it does not harm the other person, whereas an aggressive message will.

Exercises

This activity is designed to help your clients practise owning and taking responsibility for their feelings. If deemed appropriate, the client may add the word **you** after the statement. For example, I feel happy when **you** . . .

I feel ... when

I feel   happy when   _____

I feel   angry when   _____

I feel   frightened when   _____

I feel   sad when   _____

I feel   stimulated when   _____

The list can always be added to by the client.

Taken from Sutton, J. (2000). *Thriving On Stress: Manage pressure and positively thrive on it!*

Obstacles to assertiveness

- Lack of awareness that we have the option of responding in an assertive manner.

- Anxiety about expressing ourselves, even when we know what we want to say, in a way that expresses how we feel.

- Negative self-talk inhibits self-assertion by what we tell ourselves.

- Verbal poverty: A difficulty in finding the right words at the right time leads to self-consciousness and hesitancy.

- Behavioural poverty: A non-assertive, non-verbal manner hinders all assertive expression.

Self-assertiveness assessment test

Instructions

Consider each question thoughtfully and decide whether it fits with how you behave.

There are no right or wrong answers – the important thing is to be honest with yourself.

Tick whichever box you think best describes you.

	True	False
1. I can usually ask for what I want without feeling anxious	☐	☐
2. I often get treated like a doormat	☐	☐
3. I can usually say 'no' to requests without feeling guilty	☐	☐
4. I often find it difficult to express my feelings	☐	☐
5. I often keep my opinions to myself	☐	☐
6. I accept that I make mistakes and that other people make mistakes too	☐	☐
7. I try to please others all the time	☐	☐
8. I'm forever saying sorry to other people	☐	☐
9. I put other people's needs first most of the time	☐	☐
10. I often get pushed around	☐	☐
11. I find it difficult to stand up for my rights	☐	☐
12. I can usually voice my beliefs	☐	☐
13. I need to be liked and approved of by everyone	☐	☐
14. I take responsibility for my actions without blaming other people	☐	☐
15. I respect myself and show respect for other people	☐	☐
16. In a conflict situation I am prepared to work towards a compromise	☐	☐
17. I often have a subtle dig at other people	☐	☐
18. I can give compliments easily	☐	☐
19. I get embarrassed when people pay me compliments and usually shrug them off	☐	☐
20. I can give constructive criticism	☐	☐
21. I take criticism to heart and can't let go of it	☐	☐
22. I take criticism in my stride	☐	☐
23. I accept that not everyone will like me	☐	☐

24. I'm not bothered if people don't like me   □   v

25. I prefer to avoid conflict situations   □   □

26. I often use sarcasm to have a dig at people   □   □

27. I often manipulate other people to get my needs met   □   □

28. I have a tendency to humiliate other people   □   □

29. It's vital that I win   □   □

30. I sometimes violate the rights of other people   □   □

31. I can change my mind without feeling guilty   □   □

32. I can usually stand my ground in an argument   □   □

33. I never admit I'm wrong when having an argument   □   □

34. I refuse to let people get the better of me   □   □

35. I use humour to poke fun at people   □   □

36. When I feel angry I seethe inside and say nothing
    or sulk   □   □

37. When I feel angry I lash out physically or verbally   □   □

38. When I feel angry with someone I own my anger, and
    can express it directly to the person I feel angry with,
    without judging or blaming him or her. (*I'm* angry
    with you because . . . rather than, *You've* made me
    angry because . . .)   □   □

39. I demand my money back if I buy a faulty item   □   □

40. If someone jumps in a queue before me, I say nothing   □   □

Passive	Aggressive	Indirectly aggressive	Assertive
2	24	17	1
4	28	26	3
5	29	27	6
7	30	35	12
8	33		14
9	34		15
10	37		16
11	39		18
13			20
19			22
21			23
25			31
36			32
40			38

FINAL SUMMARY

This chapter has provided you with a goal setting model that can be used with clients to help them explore and resolve their problems. We have highlighted that once learned, this valuable tool can be used as a self-help method for problem solving. In addition to goal setting the section on assertiveness will give clients another skill to add to their repertoire of interpersonal skills.

This brings to an end the chapters dealing with counsellor qualities and skills, so it seems an appropriate place to map out what has been covered – an overview of the counselling process). In Chapter 9 we shall cover the termination phase of counselling, with an illustrative case study.

AN OVERVIEW OF THE COUNSELLING PROCESS

1. Counsellor provides the core conditions of:

Genuineness, unconditional positive regard, empathic understanding and non-possessive warmth.

The aim is to build a therapeutic relationship.

2. Counsellor uses the basic skills of:

Primary level empathy, active listening and attending, paraphrasing content and reflecting feelings, using open questions, summarising, focusing and concreteness,

The aim is to facilitate exploration of the problem.

3. Counsellor uses the advanced skills of:

Challenging and confronting, advanced level empathy, immediacy and self-disclosure.

The aim is to facilitate understanding of the problem.

4. Counsellor teaches the skills of:

Problem solving and goal setting

The aim is to facilitate resolution of the problem and to help the client move forward.

SOME KEY POINTS TO CONSIDER

Before we move on to discuss the topic of preparing for termination of counselling, there are two important points we consider need to be addressed:

- It is crucial to bear in mind that every client is a unique individual who comes with their own distinctive set of needs, and no particular approach or model of counselling is right for every client. Don't straitjacket the client; be flexible, listen to the client's needs and be prepared to adjust your approach if necessary.

- In practice, the skills presented in this book often overlap, and it is worth remembering that some clients work more effectively by exploring their feelings – an affective approach – while others get more from counselling by using their thinking capacity – a cognitive approach. Goal setting is more cognitive than affective; although to be truly effective both head and heart must be used.

REFERENCES

Sutton, J. (2000). *Thriving On Stress: Manage pressure and positively thrive on it!* Oxford: How To Books.

CHAPTER 9

Terminating the Counselling Relationship

In Chapter 8, one of the areas we focused on was goal setting. Ending the counselling relationship is, in itself, a goal. Counselling is a relationship with a purpose. Within it are the seeds of the ending that will come when the purpose is completed. Termination is built into the initial contract, and is kept in view throughout the entire counselling relationship. A 'weaning off' period is recommended, especially if counselling has taken place over a long time.

THE ENDING PHASE OF COUNSELLING

Charles Gerkin (1993) identifies four issues related to ending counselling:

1. How to help people make the transition from an intense, therapeutic relationship back into everyday life without that relationship. The return to the community, for many, may not be an easy journey. Where, for them, is the understanding, totally accepting, non-judgmental person to whom they have said farewell?

2. The degree of control the counsellor exercises as to the outcomes of counselling. Where the person already has allegiance to a community of faith, the aim of counselling will be to strengthen that commitment.

3. How the pastoral counsellor handles the termination of clients who do not have a relationship with a community of faith. The pastoral counsellor can never ensure the moral correctness or lasting outcome of counselling.

4. Issues concerned with care and service. The final phase of counselling is the turning away from the primary concern for self and its welfare, toward service and concern for others.

Indicators of the ending phase of counselling:

- Signals of integration and wholeness.

    Higher level of energy and the sense of well-being.

    Spontaneity of affect (feeling).

    Evidence of shared involvement.

    Self-esteem and self-criticism are more realistic.

    Fragmentation is giving way to transformation of the life story.

    Realism is replacing fantasy.

- Signals of altered behaviour and altered relationships.

    Increased understanding of behaviour and meaning.

    Congruency between behaviour in relationships.

    Signals of clearer understanding of soul issues.

    An awakening to the possibilities of the future.

    A growing awareness of one's relationship with other souls.

- Signals of openness to travelling beyond, and to, the story.

    A style of openness to life experience involving faith.

    A growing ability to go beyond the obvious and explicit.

    An openness to the flow of events in one's life.

    Changed attitude toward self and toward the world.

    No longer at war with one's life story.

    A realisation that one is a pilgrim among pilgrims.

    A greater sensitivity to the suffering of others.

PREPARING FOR TERMINATION

Termination should be well planned and worked through. Premature endings can be traumatic to both client and counsellor. Termination should be approached with as much sensitivity and caring as any stage in the counselling. When counselling has taken place over a long period, the original reason(s) may have faded into insignificance.

Counselling is like taking a journey; we know from where we have come, and roughly the route taken, but looking back, the starting point has become obscured, partly through distance, but also through time. Unlike a journey, it is necessary for both counsellor and client to look back in order to firmly establish the final position. Looking back to where and why the journey began may prove difficult; feelings, as well as memories, fade with time. Looking back is not always comfortable. It may reveal obstacles not previously recognised.

PREMATURE TERMINATION BY THE CLIENT

Clients' premature exit from counselling can be attributed to a variety of reasons. However, ending counselling early does not necessarily imply a negative experience such as the counselling not meeting the client's needs or expectations. It could be that the client has reached a stage in the process where he or she has achieved sufficient new insights and confidence to tackle some of the issues the client intended to address. The client may recognise that there are other deeper issues that are important to focus on, but feels the need to take time out before working on resolving these more complex issues.

If a pause in counselling is imminent, it remains important for counsellor and client to discuss any potential losses perceived in the client temporarily discontinuing therapy, to ascertain the client's progress and sense of personal accomplishments, to confer over key unresolved issues that the client might want to address in the future, to agree on a plan for resuming counselling at a later date and to prepare for a separation period.

TERMINAL EVALUATION

The relationship between counsellor and client is not an end in itself. Evaluation helps to establish just how the client has been able to transfer the learning into relationships outside of counselling. Evaluation helps the client to realise and acknowledge personal gains. The counsellor, in return, receives something from every counselling relationship.

A terminal evaluation should identify:

1. The different problems and how these were tackled.

2. The goals and how they have been achieved.

3. Areas of growth and insights.

A terminal evaluation gives both client and counsellor a feeling of completeness. It gives the counsellor an opportunity to look at some of those things that did not go according to plan, as well as those that did. A well carried out evaluation not only looks backward, it also looks forward. A final evaluation provides the client with something positive to carry into the future.

Success? Failure? Shared responsibility

Success is not always so easily measured. A person who comes for one session and leaves saying, 'I feel better for having talked it over, even though there is nothing you can actually do,' may then be more able to cope with life.

For example, Angela, a middle-aged woman, came to see her counsellor, William. She had multiple difficulties arising from a disastrous second marriage. She had left her first husband, 'a boring and uninteresting man', for a 'good-looking, jolly, charming man', who later turned into a criminal and who, at the time she met the counsellor, was in prison. She poured out her story, saying as she finished, 'I know there's nothing you can do. But it has helped to talk about it and not hide it.'

Success and progress or failure – whose responsibility is it?

Whose credit or whose responsibility? Unlike the engineer carrying out a bench procedure, the counsellor has no blueprint to follow and ultimately it is the client who must shoulder the responsibility for his own decisions and actions. *The counsellor can never remain absolutely neutral or unaffected by the outcome of counselling.*

It would be all too easy when counselling ends without seeing positive results to pass all the responsibility on to the client. If counsellors feel, 'If only I had been more open, more communicative, less defensive,' and so on, this should lead to them fully evaluating their own contribution.

Similarly, it may be easy, when counselling ends positively, for counsellors to accept all the credit, forgetting that whatever their contribution has been, it was the clients who were in focus throughout; and whatever was happening within the counsellors, much more was likely to be happening within the clients. If counsellors experienced growth from conflict within the counselling relationship, much more did the clients experience conflict and subsequent growth. To the client then must go the credit for whatever success has been achieved. Likewise, lack of success must remain with the client. The counsellor shares in both.

Clients who have succeeded in climbing a few hills are more likely to want to tackle mountains, and, emotionally, are more equipped to do so. Counsellors who have helped create an atmosphere of trust and respect, and have helped a client travel a little way along the road of self-discovery, are entitled to share the success the client feels.

The feeling of failure in counselling is difficult to handle. Blame should not be attributed to either counsellor or client. Both (if possible, if not the counsellor alone) should examine what did happen rather than what did not happen. *When counselling goes full term, it is unlikely to have been a failure.*

The feeling of failure, and consequent blame, is more likely when the client terminates prematurely. When counsellors have created a conducive climate, and clients are unable to travel their own road toward self-discovery, then the responsibility for not travelling that road must rest with them.

Some possible indicators of impending termination

- Abandonment; acting out, or apathy
- Decrease in intensity, denial
- Expressions of anger
- Feelings of separation and loss
- Futility
- Impotence
- Inadequacy
- Intellectualising
- Joking
- Lateness
- Missed appointments
- Mourning
- Regression
- Withdrawal.

CASE STUDY 9.1

Joan's final evaluation – continued from Chapter 1

Summary

Joan was in therapy for sixteen sessions. She and I had a warm relationship in which Joan was able to explore many of her feelings. She worked through these towards an understanding of the factors that had contributed to her loss of zest for life.

The following were the main issues identified:

- Retirement with loss of status.

- Change of identity and role.

- Loss of colleagues as friends.

- What to do with leisure time.

The following were the main feelings identified:

- Loneliness.

- As if starting to wander through a wilderness.

- Fear of the future.

- Fear of ill health.

- Anxieties about the previous surgery.

- Rejected by society.

- Fear of not having enough money to live on.

The following were the main approaches used in counselling:

- Exploration of feelings.

- Using imagery to identify feelings.

- Using force-field analysis to work towards goals.

- Homework that concentrated on matching local needs to her abilities.

The following were the main parts of the action plan:

- Discussions with various voluntary organisations and offers of help.

- Discussions with the bank manager and an investment company, on how to invest her retirement gratuity.

- Exploring the possibility of becoming a home tutor.

- To go back to studying for a doctorate.

- To take in one or two university students as lodgers.

Joan left with the understanding that further sessions would be possible if and when they were needed. The ending of therapy brings the satisfaction of having been involved with the soul of another. This is often coupled with the humbling acceptance that perhaps not all that was hoped for has been achieved. Added to this is the knowledge that in the helping, one has been helped; that in sharing the pain of another's wounds, one's own wounds have been touched and transformed. Above all, there is a sense of gratitude that whatever was changed was made possible by the spiritual presence.

William and Joan wanted the final evaluation to cover:

1. *The different problems and how these were tackled.*

2. *The goals and how they have been achieved.*

3. *Areas of growth and insights.*

William: Well, Joan, this is the last session, doesn't time fly, and we ought to spend time on evaluating the time we've been together. You'll remember that it was something we talked about at the contracting stage. So, once again, it's a joint effort. You start.

Joan: The first point on this handout you've given me is how the different problems were tackled. I appreciated the gentle, but firm way you helped me unravel the mess I was in. All I could see was a very black future, with nothing to give to anyone. You remember how early on I described this as walking in outer space, without any guideposts.

William: Yes, I remember that session very well. That was when I suggested you find yourself a guide, and then this beautiful woman appeared. You and she had a private chat that seemed to last for quite a while. Whatever she said made an immediate impression on you, for your face lit up, and you left that session with a spring in your step that I hadn't seen before.

Joan: One of these days I may tell you, though I know you're not prying. I can say, however, that it wasn't so much what she said, as what happened within me. For it was after that when the various parts of the problem really started to separate. Seeing them as parts really helped me to move on. Do you remember when you asked me to pick up one of the parts and examine it closely? I thought, 'How silly, how can I pick it up?' Yet as I did, it shrank to become a beautiful rough-cut sapphire. We both shed tears over that.

William: Yes, that was a precious moment, as you accepted that what
              you thought of as a problem was really something potentially
              precious. It seems now, looking back, that much of the stress
              you were under was tied up with the prospect of a dramatic
              change in lifestyle.

Joan: Oh, yes! I couldn't really believe that life would have any
              meaning any more. Hearing myself say that sounds really silly,
              but it only goes to show how much I'd become wrapped up in
              my job. My job had become me, and that sounds awful. Now
              that I've actually retired, I'm beginning to enjoy it, and life is so
              full.

William: On looking back, Joan, your goal was to accept retirement;
              listening to you now, it seems that you have reached your goal?

Joan: Yes, certainly. It's quite strange, really, how the fears vanished
              like a cobweb in the sunlight. Just one of them – not having
              enough to live on – is laughable now, though at the time it
              virtually kept me from sleeping. The bank manager soon sorted
              me out on that one.

William: Then there was the fear of illness.

Joan: It was practically a phobia, you know. I used to pummel
              my tummy every night to see if there was another growth
              appearing. I told you, remember, and you suggested I might like
              to talk to my GP, to put my mind at rest. I thought about that,
              but never got round to it. That's gone, too.

William: I think this is the final part, Joan, what about any leisure time,
              though listening to you, have you any?

Joan: Yes, I do, funnily enough. I did think about academic study,
              but decided against that – too near to home. Don't laugh, but
              I've just enrolled for an evening class in carpentry! I've kept
              that little bit of news until now. I knew you'd be delighted. I've
              always liked wood, and my father was a cabinetmaker, a very
              talented one. So twice a week I'll be off with my dress and on
              with the overalls.

William: We talked about other parts of the action plan, but somehow
              they no longer seem very relevant. We've journeyed together
              over some very interesting country, and even into outer space.

Thank you for allowing me to journey with you. One last thing, let's concoct a final letter to your GP.

Joan and William's letter

You referred Miss Joan— for counselling, and this is our joint letter to keep you informed. Joan and I have worked together for sixteen sessions. One of the points on which you referred her was her ebbing away of zest for life. This seemed to be linked to various fears and anxieties, which had their focus on her impending retirement from teaching.

Together we teased out the various component parts of the total problem, and, having done this, Joan found it much easier to look objectively at her life. We explored many issues which resulted in greater understanding of the nature of her difficulties. We set up an action plan, which she is still following through, though she would be the first to admit that some of the possibilities on that plan no longer have priority.

Now that Joan has retired, she finds life much more exciting and full than she could ever have imagined. We have an understanding that should she ever feel the need for further sessions, she can come direct to me.

Yours sincerely, _____

Joan left counselling with the understanding that further sessions would be possible if and when they were needed.

TRAVELLING AT THE CLIENT'S PACE

We can only take people along the road of self-discovery who are willing to travel that road, and travelling at the client's pace is crucial. Pressure brought to bear on clients to work through their difficulties too early in the process or too quickly, or probing into areas where the client is not ready or willing to go, not only carries the risk of traumatising the client, or causing emotional harm, it may bring about a sudden and unscheduled termination of counselling by the client. As Sutton (2007: 339) emphasises, 'the client needs to stay safe within the boundaries of the "bearable".'

SUMMARY

Saying goodbye can be painful and that is one of the feelings that has to be acknowledged; all endings have an echo of death and with death comes grief and loss. Often there is a desire to continue, expressed in, 'Let's meet up again, shall we?'

The longer the relationship, the deeper the exploration and the more insights gained, the more difficult it can be to end. Both client and counsellor may feel this, and sometimes both will delay the final closing of the door. Yet as we said at the start, every counselling relationship has within the seeds of its own ending. Just as a young person leaves childhood behind, and the adult leaves adolescence behind, so the client has to move forward. The counselling relationship has been but a stage in the client's journey, which the counsellor has been privileged to share, but if the ending has been kept in sight from the start, then both client and counsellor will accept it as an essential part of the overall relationship. In the next chapter we discuss the important topic of counsellor self-care, something that all counsellors need to consider seriously to alleviate the risk of suffering from burnout.

> *You give but little when you give of your possessions.*
> *It is when you give of yourself that you truly give.*
>
> Kahlil Gibran

REFERENCES

Gerkin, Charles Vincent (1993). *The Living Human Document: Revisioning Pastoral Counselling in a Hermeneutical Mode*, Abingdon Press, Nashville.

Sutton, J. (2007). *Healing the Hurt Within: Understand Self-injury and Self-harm, and Heal the Emotional Wounds.* 3rd revised edition. Oxford: How To Books.

CHAPTER 10

Counsellor Self-Care

To keep a lamp burning we have to keep putting oil in it.
Mother Teresa of Calcutta (1910–97)

Counselling is essentially creative and if we don't care for ourselves, we may find that our creative spirit declines.

In Chapter 9, we emphasised the importance of planning for the termination of counselling, and the potential effects of premature endings on both client and counsellor. In this final chapter, we focus our attention on yet another noteworthy topic – the need for counsellor self-care. Constant empathic engagement and giving our all to our clients, particularly traumatised or resistant clients, is emotionally demanding, and if the counsellor does not recognise the warning signs of emotional and physical exhaustion, and manage them effectively, the consequences can prove extremely costly. Depleted personal resources and exhaustion not only show themselves in reduced client empathy, they can affect every area of our life – from snapping inappropriately at the kids or our partner, to being forever tired and irritable, or not sleeping properly because we cannot switch off, or detach from, worrying about whether we are doing the right thing with our clients and keep replaying things over and over in our mind. Ignoring what is happening within us, or burying our head in the sand to the pressure we feel under, and failing to nip it in the bud, invariably leads to decreased functioning and burnout, defined in the Merriam-Webster's Online Dictionary as 'exhaustion of physical or emotional strength or motivation usually as a result of prolonged stress or frustration.' http://www.merriam-webster.com/dictionary/burn+out

WHY COUNSELLORS NEED SUPERVISION

For counselling to be productive, counsellors must be continually moving forward towards increased understanding of themselves in relation to other people.

Repeatedly they will be brought into contact with clients whose problems will awaken within them something that will create resistance or conflict *within that relationship and specific to it*. The client's difficulty will not be adequately resolved until the counsellor's own resistance or conflict is resolved.

The client may seek help from other sources, but if she does the counsellor's personal development may be retarded. When faced with a situation where their own emotions are thrown into turmoil or where counselling appeas to have reached stalemate, there are three courses of action that counsellors may take. They can pull the blanket over their heads and hope that the problem will go away, they can work at it on their own or they can seek help.

There is an element of truth in what people say – one must have experienced something before one can really help others. This does not mean that the counsellor must have passed through an *identical* experience, but it is important that every person who engages in counselling has been the recipient in a helping relationship. Many people who counsel have personal experience of what it is like to be a client, and it has been this experience that has prompted them to become counsellors. Not everyone has had this first-hand experience and yet it is possible to experience similar feelings when it becomes necessary to seek the help of someone else during counselling.

In counselling, we hope that clients will achieve a degree of insight in order to see their problem more realistically. If insight is essential for the client, how much more essential is it for the counsellor? If it is necessary for clients to seek help from someone to work through their problems, it is equally important for the counsellor.

People in need of counselling have probably put off seeking help and have tried to work it out for themselves, but to no avail – the problem is still there. They may feel inadequate; that they should have been able to manage. They may think, 'Can this other person really help?' Counsellors may experience similar feelings when it is obvious that the counselling relationship has turned sour; that the client is being difficult, resistant, hostile or whatever. Is it easier for the counsellor in this position to go to someone else for help than it was for the client to approach the counsellor in the first instance? At that stage counsellors, in their heart, know how the client feels. Counsellors may resist it, and rebel against it, but only if they submit to this experience, when it becomes necessary, will their counselling once more assume accurate empathy.

The supervisor assumes an important role in counselling. The supervisor will assist the counsellor to resolve the difficulty that has arisen between the counsellor and the client, mainly because the supervisor can stand outside and explore with the counsellor what is happening within the client, within the counsellor and in the relationship between counsellor and client.

The supervisor will be able to use what happens between him or herself and the counsellor – the supervision relationship – to point to what may be happening between the counsellor and the client. This is similar to how the counsellor may be able to point out to the client that what happens between them may be similar to what happens between the client and other people. For the counsellor who has such a mentor relationship the potential for personal awareness is infinite. Counsellors who choose to disregard such a relationship will lose out and run the risk of eventually becoming ineffective in their counselling.

Supervision helps counsellors to increase their skills and develop understanding and sensitivity of their own and the clients' feelings. The supervisory relationship is not primarily a therapeutic one; the task of the supervisor falls somewhere between counselling and tutoring. Supervision is developmental, helping the counsellor examine her relationship with particular clients and the counselling process.

The supervisory relationship forms a three-way relationship of client, counsellor and supervisor. Supervision is often resisted, because people don't use it fully. Counsellors who disregard the supervision relationship will lose out and run the risk of their counselling becoming stale.

Ongoing supervision is a professional requirement for all BACP members who are practising counsellors. (http://www.bacp.co.uk/) The function of supervision is to facilitate the enhancement of the counsellor's theoretical knowledge, skills and personal development as a practitioner – it is not aimed at providing personal therapy. Thus, the task of the supervisor falls between the polarities of expert and apprentice.

Increasing self-understanding

Supervision is the first 'port of call' when concerned about a client's problems or feeling 'stuck' and unable to see the best way forward. Just as counsellors enable their clients to unravel their concerns, view things in a different light, make informed decisions and take strides forward, so it is with supervision.

Seeking supervision if a counselling relationship appears to have turned 'sour', if the client is actively being resistant, hostile or difficult, if the counsellor feels out of their depth or if counselling has reached stale-mate, is an absolute must to prevent what could potentially result in the counselling relationship degenerating into a recipe for disaster for both client and counsellor.

Understanding the supervisor's role in counselling

Supervisors can provide valuable guidance to counsellors by offering a one-step-removed perception on any difficulties that are arising between counsellor and client. In other words, the supervisor can offer an objective, rather than subjective, view of what might be happening in the interaction between the two, based on counsellor reporting of the situation as opposed to being 'in the room' with the client.

A supervisor is a non-participating interested spectator/observer standing on the outside looking in. Additionally, the supervisor may be able to use what is happening within the supervisory relationship to point to what may be happening between the counsellor and the client and between significant others in their outside world. As such, the engagement in a fruitful supervisory relationship has infinite potential for the counsellor to grow and develop. Counsellors who choose to disregard such a relationship will lose out and run the risk of eventually becoming ineffective in their counselling.

The essence of the supervisory relationship is simple:

> I proceed with a case of counselling and, on a regular basis, report back to another counsellor with whom I discuss what transpired in the counselling of the client and how the supervisory relationship affects me personally.

Components of the supervisory relationship

- To support and encourage the counsellor.
- To teach the counsellor to integrate theoretical knowledge and practice.
- To assess the maintenance of standards.
- To transmit professional values and ethics.
- To help the counsellor develop through insight.
- To enable the counsellor to develop skills and build self-confidence.

- To enable the counsellor to share vulnerabilities, disappointments and to be aware of his limitations.

- To help the counsellor move forward with a client if she feels stuck.

- To enable the counsellor to evaluate his work and effectiveness.

- To share ideas and explore different counselling approaches.

- To report on the client's progress or lack of progress.

- To recharge the counsellor's batteries.

Types of supervision

Supervision can be achieved in several ways:

1. One-to-one supervision

Individual supervision is a formal arrangement between counsellor and supervisor wherein they meet on a regular basis to discuss the counsellor's casework. The advantages of one-to-one supervision are that the time is wholly the counsellor's, and the entire session is totally confidential and related to the counsellor's client(s). The main disadvantage is that the counsellor only gets the perspective and experience of the supervisor and works with only one approach.

2. Co-supervision or peer supervision

This is usually recommended for experienced counsellors who meet on a regular basis. The advantages are the mix of different views and hearing about different cases and the skills used. The insights gained are increased as each case is explored and as different skills and techniques are shared. The disadvantages are that sessions need to be longer and each person's time is limited. Another disadvantage for some people is the lack of structure.

3. Peer group supervision

This is a small group typically comprising experienced counsellors who meet together at regular intervals to present their cases, discuss any difficulties encountered in their client work, enhance their practice, and for mutual support. In this form of supervision, group members may temporarily take on the role of supervisor on a rotating basis. BACP does not advocate this supervision approach for counselling trainees or recently qualified counsellors.

4. Group supervision

Group supervision is a formal arrangement between a small group of counsellors and a designated supervisor, who meet on a regular basis. Typically, the supervisor assumes responsibility for dividing the supervision time among group members. The advantages of group supervision are that members benefit from feedback on the quality of their practice from both supervisor and their peers, and the opportunity to listen to other members present their casework, which can provide valuable learning. The disadvantage is that the shared time may prevent in-depth discussion of a case that an individual counsellor has concerns about.

Three approaches to supervision

Focus on the case – characteristics of this approach:

(a) Exploration of case material.

(b) Concentrated mainly on what took place, with little if any exploration of the counsellor's feelings.

(c) Little exploration of the counselling relationship.

(d) A teacher/pupil relationship.

(e) Discussion is more in the 'then-and-there' than in the 'here-and-now'.

This approach may create a relationship of the expert and the novice who seeks to please. Because there is often a climate of criticism in this case-centred style of supervision there may be a tendency for the counsellor to skate over the events he is ashamed of or doubtful about revealing – so there may be an 'evasion factor' in the discussion.

Focus on the counsellor – characteristics of this approach:

(a) The counselling relationship and what is happening within the counsellor.

(b) Feelings are more readily acknowledged.

(c) Carried out in an uncritical atmosphere.

The belief that underpins this approach is that learning is only meaningful if it is personal, so it is advocated that links are made between situations in casework and the counsellor's own personal circumstances. With this approach, the counsellor is likely to feel less criticised and so more supported and thus the ability to learn from the teaching offered may be greater.

Focus on the interaction – characteristics of this approach:

(a) Takes into account both the case and the counselling relationship.

(b) The interaction between client and counsellor may, in some way, be reflected in the supervisor relationship. Recognising the interaction, and working with it, is likely to provide the counsellor with invaluable first-hand experience.

The key to this interactive approach is that the counsellor's behaviour with the case is not taken up directly, but always in relation to the effect the client is having on them. The interactive supervisor knows that the counsellor normally manages his cases thoughtfully and assumes, therefore, what has happened tells him something about the dynamics of the case. Clearly not everything a counsellor does is a reflection of the case, and the supervisor would need to draw attention to how the counsellor is using defences to avoid dealing with a particular issue. Perhaps in certain circumstances he or she might even suggest therapy elsewhere to help, but would not deal with the problem personally.

BURNOUT AND HOW TO PREVENT IT

Burnout is a term used in two ways: to describe the injurious effects of the stress of counselling upon counsellors; and to describe the injurious effects of stress, particularly related to work.

Counsellor burnout

In counselling, burnout, resulting in physical or psychological withdrawal, is characterised by:

- chronic low levels of energy
- defensive behaviour
- distancing emotionally from people.

Counsellors often look forward to sessions where there is progress and dread sessions that don't go anywhere. Sessions that go badly have a debilitating effect on the counsellor, because prolonged client resistance depletes energy. Burnout may also be associated with the relationship in which there is a high level of empathy and with the high level of concentration that goes with giving full attention.

Counsellors who feel that they are starting to be impatient with clients or with members of the family, who are having difficulty sleeping, who feel that there are never, ever, enough hours in the day and that they simply could not face taking on another client, are probably heading for burnout.

If counsellors suggest that their clients take stock of their lives, can they do less with theirs? Finding satisfying ways to recharge the batteries is essential in order to prevent burnout.

To avoid the risk of burnout, or whatever term we choose to use, invariably poses the question of what counsellors can do to minimise the hazard of falling foul of what can be a debilitating experience. Certainly, there are two positive routes that counsellors can take – one being supervision to ensure professional, ethical and competent practice and the second being to devise a personal action plan to safeguard against falling victim to the disabling consequences of feeling 'sucked dry' and unable to cope. These two themes are therefore the primary focus of this chapter. We start by looking at supervision, and discussing several approaches to supervision. This is followed by suggestions to prevent the risk of burnout, and three case studies.

CASE STUDY 10.1

Tom's account of how he survived burnout at work

I work as a counsellor in a large college. I was finding myself getting tired and irritable, not at work but at home. Always biting the children's heads off. I had to take stock. So I asked myself some searching questions.

Goals

I decided that the goals I had originally hadn't changed. I still enjoyed my work with the students as well as my teaching role. I do experience some conflicts, in that sometimes the college want me to put their needs before the individual needs of the students who are my clients.

Resources

I fit in well with the other staff and they accept me and the job I do, and are ready to help if I need help. They also ask me for help. I don't experience any difficulty with the things like health and safety, or environmental factors. I do have difficulty sometimes getting access to photocopying facilities, and that annoys me. The college allows me supervision time and that's crucial.

Compare goals with resources

Overall, I consider I am well catered for. I feel a trusted and valued member of the team.

I know that my quarterly reports are read and absorbed.

Time to plan

An essential part of planning is thinking, and I am given a lot of leeway in planning my time so that I can be effective.

So why do I feel stressed?

The main reason is that I don't allocate enough time for me. I have to travel twenty miles each way every day. I like driving, but the traffic winds me up. If I left earlier, I could beat some of the worst of the traffic. I often have to do teaching preparation at home. If I cut the number of counselling sessions by one, I could have that hour for preparation and I wouldn't need to bring it home. Problem: I find it difficult to say no! Must discuss that with my supervisor. I think I've worked out how I can reduce some of the stress. If I can, then I can survive.

CASE STUDY 10.2

Burnt-out Bernice

Bernice set up her own aromatherapy practice. She loved helping people and enjoyed talking to her clients. Initially she was full of enthusiasm, had boundless energy and put her all into her work. Her hard work paid dividends; within a year, she had built a very successful business.

However, after about three years she noticed that she was feeling very tired and her enthusiasm was waning. As her energy levels decreased so did her ability to sleep. Everyday tasks became more difficult to cope with, and she started feeling an element of resentment towards her clients for making so many demands on her energy and time. She began to get headaches and backache, and on waking each morning felt as if she'd hardly slept a wink. Normally a calm and relaxed person, she was surprised at what a short fuse she was on. She would suddenly explode at her husband for no reason, and was rather cool towards her clients.

She pushed herself harder and harder to try to cope with her increasing workload, despite a large part of her wanting to run away and say 'to hell with everything'. After pushing herself in this way for a further six months, Bernice collapsed. She was admitted to hospital suffering from burnout. Bernice had become starved of vital fuel. She had nothing left in reserve to keep her going, rather like a car that's run out of petrol and hasn't been properly maintained.

(Taken from Sutton, J. [2000:17]).

CASE STUDY 10.3

Andy talks to his supervisor

(For a verbatim account of the whole session see Tom Jenkins in William Stewart (1979) *Health Service Counselling*, Pitman Medical.)

This is the second session between Tom, a laundryman, and Andy, his manager. Tom has been in trouble over causing a machine failure. Andy is interested in counselling, having attended a course on counselling at work. The early counselling relationship was strained; Andy's attempts to make emotional contact with Tom proved difficult, as Tom was very suspicious of Andy's motives.

Partway through the session, Tom had been talking about how miserable he felt most of the time and when Andy responded with empathy, Tom rose up and looked out of the window. After an inward struggle, he revealed that he was born out of wedlock and that he was not his father's son. Tom discovered this by accident when he was aged fifteen; after that his schoolwork slid into decline and he joined the army at sixteen, but was a rebel. Andy felt out of his depth and asked Tom if he could consult his supervisor, Dennis.

In his notes Andy said:

> *Never felt so helpless in my life; couldn't think clearly; wanted desperately to weep. Glad I persuaded him not to leave; I would have felt really bad. He did seem happier when he left. What would I have done if he had started to cry? Can I help him to get through this? How is he coping away from me? Even if I can help him, what will happen in his work? What's he going to do with his life? Right now, I feel I can't carry the responsibility. I might make a hopeless mess of it and then what would happen?*

Andy rang Dennis and they arranged to meet. Dennis asked him to write down as much as he could remember of the two sessions and to bring the notes with him.

The supervision session

Dennis read Andy's notes and encouraged him to relate his own feelings. Dennis took Andy through the session bit-by-bit and the main point related to when Andy described how Tom stood gazing out of the window. 'I felt very lonely at that stage, isolated, an onlooker. I sensed he was struggling with something. Strange, Dennis, I'm not particularly religious yet I found myself praying, "Oh God, help him; help me." He looked so forlorn, all hunched up. I didn't really see him as a man; he was just a little boy. But at the same time, *I* felt lonely. I wanted someone to hold *me* and comfort *me*. My feelings were all jumbled up; I wanted to cry with him. Tom sensed this, I'm sure, yet at the same time, I was angry. I felt it was happening to me. Why was that?'

In response to Dennis's question, 'Do you think he could have been looking out of the window or possibly looking in, or do you . . .', Andy interrupted and sat and wept. Dennis had opened an emotional window for Andy. After the catharsis, Andy told Dennis that he was adopted and how lonely he felt as a child and 'I think I must have made a nuisance of myself for I became quite possessive of my friends. I wanted them exclusively to myself and didn't want to share them. It wasn't until I went into the army that I was able to relate to groups of people.' The session continued talking about Andy and Tom and how an event like Tom looking out of the window can trigger something deep within the counsellor, and the need to spend time exploring that.

Discussion

This session between Dennis and Andy demonstrates the value of the supervision relationship. This was a fairly dramatic example, probably because it was a strong emotional reason that prompted Andy to seek help from Dennis. It is important to point out that this was supervision and not therapy, although what took place was definitely therapeutic and Dennis kept on returning to the relationship between Andy and Tom. If, in the process of helping Andy work through some of the issues with his client, he develops insight and more self-awareness then the outcome is doubly positive. Andy certainly found that what takes place in counselling sets up reverberations that might only be heard clearly during supervision.

Dennis was quick to realise that in this particular instance it was not the process of counselling – what Andy did – on which he should concentrate but on Andy himself (counsellor-centred). This also illustrates how vulnerable we make ourselves when counselling others. We can never know, at the start of a counselling session, just how it will progress or how it will end. But it is also true that only as we make ourselves vulnerable can we achieve increasing understanding of ourselves and other people. It is doubtful if Andy could have achieved insight into this part of himself if he had not persisted with Tom. It was Tom and his problem that triggered this in Andy.

Sixteen tips to ward off burnout

1. Be gentle with yourself!

2. Remind yourself that you are an enabler not a provider. You cannot change anyone else – you can only change how you relate to them.

3. Find a quiet spot, and use it daily.

4. Give support, encouragement and praise to peers and to management. Learn to accept praise in return.

5. Remember that in the light of all the pain we see, we are bound to feel helpless at times. Admit it without shame. Caring and being there are sometimes more important than doing.

6. Change your routine often and your tasks when you can.

7. Learn to recognise the difference between complaining that relieves and complaining that reinforces stress.

8. On the way home, focus on one good thing that occurred during the day.

9. Be a resource to yourself! Be creative – try new approaches. Be an artist as well as a technician.

10. Use a mentor regularly as a source of support, assurance and redirection.

11. Avoid 'shop-talk' during breaks and when socialising with colleagues.

12. Schedule 'withdraw' periods during the week – limit interruptions.

13. Say 'I choose' rather than 'I should', 'I ought to' or 'I have to'. Say 'I won't', rather than 'I can't'.

14. If you never say 'No', what is your 'Yes' worth?

15. Aloofness and indifference are more harmful to people than admitting you can't do something.

16. Laugh and play.

(Adapted from an unknown source.)

DRAWING THE THREADS TOGETHER

Creating this fourth edition has been a stimulating and challenging experience for the authors. We hope you too will find it inspiring and thought-provoking.

Counselling is not merely learning theories and techniques – there is so much more to it than that. Counselling is a unique relationship within which many secrets, emotions, unresolved painful experiences, personal struggles and intimate details of clients' lives are given a voice – it is a hugely privileged position to be in. Each client who enters the counsellor's door provides a precious opportunity for the development of knowledge on human behaviour, and a step forward on the path to increased self-awareness. Wherever you are on your counselling journey, whether considering training, in training, or practising as a counsellor, our sincere hope is that this book will add something of value to your ongoing journey of learning to counsel.

To conclude this chapter we include a particularly poignant poem presented to Jan by a client – reprinted from *Healing the Hurt Within* (Sutton, 2007: 402) – which in our view, speaks for itself:

Be with me (please)

Can I trust you with my pain?
To treat it with kindness and respect?
To listen to it,
So I can speak the unspoken?

Will you help me catch the tears
As the floodgates open?
Swim with me into the unknown?
Save me from drowning in my sorrow?

If I entrust you with my grief,
will you help me take care of it?
Console it? Soothe it? Make it feel safe?
Will you accept it as a gift to be protected?

If I take the risk and end the drought,
will you leave me alone and sodden after the storm?
Will you reach for your umbrella,
and just walk away?

I feel my need and I fear it
as I fear all that I do not understand,
yet I ask you to be with me,
for I am tired of walking alone.

REFERENCES

Figley, C.R. (Ed.) (1995). *Compassion Fatigue: Coping with Secondary Traumatic Stress Disorder in Those Who Treat the Traumatized.* New York: Brunner/ Mazel.

Hawkins, P., & Shohet, R. (2012). *Supervision in the helping professions.* Milton Keynes: Open University Press.

Pearlman, L.A., & Saakvitne, K.W. (1995). *Trauma and the Therapist: Countertransference and Vicarious Traumatization in Psychotherapy with Incest Survivors.* New York: W.W. Norton.

Sutton, J. (2000). *Thrive On Stress: Manage pressure and positively thrive on it!* Oxford: How To Books.

Sutton, J. (2007). *Healing the Hurt Within: Understand Self-injury and Self-harm, and Heal the Emotional Wounds.* 3rd revised edition. Oxford: How To Books.

RECOMMENDED READING

Cherniss, C. (1980). *Staff Burnout: Job stress in the human services.* London: Sage Publications.

Corey, G. (2001). *Theory and Practice of Counselling and Psychotherapy.* 6th edition. Pacific Grove, CA: Brooks/Cole-Thompson Learning.

Faber, B. A., & Heifetz, L. J. (1982). The process and dimensions of burnout in psychotherapists. *Professional Psychology: Research and Practice*, 13, 293–301.

CHAPTER 11

Introduction to Four Counselling Approaches

In Chapter 1, we introduced three counselling approaches – psychodynamic, person-centred and CBT. This concluding chapter introduces four other approaches, which we hope will help to broaden your counselling base and inspire you to add them to your repertoire of skills. They are behaviour therapy, gestalt therapy, psychosynthesis and transactional analysis (TA).

BEHAVIOUR THERAPY

This is the applied use of behavioural psychology to bring about changes in what people are doing and thinking. In behaviour therapy, the central principle is that all behaviour is learned and maintained as a result of the person's interaction with the environment.

A useful definition is, 'A mode of treatment that focuses on modifying observable and, at least in principle, quantifiable behaviour by means of systematic manipulation of the environment and variables thought to be functionally related to the behaviour. Some behaviour therapy techniques are operant conditioning, shaping, token economy, systematic desensitisation, aversion therapy, and flooding (implosion).' *American Psychiatric Glossary*, American Psychiatric Press, Inc. Washington, DC.

Rewarded behaviour will tend to increase in frequency, while behaviour not rewarded, or punished, will tend to decline. Behaviour therapy is a major form of therapy practised by clinical psychologists.

In the treatment of phobias, behaviour therapy seeks to modify and eliminate the maladaptive response that the person uses when confronted with a phobic object or situation. Although avoiding the feared situation, responding in this way reinforces the belief that whatever it is cannot be coped with in any other way and, unless challenged, will frequently persist.

Behaviour therapy interrupts this self-reinforcing pattern of avoidance behaviour by presenting the feared situation in a controlled manner so that it eventually ceases to produce anxiety.

The behavioural therapist is concerned with what can be observed – with what is said and done – not with experiences in the past that may have caused it nor with any postulated intrapsychic conflict – what must be inferred – unconscious motives and processes and symbolic meanings.

Although the focus is on changing behaviour, the therapeutic relationship is important, not in itself, but to support the client through the difficult times of change and discomfort. In contrast to, for example, person-centred counselling, the behavioural counsellor is directive and active; but a relationship without warmth and empathy will be less likely to succeed than one where these are evident.

THE ROOTS OF BEHAVIOUR THERAPY

The behavioural approach has its roots in the 1950s and early 1960s as a radical reaction to the dominant psychoanalytic perspective. During the 1970s, behaviour therapy emerged as a major force in psychology and made a significant impact on education, psychotherapy, psychiatry and social work. Behavioural techniques were developed and expanded, and they were also applied to fields such as business, industry and child-rearing. This approach was now viewed as the treatment of choice for certain psychological problems.

Moving into the present, two of the most significant developments in the field are:

- the continued emergence of cognitive behaviour therapy as a major force

- the application of behavioural techniques to the prevention and treatment of medical disorders.

The main contributors are:

- Joseph Wolpe's work on experimental neuroses in cats and the clinical work that developed from that research; the most important technique is systematic desensitisation.

- B. F. Skinner's contribution of operant conditioning.

- Albert Bandura's social learning theory.

- Albert Ellis's creation of rational emotive behaviour therapy.

- Aaron Beck's development of cognitive therapy.

- Donald Meichenbaum's treatments such as stress inoculation and self-instructional training.

- Hans Eysenck's contribution to learning and trait theories of personality.

Systematic desensitisation

Desensitisation is the reduction or the extinction of sensitivity to something specific that causes a problem, e.g. allergies. The same behavioural principle is applied in the treatment of anxiety and phobic behaviours by counter-conditioning.

The behaviour therapy technique:

The client is exposed, under relaxed conditions, to a series of stimuli that increasingly approximate to the anxiety-provoking one, until the stimuli no longer produce anxiety.

The stages:

1. Relaxation training, which the client is urged to practise twice daily.

2. The construction of a hierarchy of anxiety-provoking stimuli, ranked according to the level of anxiety they evoke from least to greatest.

3. Presentation of scenes during relaxation, starting with the least anxiety-provoking and working in a step-by-step progression through the hierarchy.

Some people find it very difficult to relax, to carry out visualisation or to produce hierarchies that accurately reflect their problem.

Variations on the theme

Some therapists get their clients to listen to recorded instructions for home desensitisation. Some work in groups, while others carry out the process in real situations.

The main features of behaviour therapy

1. It concentrates on behaviour rather than on the underlying causes of the behaviour.

2. Behaviour is learned and may be unlearned.

3. Behaviour is susceptible to change through psychological principles, especially learning methods.

4. Clearly defined treatment goals are set.

5. Classical personality theories are rejected.

6. The therapist adapts methods to suit the client's needs.

7. The focus is on the 'here and now'.

8. There is a belief in obtaining research support for the methods used.

The stages of behaviour therapy

1. A detailed analysis of the client's problems and behavioural factors.

2. Specific treatment goals.

3. Treatment plan using appropriate behavioural techniques.

4. Implementation of the plan, including full discussion with the client.

5. Evaluation.

Therapeutic techniques used

● **Exposure:** The aim is to extinguish the anxiety, and its associated behaviour, by systematic exposure to the feared situation. This may include modelling – observing someone carrying out the desired behaviour before attempting it.

● **Contingency management:** This means reinforcing positive behaviour but not reinforcing negative behaviour. Rewards in the form of tokens is an example.

● **Cognitive behaviour therapy:** Concerned with thoughts and beliefs.

● **Assertive and social skills training.**

● **Self-control:** Behaviour therapy aims to teach people methods of self-control and self-help, to enable them to cope with situations they find difficult. For example, exposure to the feared situation – rehearse the difficult situation and arrange for positive reinforcement when the task has been done.

- **Role-play:** Clients may be asked either to replay an actual situation or to imagine one.

- **Guided imagery:** Clients symbolically create or recreate a problematic life situation.

- **Physiological recording.**

- **Self-monitoring:** For example, recording daily calorie intake.

- **Behavioural observation:** Assessment of problem behaviour is more accurate when based on actual observation.

- **Psychological tests and questionnaires:** Behaviour therapists will not generally use tests based on psychodynamic theories. They will use tests that yield the information necessary for a functional analysis or for the development of an intervention strategy.

- **Stress management:** Particularly the use of progressive relaxation.

Behaviour therapy does not ignore the importance of the therapeutic relationship. The client who is in a trusting, supportive relationship will generally work conscientiously through the therapy.

Behaviour therapy is tailor-made to suit individual clients' needs. Much of behaviour therapy is short-term – twenty-five to fifty sessions. Behaviour therapy is applicable over a full range of problems, for example:

- anxiety disorders
- cardiovascular disease
- childhood disorders
- depression
- hypertension
- interpersonal/marital problems
- obesity
- sexual disorders
- speech difficulties
- stress management
- substance abuse
- tension headaches.

While behaviour therapy is generally considered to be unsuitable in psychotic conditions, it is used in the treatment of people with chronic mental illnesses.

SELF-MANAGEMENT PROGRAMMES AND SELF-DIRECTED BEHAVIOUR

Over the past two decades in particular, we had seen a growing trend to help people manage their own problems, teaching them to manage their lives more effectively. However, the roots of this can be traced as far back as 1942 with Karen Horney's *Self-analysis*. At the time, this approach was revolutionary, possibly equated with 'giving away secrets'.

Self-helpers are encouraged to control smoking, drinking and drugs; time-management skills; and dealing with obesity and overeating.

Counsellors can encourage clients to take control by engaging them in a relationship that helps them to believe in themselves – that they can do it – and by helping clients set realistic goals. However, clients and counsellors have to realise that change takes time and effort and will not be achieved quickly.

USEFUL WEBSITES

http://www.simplypsychology.org/behavioral-therapy.html

http://www.britannica.com/topic/behaviour-therapy

http://www.bing.com/videos/h?q=youtube+behaviour+therapy&qpvt=youtube+ behaviour+therapy&view=detail&mid=0EB693B490D578761F110EB693B490 D578761F11

FURTHER READING

Cormier, W. H. and Cormier, L. S. (1979). *Interviewing Strategies for Helpers: A guide to assessment, treatment and evaluation*, Brooks/Cole, Monterey, CA.

Corey, G. (2001, 6th edition.) *Theory and Practice of Counselling and Psychotherapy*, Wadsworth. Brooks/Cole. On pp 280–2 of Corey's book, you will find the detailed case study of how Corey applies behavioural therapy to Sam, one of his clients.

See also, Corey, G. (2001, 5th edition.) *Case Approach to Counselling and Psychotherapy*. Wadsworth. Brooks/Cole.

Horney, K. (1942, reissued 1994). *Self-analysis*. W. W Norton & Co, Inc. New York.

O'Sullivan, G. (1996). Behaviour therapy. In: *Handbook of Individual Therapy*, (ed. W. Dryden), Sage Publications, London.

Trower, P., Casey, A. and Dryden, W. (1988) *Cognitive Behavioural Counselling in Action*, Sage Publications, London.

GESTALT THERAPY

Gestalt is a German word which, when translated loosely, means 'pattern' or 'form'. When the pattern, or *Gestalten*, is incomplete, we talk of 'unfinished business'. Gestalt psychology sprang out of dissatisfaction over the inability of both psychoanalysis and behaviourism to deal with the whole person.

The chief tenet of Gestalt psychology is that analysis of parts, however thorough, cannot provide an understanding of the whole. An analogy is the human body, each part of which has its distinct function yet all are integrated to make up the body. Parts are not understood when analysed in isolation. Mental processes and behaviours come complete. An example is that we hear a melody as a whole and not merely as a collection of individual notes.

Fritz Perls (1893–1970), the 'father of Gestalt therapy', aided by his wife Laura, brought on a revolution in psychiatry. He provided a foundation from which humanistic and transpersonal psychology was built. Gestalt therapy aims to help the person to be self-supportive and self-responsible, through awareness of what is going on within the self at any given moment, the 'here-and-now'. Gestalt therapy is heavily influenced by existentialism, psychodrama and body therapies.

The theory is based on the principle that mental processes and behaviour cannot be analysed into elementary units. They come complete. The core of Gestalt therapy is the belief that people split off from the experiences, thoughts, sensations and emotions that are uncomfortable. This splitting off creates a fragmentation of the personality. Perls's focus was to assist people in owning their experiences and developing a healthy gestalt or wholeness. According to Perls, there are six factors causing psychological discomfort:

1. The lack of contact: no social support.

2. Confluence: the environment takes control.

3. Unfinished business: inability to gain closure.

4. Fragmentation: denied or fragmented self.

5. Winner/loser: conflict of values and expectations.

6. Polarities: never seeing grey, always black or white.

Gestalt therapy is usually performed in groups, though many of the techniques are applicable in individual work. The aim of therapy is to get clients to move from environmental support to self-support through their increased ability to use the world actively for their own development instead of manipulating the environment by playing neurotic roles.

KEY AIMS OF GESTALT THERAPY

Perls rejected the belief that human beings are determined and controlled by external and/or internal factors. This belief is reflected in two of his basic ideas:

1. That human beings are responsible for themselves and their lives and living.

2. That the important question about human experience and behaviour is not why but how. The more we strive to be what we are not, the more entrenched we become in not being who we are meant to be.

Implicit in these ideas is the belief that human beings are free and can change. He rejected the dualities of mind and body, body and soul, thinking and feeling, thinking and action, and feeling and action. The rejection of dualities is inherent in the concept of holism. Human beings are unified organism, and always function as a whole.

The emphasis of Gestalt counselling is on

- change through activity
- the central meaning of present experience
- the importance of fantasy and creative experimentation, particularly using the right, creative hemisphere, though not ignoring the contribution of the left, structured hemisphere
- the significance of language.

Here-and-now awareness

The Gestalt therapy slogan is 'I and Thou, Here-and-Now'. Only the 'now' exists. Problems solved in the present solve problems of the past. The client is not allowed to talk 'about' problems in the past tense or in terms of memories. The client is asked to experience them now in his breathing, gestures, feelings, emotions and voice. The manner of expression, not the content or the words, is what is important. The basic sentence the client is required to repeat is, 'Now I am aware . . .'. Variations are:

- 'What are you aware of now?'
- 'Where are you now?'
- 'What are you seeing? Feeling?'
- 'What are you doing with your hand? Foot?' or
- 'Are you aware of what you are doing with your . . . ?'
- 'What do you expect?'
- 'What do you want?'

Draw attention to the client's behaviour, feelings and experiences, do not interpret them and discover how he is preventing awareness of unfinished business, of holes or missing or rejected parts of his personality. Awareness, or formation of gestalts, cannot be forced.

The therapist makes the client responsible by getting him to use 'I' not 'it' when referring to parts of his body and activities. Any statement or behaviour that does not represent self is challenged.

Peeling the onion

Perls likens the unfolding of the personality to peeling five layers of an onion:

- **The phoney.** Reacting to others in stereotyped and non-genuine ways, and playing games instead of being real.

- **The phobic.** Where we strive to avoid emotional pain by keeping parts of ourselves out of sight.

- **The impasse.** This is where our maturation is stuck and we do not feel alive.

- **The implosive.** This is where we fully experience our deadness. Where we expose our defences.

- **The explosive.** Where we let go of phoney roles and pretences. Energy is released and we become alive and authentic.

The counsellor draws attention to:

- what the client says
- how it is said
- the client's behaviour
- non-verbal communication
- breathing pattern
- tensions within the session.

Clients are encouraged to act out various roles in life that they, and others, have played or are currently playing and to take responsibility for their own conflicts.

Counselling goals

- to re-establish contact and normal interaction; restore ego function and restore the whole

- to foster:

  maturation and growth
  independence
  self-support
  awareness

- to help the client:

  deal with unfinished business
  learn to live in the 'here and now'.

THE COUNSELLING PROCESS

Clients are asked, and sometimes actively encouraged, to experience as much of themselves as possible – gestures, breathing, voice, and so on. In so doing they become aware of the relationship between feelings and behaviours and are thus able to:

- integrate their dissociated parts

- establish an adequate balance and appropriate boundaries between self and the environment.

Clients are constantly required to repeat and complete the basic sentence, 'Now I am aware . . .' and its variations:

- 'What are you aware of now?'
- 'Where are you now?'
- 'What are you seeing? Feeling?'
- 'What is your hand/foot doing?'
- 'What do you want?'
- 'What do you expect?

Integration means:

- Owning disowned parts of oneself.

- Being responsible for one's own life goals.

- Expressing everything that is felt in the body.

- Expressing the vague feelings associated with shame and embarrassment about expressing certain thoughts and feelings. Shame and embarrassment are the prime tools of the defence mechanism of repression. Endurance embarrassment brings repressed material to the surface.

Disowned parts of the personality are integrated into the whole to complete that person's Gestalten. When a need is satisfied, the situation is changed and the need fades into the background. If a need is not fulfilled – if a Gestalten is not completed – it may produce a conflict that is distracting and draining of psychic energy.

The awareness of, and the ability to endure, unwanted emotions is the precondition of a successful outcome. It is this process and not the process of remembering that is the royal road to health.

Critics of Gestalt therapy say that it may help clients get in touch with their needs but does not necessarily teach them the skills or wisdom to deal with those needs.

The 'Gestalt prayer' is generally taken as a classic expression of the kind of individualism associated with the American culture of the 1960s. The key idea of the statement is the focus on living in response to one's own needs. It also expresses the idea that, by fulfilling their own needs, people can help others do the same, i.e. when they 'find each other, it's beautiful'. The principles of Gestalt therapy are found in most current schools of psychotherapy and provide the springboard for eclectic psychotherapy.

See Corey (pp 217–19) for a case study of applied Gestalt therapy.

For more on gestalt therapy, see http://www.gestalt.org/yontef.htm

https://www.youtube.com/watch?v=8y5tuJ3Sojc

FURTHER READING

Brownell, Philip (2008). *Handbook for Theory, Research, and Practice in Gestalt Therapy*, Cambridge Scholars Publishing.

Clarkson, Petula (2004). *Gestalt Counselling in Action*, Sage Publications, London.

Corey, G. (2001, 6th edition.) *Theory and Practice of Counselling and Psychotherapy*, Wadsworth. Brooks/Cole.

Houston, Gaie, (2012). *Gestalt Counselling in a Nutshell.* Sage Publications.

Patterson C. H. (1986). *Theories of Counselling and Psychotherapy*, 4th revised edition. Longman.

Perls, Frederick, S. (1992). *Ego Hunger and Aggression: A Revision of Freud's Theory and Method.* Gestalt Journal Press, U. S.

—. (1992). *Gestalt Therapy Verbatim.* Gestalt Journal Press, U.S.

—. (1992). *In And Out Of the Garbage Pail*, Gestalt Journal Press, U.S.

—. (1994). *Gestalt Therapy: Excitement and Growth in the Human Personality*, Souvenir Press

PSYCHOSYNTHESIS

Psychosynthesis was developed by Roberto Assagioli (1888–1974), an Italian psychiatrist who broke away from Freudian orthodoxy early in the twentieth century and developed an integrated approach to psychiatry.

Psychosynthesis – beginning around 1910 and continuing to the present day – is a synonym for human growth, the ongoing process of integrating all the parts, aspects and energies of the individual into a harmonious, powerful whole. Assagioli draws upon psychoanalysis, Jungian and existential psychology, Buddhism and yoga, and Christian traditions and philosophies, and affirms the spiritual dimension of the person, i.e. the 'higher' or 'transpersonal' self. The higher self is seen as a source of wisdom, inspiration, unconditional love, and the will to meaning in our lives. Each person's life has purpose and meaning within this broader context and it is possible for the individual to discover this. Psychosynthesis has had a profound impact on the human potential movement. For example, the use of guided imagery and the concept of subpersonalities originate in psychosynthesis.

THE FUNDAMENTALS OF PSYCHOSYNTHESIS

Psychological pain, imbalance and meaninglessness are caused where the various elements of the psyche are unconnected or clash with one another. When these elements merge, we experience a release of energy, a sense of well-being and a deeper meaning of life.

*   *   *

Assagioli's map of the human psyche has seven areas:

- *The lower (infra) unconsciousness* – Here are stored all our unconscious drives and instincts.

- *The middle unconsciousness* – To which we have access during our waking state.

- *The higher unconsciousness* – From where all our higher feelings and thoughts enter consciousness.

- *The field of consciousness* – Accessible to us during the waking state: the field of consciousness lies within the middle unconscious. It is the part of which we are directly aware and contains sensations, images, thoughts, feelings, desires and impulses. It also includes power to observe, analyse and make judgments.

- *The conscious self or ego* – The centre of our consciousness. The conscious self or 'I' lies in the centre of the field of consciousness. The client's task is to gain experience of the essence of self or 'I'. Awareness of the conscious self is essential for psychological health. The personal self is a reflection of the transpersonal self, in much the same way as the moon is lit up by the sun's rays. Since this 'self' has two aspects – the personal and the transpersonal – synthesis happens in two stages: first the personal, followed by the transpersonal.

- *The higher self* – The self that keeps our consciousness alive, when we cannot control it. The higher unconscious or super conscious is an autonomous realm, from where we receive our higher intuitions and inspirations – altruistic love and will, humanitarian action, artistic and scientific inspiration, philosophic and spiritual insight, and the drive toward purpose and meaning in life. The higher or transpersonal self is the true self, the permanent centre, situated beyond or above the conscious self. Identification with the transpersonal self is a rare occurrence.

- *The collective unconsciousness* – Where there is a constant exchange going on between the world inside individual consciousness and consciousness surrounding it. The psyche is bathed in the sea of the collective unconscious of dreams, myths, legends and archetypes.

The lines that delimit the various parts of the diagram are analogous to permeable membranes, permitting a constant process of 'psychological osmosis'.

Assagioli's map of the psychological functions (in diagrammatic form, star-shaped) is made up of three dimensions:

- Sensation – Intuition
- Thought – Emotion-feeling
- Impulse-desire – Imagination

Key values that psychosynthesis holds in the process of psychotherapy:

- Creating a bridge between the psychological and spiritual realities that many new psychologies now follow.
- A deep spiritual understanding of the relationship between parts and wholes and how a spiritual perspective can deepen the experience of self.
- An openness, lack of dogma and inclusiveness to whatever approaches, from Raja Yoga and esoteric spirituality to humanistic psychology, which fit a holistic perspective.
- An optimistic emphasis on the unfolding potential of humans.
- Practices such as 'dis-identification' to loosen the bonds of outdated personal beliefs and open to being part of a greater sense of self.
- A utilisation of imaginative guiding to bring clients to points of higher awareness.
- The use of evocative imagery to awaken clients to their own inner wisdom.
- An understanding of the importance of meaning and purpose in any individual's life.
- An appreciation of the importance of Will in terms of self-responsibility and choice.
- A dramatic and easily engaged method of working with personality dynamics called sub-personalities.

ASSAGIOLI'S CONCEPT OF SUB-PERSONALITIES

Sub-personalities are distinct, miniature personalities, living together within the personality, each with its own cluster of feelings, words, habits, beliefs and behaviours. They are often in conflict with one another and engaged in a constant jockeying for position.

They are remnants of helpful and unhelpful influences left over from a time when they were needed for survival to meet lower level needs. For example, a policeman sub-personality is helpful in keeping you on the right side of the law, but becomes tyrannical when it always pushes you into punishing other people for minor breaches of your self-imposed standards.

Sub-personalities are expressions of different parts of us, as Andrew found out. He confronted a stern, rigid and unyielding priest. This inner rigidity interfered in their relationship, because the priest was prone to be judgmental and critical. What this study stresses is that it is essential to 'dis-identify' from the sub-personality or sub-personalities by affirming, 'I sometimes play the role of [Andrew might say] "Judge", but I am not that Judge. I am more than that Judge. I am self-identified.' (Adapted from Assagioli 1990.) (See *On Spiritual Psychology – What Are Subpersonalities?* http://www.plotinus.com/what_are_subpersonalities.htm.) Dis-identification takes place when we can 'step away' from rather than 'into'.

Sub-personalities are a mixture of helpful and unhelpful; they become unhelpful when they start to control us.

THE GOALS OF PSYCHOSYNTHESIS

- To free ourselves from the infirmity of illusions and fantasies, unrecognised complexes, of being tossed hither and thither by external influences and deceiving appearances.

- To achieve a harmonious inner integration, true self-realisation and a right relationship with others.

- To recognise when we have identified with one or another sub-personality and dis-identify from its control.

These goals are achieved through knowledge of one's personality, control of the various elements of the personality and working with the sub-personalities to free yourself from their tyranny. Psychosynthesis speaks of 'guiding', not therapy.

Psychosynthesis is an evolutionary psychology, to help us to become increasingly aware of our vast potentials and to bring them into service in the world. It can help us to balance all aspects of the human personalit: intellect, emotion, body, intuition and imagination.

Psychosynthesis can facilitate courage and patience, wisdom and compassion. It refers to the ongoing synthesis of the psyche, a process that transcends specific models and methods.

For more on psychosynthesis, see http://synthesiscenter.org/ps.htm

http://psychosynthesiseastwest.com/

FURTHER READING

Assagioli, Roberto (1969). *Symbols of Transpersonal Experiences*, Institute of Psychosynthesis, and at http://two.not2.org/psychosynthesis/articles/symbolstp.pdf

—. (1983). *Psychosynthesis Typology*, Institute of Psychosynthesis.

—. (1999). *Psychosynthesis: A manual of Principles and Techniques*, Thorsons.

—. (1999). *The Act of Will: A Guide to Self-actualisation and Self-realisation*, The Psychosynthesis & Education Trust (new edited edition).

—.(2008). *Transpersonal Development: The Dimension Beyond Psychosynthesis*, Inner Way Productions.

Ferrucci, Piero (2000). *What We May Be: Techniques for Psychological and Spiritual Growth*, Jeremy P Tarcher (new edition).

Firman, John, & Gila, Ann (2002). *Psychosynthesis: A Psychology of the Spirit*, State University of New York Press.

Parfitt, Will (2006). *Psychosynthesis: The Elements and Beyond*, P. S. Avalon.

Whitmore, Diana (2004). *Psychosynthesis Counselling in Action*, Sage Publications Ltd.

For more books on psychosynthesis see The Institute of Psychosynthesis http://www.psychosynthesis.org/html/bookshop.htm

TRANSACTIONAL ANALYSIS

Transactional analysis (TA) is a system of analysis and therapy developed by Eric Berne (1919–70), and comprises a theory of personality, a theory of social interaction and an analytical tool for psychotherapy.

PHILOSOPHY AND CONCEPTS

Although infants start off from the position of being OK, obstacles and difficulties often prevent them from developing their potentialities to their best advantage and to the advantage of others. These obstacles and difficulties also interfere with their ability to be able to work productively and creatively, and to be free from psychological disturbances. TA is also a method of group work that emphasises the person's ability to change, the role of the inner Parent in the process of change and the person's control of the ego states.

Berne identifies four forms of hunger-need

1. *Tactile* – intimacy and physical closeness. This need continues through life.

2. *Recognition* – 'I cannot physically touch you, but I will verbally *stroke* you.' (The stroke is a basic unit of social interaction.) A *transaction* is an exchange of strokes.

3. *Structure* – 'I must fill my time to prevent boredom.'

4. *Excitement* – 'I must fill my life in interesting and exciting ways.' Leaders provide structure for others to fill their time. However, many of us are brought up to believe that seeking excitement is bad and should be shunned.

Intimacy

Intimacy is the most satisfying solution to stimulus, recognition and structure hunger. To be able to enter into intimacy, a person must have awareness and enough spontaneity to be liberated from the compulsion to play games.

Personality structure comprises:

- Three various 'selves' or ego states: Parent; Adult; Child. (Parent, Adult, Child are capitalised to identify them as distinct states). We all incorporate all three. At any given moment we will exhibit one (and only one) or another of these states. An ego state involves thinking, feeling and behaving.

- Transactions between people and between our various selves

- An individual existential position

- A preconscious life plan or 'script'.

1. The Parent ego state

A set of feelings, thoughts, attitudes and behaviours that resemble those of parental figures, characterised by postures, gestures, verbalisations and feelings. The function of the Parent is to conserve energy and to diminish anxiety by making certain decisions 'automatic'. The Parent in you feels and behaves in the same ways you perceived the feelings and behaviours of your mother, father or significant others who raised you. The Parent state consists of:

The critical Parent

- The basic need of the critical Parent is power.

- Critical Parent functions are to set limits, discipline, make rules and regulations about how life should be; the do's and don'ts.

- The critical Parent ego state criticises and finds fault and is contrasted with the nurturing Parent.

- The critical Parent may also be assertive and self-sufficient.

- The critical Parent uses such words as 'always', 'never', 'should', 'should not', 'must', 'ought to', 'have to', 'cannot', 'good' and 'bad'.

- The critical Parent judges and criticises and uses such language as 'Because I said so', 'Brat', 'Childish', 'Naughty', 'Now what?', 'what will the neighbours say?'

- Some typical gestures and postures: Eyes rolling up in disgust, finger-pointing, folded arms, tapping of feet in impatience.

- Some typical voice tones: Condescending, punishing, sneering.

- Some typical facial expressions: Angry frown, disapproving, furrowed brow, hostile, pursed lips, scowl, set jaw.

The nurturing Parent

- The basic need of the nurturing Parent is caring.

- Nurturing Parent functions are to give advice, guide, protect, teach how to form and keep traditions – group work helps people become aware of the influence of the Parent, then to sort out what makes sense and what does not.

- The nurturing Parent ego state is characterised by warmth, support, love.

- Some typical words and phrases: 'Don't worry', 'Good', 'Darling', 'Beautiful', 'I'll take care of you', 'Let me help you', 'Smart', 'There, there'.

- Some typical gestures and postures: Consoling touch, head nodding – 'Yes', pat on the back.

- Some typical voice tones: Encouraging, supportive, sympathetic.

- Some typical facial expressions: Encouraging nod, loving, sympathetic eyes.

2. The Adult ego state

The Adult is the part of you that figures out things by looking at the facts. It is the part that computes, stores memories and uses facts to make decisions. The Adult is unemotional and is concerned with 'what fits' or what is most expedient and useful. *Adult* does not mean *mature*.

- The basic need of the Adult is rationality.

- Adult functions are to work on facts, to compute, store memories and feelings, to use facts to make decisions

- The Adult decides what fits, where, and what is most useful.

- The Adult gathers data on the Parent and the Child, makes decisions based on available data and plans the decision-making process.

- The Adult is an analytical, rational and non-judgmental ego state.

- The Adult problem-solves and obtains information.

- Some typical phrases: 'According to statistics', 'Look for alternatives', 'Check it out', 'Have you tried this?', 'What do the results suggest?', 'How do you arrive at that?'

- Some typical gestures and postures: Active listening, checking for understanding, giving feedback, pointing something out.

- Some typical voice tones: Calm, clear (with appropriate emotion), confident, informative, inquiring, straight.

- Some typical facial expressions: Attentive, confident, eyes alert, direct eye contact, lively, responsive, thoughtful.

3. The Child ego state

Every adult was once a child. Feelings, thoughts and behaviour patterns exist in later life as relics of the individual's childhood. Berne considers that we all carry within ourselves a little boy or girl who feels thinks, acts and responds just as we did when we were children of a certain age. The behaviour of the Child is not childish but *childlike*.

It is a basic ego state consisting of feelings, impulses and spontaneous acts. As a result of learning, the Child ego state takes the form of the adapted Child or the natural Child.

The natural (or free) Child

- The basic need of the natural Child is creativity.

- The natural Child is loving, spontaneous, carefree, fun-loving and exciting.

- The natural Child is adventurous, curious, trusting and joyful.

- The natural Child describes the spontaneous, eager and playful part of the personality.

- People whose natural Child is too dominant generally lack self-control.

- Some typical words: 'Eek', 'Gee whiz', 'Gosh', 'I'm scared', 'Let's play', 'Look at me now!', 'Wow!'

- Some typical gestures and postures: Joyful, skipping, curling up, pretending.

- Some typical voice tones: Belly-laughing, excited, giggling, gurgling, whistling, singing.

- Some typical facial expressions: Admiration, wide-eyed and curious, excited, flirty.

The adapted Child

- The basic need of the adapted Child is approval.

- Adapted Child functions are being angry, rebellious, frightened and conforming.

- The adapted Child functions are to conform to, or rebel against, what another person wants.

- Some typical words and phrases: 'Can't', 'Did I do all right?', 'Do it for me', I didn't do it', 'It's all your fault', 'It's all my fault', 'Nobody loves me'.

- Some typical gestures and postures: Batting eyelashes, dejected, nail-biting, obscene gestures, temper tantrums.

- Some typical voice tones: Asking permission, annoying, spiteful, sullen silence, swearing, whining.

- Some typical facial expressions: Eyes directed upward/downward, helpless, pouting, woebegone.

In other words:

- Parent is our 'Taught' concept of life.
- Adult is our 'Thought' concept of life.
- Child is our 'Felt' concept of life.

Berne considered the natural Child to be the most valuable part of the personality. The proper function of a 'healthy' Child is to motivate the Adult so as to obtain the greatest amount of gratification for itself. This it does by letting the Adult know what it wants and by consulting the Parent about its appropriateness. The Adult can turn off either or both of the other ego states. Control is not repression; it means changing the ego state. Control is about choice and decisions.

A variation of the PAC (Parent/Adult/Child) states

Parent	Nurturing	Nurturing (positive)
		Spoiling (negative)
	Controlling	Structuring (positive)
		Critical (negative)
Adult	Adult remains as a single entity, representing an 'accounting' function or mode, which can draw on the resources of both Parent and Child.	
Child	Adapted	Co-operative (positive)
		Compliant (negative)
	Free	Spontaneous (positive)
		Immature (negative)

www.businessballs.com/transact.htm

Personality function

The three systems of personality react in the following ways:

- the Parent judgmentally attempts to enforce external standards;
- the Adult is concerned with processing and storing information;
- the Child reacts more impulsively on poorly differentiated perceptions.

Transactional analysis recognises four basic life positions (Table 1).

Table I Transactional analysis's four life positions

I'm OK, You're not OK The basic attitude is, 'I'm going to get what I can, though I'm not much. Your life is not worth much; you are dispensable. Get out of my way.' This is a distrustful position and is taken up by a Child who is suspicious of people.	Words to describe this state: Arrogant, do-gooder, distrustful, bossy.
I'm not OK, You're OK The basic attitude is, 'My life is not worth much; I'm nothing compared to you.' The position of the Child who usually feels low or depressed.	Words to describe this state: Depression, resignation, suicide.
I'm not OK, You're not OK The basic attitude is, 'Life is not worth anything at all; we might as well be dead. So, it doesn't matter what we do or who we hurt.' Such people may yearn for warmth, but cannot accept it and cannot trust the person who gives it. The position of a Child who feels that life just isn't any good and that there is no escape from it.	Words to describe this state: Futility, alienation, severe withdrawal.
I'm OK, You're OK The basic attitude is, 'Life is for living; let's live it to the full.' Only this state puts people on equal terms. The healthy position.	Words to describe this state: Good, healthy, successful, competent, confident, challenging, creative.

Transactions

Transactions are the basic units of human communication; any exchanges between the ego states of any two people. Transactions may be verbal and non-verbal. Transactions operate at an overt social level and at a covert psychological level.

Transactions may be:

- Parallel, e.g. Parent to Parent and Parent to Parent.

- Crossed, e.g. Parent to Parent and Parent to Child.

- Ulterior, e.g. Adult to Adult and Child to Adult.

Contamination

This is where the Child takes on the values, prejudices, opinions and feelings of significant others without filtering them through the Adult.

Strokes

Strokes describe the recognition we receive from others. Strokes can be verbal, non-verbal or both. A wave of the hand. 'Hello, how are you today?' A slap.

We need positive strokes to maintain physical and mental well-being. Institutionalised infants have been known to die when deprived of stroking. As we grow, words are often substitutes for the physical stroking we received as children.

So often, strokes are given when we have done something. We also need strokes just for being who we are. We also need to learn to ask for strokes when we need them. 'I'd really appreciate a big hug right now.' 'Give me a kiss, darling.'

A positive self-esteem makes it in order to stroke oneself: 'I did a really good job and I'm pleased with myself.' Recognition from others may be:

- Positive – evoking the feeling of 'I'm OK, You're OK'.

- Negative – evoking the feeling of 'I'm not OK, You're OK'.

- Conditional strokes are given for something done – 'I will love you if . . .'

- Unconditional strokes are given just for being.

- Positive, unconditional stroking benefits the giver as well as the receiver.

People whose Child feels 'not OK' become more used to negative strokes than to positive ones. They may yearn for compliments, but cannot accept them and cannot trust the person who gives them.

Existential or basic positions (scripts)

A script is our preconscious life plan by which we structure our time, decided by the Child before the age of six or seven. It is based on injunctions ('don't do . . .') and counter-injunctions (usually in the form of slogans). A counter-script is a preconscious life plan decided by the Child's Parent.

Scripts determine our destinies, including our approach to relationships and to tasks. They are based on childlike illusions which may persist throughout life. Very often, we live under the illusion that we live our lives autonomously. In reality, much of what we do as Adults bears parental and other influences. The aim of therapy is to free people from following their scripts and counter-scripts.

Stamps and Rackets

'Stamp collecting' is storing bad feelings as an excuse for doing things you might not otherwise do. Stamps are not needed if the basic position is 'I'm OK, You're OK'.

Rackets is a term to describe the habitual ways of feeling bad about oneself, learned from parents and other significant people. They are the feelings of our parents; they do not rightly belong to us, but we act as if they do.

An example would be that, when our parents were under pressure, they may have become anxious, depressed, confused or nervous. If they did not take appropriate Adult action to eliminate the tension or pressure, the likelihood is that we learned a racket by responding in the same way. Rackets originate from the 'not OK' Child of our parents; our Child then repeats these to avoid taking constructive action.

Games

- Games describe unconscious, stereotyped and predictable behaviours. When games are conscious, it is manipulation. The transactions in games are ulterior and result in negative payoffs for the players.

- Games are classified as first-, second- or third-degree depending on the seriousness of the consequences. They allow the player to collect 'stamps'. Stamps are stored-up feelings, positive or negative. When we have amassed enough stamps, we may cash them in for a 'prize': letting fly at someone with whom we have been really tolerant over a long period; allowing yourself a period of relaxation, for example.

- Brown stamps are for negative feelings; gold stamps are for positive feelings.

- Stamp collecting is a way of trying to help the Child to feel OK.

A game consists of:

- An apparent (conscious) transaction (usually Adult–Adult).

- A hidden (unconscious) transaction (usually Parent–Child or Child–Child).

- A sudden and unpleasant reaction (a stamp).

The most common games are:

- 'If it weren't for you.'

- 'Kick me.'

- 'I'm only trying to help.'

Injunctions, attributions and discounts

Although directives from parents can be nurturing and conducive to the child's emotional development, they can also be restrictive, reflecting the fears and insecurities of the Child in the parent. Injunctions are irrational negative feeling messages expressed pre-verbally and non-verbally. They are restrictive, reflecting fears and insecurities.

Examples of injunctions:

- Don't be you, be me, or someone else.

- Don't grow up.

- Don't be well, be sick.

- Don't be a child, be grown up.

- Don't make it, don't be a success.

- Don't be close to people.

- Don't be sane, be crazy.

- Don't count, be unimportant.

- Don't think/feel what you think/feel (angry, sexy, happy, or good). Think/feel only what I think/feel.

Examples of slogans as injunctions:

- Be a man, my son.

- God helps those who help themselves.

- Raise yourself up by your own bootlaces.

The following injunctions block intimacy:

- Do not give strokes if you have them to give.

- Do not ask for strokes when you need them.

- Do not accept strokes even if you want them.
- Do not reject strokes even if you do not want them.

Attributions

Being told what we are, what we must do and how we must feel. Family reinforcement schedules tend to reward children who follow attributions and punish children who disobey injunctions.

Where children (pre-school development) are given unconditional protection, they are less likely to develop a restrictive script. When parents make their nurturing conditional on their child's submission to their injunctions and attributions, the child may make a conscious decision to adhere to parental wishes even though this means the sacrifice of autonomy.

Attributions are:

- being told what we are, what we must do and how we must feel
- generally approving of obedience and disapproving of disobedience.

Injunctions and attributions lie at the heart of a judgmental attitude. The developing child's autonomy may be sacrificed on the altar of parental control.

Scripts

- A script is a preconscious set of rules by which we structure our life plan.
- Scripts are decided by the age of 6 or 7 years.
- Scripts are based on injunctions and attributions.
- Scripts determine how we approach relationships and work.
- Scripts are based on childlike illusions that automatically influence our lives.

When we attempt to move out of script discomfort is produced. Comfort is re-established when the script is picked up, when once again there is acquiescence to parental wishes.

Berne proposed that the parent of the opposite sex tells the child what to do and the parent of the same sex demonstrates how to do it.

CONSIDERATIONS FOR COUNSELLING

1. Assumptions

Therapist cannot change clients; they can only:

- bring clients to an awareness of how they make themselves and others sick, bad, stupid or crazy

- help them develop permission to change

- give them protection while they change.

If clients are aware of how they hurt themselves, they are aware of the changes they need to make, if they wish to. The counsellor may need to help the person give himself permission to make the change.

2. Bases for change

Therapeutic change is based on decisions and action. If the person does not do this, no one else will; hence the necessity to emphasise:

- the Adult's ability to turn off inappropriate Child and Parent states

- permission

- protection

- decision

- what the client can do. If counsellors accept a 'can't', they agree with the person that he is helpless and/or hopeless.

3. Contract

The client commits himself to a plan for behaviour change. Important contracting conditions:

- The person makes the contract with himself: the facilitator is only a guide and a witness. With a dishonest contract, the person thus defeats only himself.

- The more explicit the contract the better. The person has the right to refuse a contract, which is another way of clarifying his readiness for change.

- The more operational the contract the better (e.g. 'happiness' is not operational; there are no criteria to measure it by). You might ask the person:

  What would you be doing better if you were happier?

  How do you make yourself unhappy?

  What do you want to stop doing?

The contract can be renegotiated.

Contracts are most useful if satisfactory to all of the three ego states of both the facilitator and the person.

The contract is one way of assuming that what goes on between the facilitator and the person is more likely to be an activity which promotes growth toward personal fulfilment.

Drama triangle (also known as the rescue triangle)

A significant part of transactional analysis is identifying the games people play. One of these games is the rescue triangle of Rescuer, Persecutor and Victim.

- We adopt the role of Rescuer by helping and keeping others dependent on us.

- We adopt the role of Persecutor when we set unnecessarily strict limits on behaviour or are charged with enforcing the rules, but do so with brutality.

- We adopt the role of Victim when (without cause) we feel we are being unjustly treated.

All three roles are interchangeable and we may play them all in turn.

Caught in the drama triangle trap

Selflessness, doing for others, generosity and co-operation are encouraged, even when people are selfish, stingy and do not co-operate with us. This is exploitation and characteristic of the Rescuer role.

Being one-down in a relationship is the experience of many women, while the reverse is true of many men. Women are more likely to be trained into the playing of the Rescuer role, to always be available.

Don't rescue me! If we don't want to be a Victim, we must demand not to be rescued. We may have to repeat our demand many times, because people who are confirmed Rescuers experience tremendous feelings of guilt if deprived of the Rescuing role.

Counsellors, too, can be caught up in the game. The client who ends a long recital of what is wrong in her life by saying, 'I really don't know what to do. I feel so helpless. It's not my fault, is it?' is casting herself in the Victim role. The unwary counsellor – intent on action rather than on exploring and challenging – who agrees that life is cruel and that the client is entirely innocent is falling into the role of Rescuer. A simple, 'You feel as if you are an innocent victim in all this. Perhaps it would be productive to look at your part in the break-up of your marriage,' would be enough to convey to the client that she has the resources within her to challenge herself and the counsellor would not become the Rescuer and run the risk of the client becoming the Persecutor.

An example of rescuing (William speaking)

I was a member of a small study group. Sheila was another member of the group. When we were discussing going back into the large group, Sheila said she didn't think she could say how she felt. When it came to her turn, the deadly silence was unbearable. Sheila looked at me imploringly. I said, 'Sheila said this would happen. I think we shouldn't press her.' The group leader, after a pause, said, 'That is a classic example of rescuing someone.' What I could have done was to maybe hold her hand and encourage her to contribute. What I did was to announce that I was stronger than Sheila.

SUMMARY

TA helps clients to become aware of how they hurt themselves, the changes they need to make and the inner forces that hinder change. Therapeutic change is based on decisions and action. If we do not decide or act, no one will or can do it for us. When we accept a 'can't' we agree with clients that they are helpless. Clients make a contract with themselves to work toward specific changes in behaviour. Change is for the purpose of the client assuming responsibility for her life and achieving a degree of self-actualisation.

TA is an ideal model for eclectic counsellors to add to their repertoire, mainly because it does not clash with other models and secondly because clients readily understand the basic principles of the Parent–Adult–Child ego states and are normally adept at identifying which ego state they are speaking from, and the drama triangle makes sense.

Intimacy is the most satisfying solution to the need for positive stroking. To be able to enter intimacy, a person must have awareness and enough spontaneity to be liberated from the compulsion to play games. Intimacy is like a harp. The music it produces comes from all its strings. Intimacy means discovering the particular harmony and melody that is enjoyed by the people involved. Sometimes the melodies will vary. Sometimes a minor key will be more appreciated than a major one. But, as with music, it is all there to be enjoyed. Within the intimacy of the counselling relationship, the client will learn how to ask for and receive positive strokes.

For more on TA, see http://www.ericberne.com/transactional-analysis/ http://www.ericberne.com/transactional-analysis/

http://www.businessballs.com/transactionalanalysis.htm

http://www.bing.com/videos/h?q=transactional+analysis+youtube&qpvt=TRANSACTIONAL+ANALYSIS+youtube&FORM=VDRE

FURTHER READING

Berne, E. (2001) *Transactional Analysis in Psychotherapy: The Classic Handbook to its Principles*, Souvenir Press.

Berne, E. (2010) *Games People Play: The Psychology of Human Relationships*, Penguin.

Harris, Thomas A. (2012) *I'm OK – You're OK*, Arrow.

Stewart, Ian (2013) *Transactional Analysis Counselling in Action*, Sage Publications Ltd.

Stewart, W. (1998) *Building Self-esteem*, How To Books, Oxford.

—. (2008) *A Biographical Dictionary of Psychologists, Psychiatrists and Psychotherapists*, McFarland.

Tudor, Keith (2007) *The Adult Is Parent to the Child: Transactional Analysis with Children and Young People*, Russell House Publishing Ltd

Useful websites for the drama triangle:

The Drama Triangle City Vision University www.cityvision.edu/courses/coursefiles/419/**DRAMA_TRI . . .** · DOC file · Web view by **Steve Karpman** with Comments by **Patty E. Fleener** M.S.W.

http://www.lynneforrest.com/html/the_faces_of_victim.html

FINALE

This book has been a mix of theory and practice, and in every chapter, the aim has been to engage you in all that is taking place. Just how far we have succeeded in doing that we may never know, but if you have added some insights, and learned some skills in becoming a counsellor, then there has been some engagement or involvement.

Engaging someone is like driving a car. For the car to move, the gears have to be engaged. Just so in this process of counselling. In counselling, if there is no involvement, there will be no movement. There has to be a meeting of minds and spirits of the two people, and together they move forward.

As you end this book, try to apply the skills and insights to your life. Counselling involves change and counselling training also involves change. The route of change might not be easy; in fact, it could be incredibly difficult. But don't let the prospect of difficulty put you off. Think of the future; imagine the future; imagine what the view will be like from the top of the mountain, as you look back and see how far you have come. As the panorama stretches out before you, you can say, 'I've done it! I am here!'

But then look up, and you will see there is more; further heights to climb. Never be satisfied with what you have achieved thus far. Your life and the lives of those you touch will be the richer for all the hard work you have put in to get to where you are.

Jan Sutton
William Stewart

Sample Forms and Letters

Sample form 1
Assessment for counselling
All information with be treated in the strictest confidence

Please complete this form and return to: _____

Surname: _____ First name(s): _____

Address: _____

_____

_____ Postcode: _____

Telephone numbers: Work _____ Home _____ Mobile _____

Can we leave a message on these numbers? ☐ Yes ☐ No

Email address: _____

Can we contact you by email? Yes ☐ No ☐

If not, how would you like us to contact you? _____

Title *(please tick)* ☐ Mr ☐ Mrs ☐ Miss ☐ Ms ☐ Other ☐ Gender:
☐ Male ☐ Female

Date of Birth: /   /

Marital status:

(please tick) Single ☐ Married/Civil partnership ☐ Widowed ☐ Separated
☐ Divorced ☐

Ethnic Category

(please tick)

White ☐ Indian ☐ Pakistani ☐ Bangladeshi ☐ Chinese ☐ Black-African ☐ Black-Caribbean ☐ Asian-Other ☐ Black-Other ☐ Other ☐

What is your first language: _____

Appointment availability

Appointments last one hour and are offered on the hour between 9.00am and 5.00pm Monday to Friday *(please tick days available)*. The more flexible you can be the earlier we may be able to offer you an appointment.

Monday ☐ Tuesday ☐ Wednesday ☐ Thursday ☐ Friday ☐

Counsellor preference

(please tick)

If we can accommodate your choice would you prefer to see a:

Male counsellor ☐ Female counsellor ☐

General Practitioner

Name of GP: _____

Address: _____

_____

Postcode : _____ Telephone number: _____

Note: We respect your privacy and will not contact your GP without your permission.

Physical disabilities

(please tick)

Do you suffer from any physical disabilities? Yes ☐ No ☐

If yes, please provide details _____

Mental health issues

(please tick)

Have you ever suffered from a mental illness? Yes ☐ No ☐

If yes, have you received a diagnosis? Yes ☐ No ☐

If yes, please provide details _____

Have you ever been admitted to hospital suffering from a mental illness?
Yes ☐ No ☐

If yes, please provide dates _____

Medication

Are you currently taking prescribed medication? Yes ☐ No ☐

If yes, please provide details _____

Are you currently taking any non-prescribed medication? Yes ☐ No ☐

If yes, please provide details _____

Reason for seeking counselling

Is it your decision to seek counselling? Yes ☐ No ☐

Please describe briefly in the space below the issue(s) you are seeking
counselling for, eg: depression, anxiety, bereavement, eating concerns, self-
injury, drugs, alcohol, relationships, sexual problems.

Goals for counselling

Please describe briefly in the space below what you hope to gain from
counselling

Previous counselling

(please tick)

Have you been for counselling before? Yes ☐ No ☐

If yes, please provide dates, details and reason for termination in the space below

Referral:

Did anyone suggest that you came to see a counsellor? Yes ☐ No ☐

Employment status

Are you currently in employment/self-employed? Yes ☐ No ☐

Are you currently in receipt of any benefits? Yes ☐ No ☐

Cost of assessment

£_____ if in full-time employment

£_____ if in part-time employment

£_____ if unemployed

Privacy

We will ensure that all personal data supplied is held in accordance with the Data Protection Act 1998.

Sample form 2
Supervision presentation form

Client's reference _____   Date of presentation _____

Counselling commenced _____   Number of sessions to date _____

Counselling sessions presented _____   Supervisor _____

Issues raised in supervision

_____

_____

_____

_____

_____

_____

_____

_____

Feedback received from supervisor and interventions recommended

_____

_____

_____

_____

_____

_____

_____

_____

Sample form 2: Supervision presentation form.

Sample form 3
Counsellor case note form

Client's reference _____ Session number _____ Date _____

Changes observed in the client since the previous session

_____
_____
_____
_____

Issues explored in the session

_____
_____
_____

Homework activities agreed

_____
_____
_____

Counsellor interventions and comments about the session

_____
_____
_____

Issues to be raised in supervision

_____
_____
_____

Date of next session _____ Counsellor _____

Sample form 3: Counsellor case note form.

Sample letter 1
Confirmation of counselling consultation letter
Counsellor's Name
Qualifications

[Counsellor's address]_____

_____

Tel: _____

Mob: _____

Email: _____

Confidential

Date: _____

[Recipient's name and address]_____

_____

Dear _____

This letter confirms your appointment for an initial counselling consultation on _____ at _____ . This consultation, which will last fifty minutes, aims to provide us with an opportunity to discuss whether counselling is appropriate for the issue(s) that are causing you concern, to gauge if I have the relevant skills and experience to suit your needs and to consider whether we can work together should we conclude that counselling is the best option for you.

Confidentiality and anonymity are vital to building trust and safety. It is essential therefore that you arrive for your appointment at the exact time stated. If you are unable to attend, or decide not to keep this appointment, twenty-four hours' notice would be appreciated.

As discussed via the telephone, the initial consultation is free. Should we deem counselling appropriate for you following the consultation, we will agree a contract (number of sessions, day, time, fee, etc.). To clarify, my standard fee is £35.00 per fifty minute session for individuals, but I am willing to negotiate a sliding fee scale according to income.

A map giving directions to my premises is enclosed together with my counselling brochure, which explains more about counselling and the approach I use.

I trust this information is of assistance and look forward to meeting you. If you have any queries, please contact me.

Yours sincerely

[Signature]

Enclosures (2) Map of directions, Counselling brochure.

Sample letter 1: Confirmation of counselling consultation letter.

Sample letter 2
Referral letter to a General Practitioner
Counsellor's Name
Qualifications

[Counsellor's address] _____

_____ _____

Tel: _____

Mob: _____

Email: _____

Confidential

Date: _____

[GP's name and address] _____

_____

Dear _____

Re: Your Patient _____

Address: _____

_____ _____ _____

I am writing to inform you that _____ attended a counselling
consultation on _____. She is seeking help for self-injury,
which started five years ago, and has become more serious and frequent
over the past six months. We have talked at length and as much as I
would like to help her, I do not consider I have the relevant skills or
experience to adequately address this issue. She has assured me that she
is not experiencing suicidal thoughts, and that she uses self-injury as a
coping mechanism to deal with difficult feelings and emotions following a
traumatic experience five years ago.

In the circumstances, I should be grateful if you could kindly arrange a psychiatric assessment referral for her as soon as possible.

_____ is in agreement with this course of action, and she has been given a copy of this letter. She will contact the surgery tomorrow to make an appointment to see you to discuss the matter further.

Thank you for your assistance in this regard.

Yours sincerely

[Signature]

Sample letter 2: Referral letter to a General Practitioner.

Suggested Responses to Exercises

Chapter 6

Exercise 6.1 Primary level empathy

Case study 1 – Julie

Feelings: Discouraged, disintegration, drained, frightened, pain, probing, scared, vulnerable.

'You feel drained and frightened because we're getting into some painful areas. What's happening to your friends outside of the group makes it too hot to handle your feelings now, and you'd rather be anywhere than here.'

Case study 2 – Margaret to Keith

Feelings: Appreciation, attention, caring, doubts, expectations, need to prove, pressures, uncertain, worth.

Keith says, 'Margaret, you feel both appreciation and doubt because I don't say the right things, even though, at the same time, you recognise that's the way I am.'

Case study 3 – Matthew

Feelings: Able to risk, at home, accepted, confident, edgy, hopeful, open, pretty good, relieved, safe, secure.

'Matthew, you feel both secure within the group yet uncertain, because of your sexuality and how we will respond to you now you've disclosed this about yourself.'

Exercise 6.2 – correct answers to listening exercise

1. Not listened to.
2. Listened to.
3. Listened to.
4. Not listened to.
5. Listened to.
6. Listened to.
7. Not listened to.
8. Listened to.
9. Not listened to.
10. Not listened to.
11. Listened to.
12. istened to.
13. Not listened to.
14. Listened to.
15. Not listened to.
16. Listened to.
17. Not listened to.
18. Listened to.
19. Not listened to.
20. Listened to.
21. Listened to.
22. Not listened to.
23. Listened to.
24. Not listened to.
25. Not listened to.
26. Not listened to.
27. Not listened to.
28. Not listened to.
29. Not listened to.
30. Not listened to.
31. Listened to.
32. Listened to.
33. Listened to.
34. Listened to.
35. Listened to.
36. Listened to.
37. Listened to.
38. Listened to.
39. Listened to.
40. Listened to.
41. Listened to.
42. Listened to.
43. Listened to.
44. Not listened to.
45. Not listened to.
12. Listened to.

Exercise 6.3 Paraphrasing

Case study 1 – Alex

Key words and phrases: have to, cope, own life.

The counsellor says: 'You're saying, Alex, that something is forcing you into making a break from your parents, even though living on your own might not be easy for you, and you're not quite certain you can manage by yourself. You also have difficulty getting your parents to see that you need more independence.'

Case study 2 – James

Key words and phrases: nursing, mates, queers, hard time, really want, what should I do?

The counsellor says: 'Life is not easy at the moment, James. Your mates are ribbing you because you want to become a nurse, yet you're convinced, in spite of what they think about you, that this is the career for you. You would like me to help you make up your mind.'

Exercise 6.4 Alternative words and phrases

Abandoned	Deserted	Forsaken	Cast out	Neglected
Afraid	Fearful	Anxious	Scared	Terrified
Aimless	Directionless	Purposeless	Goal-less	Pointless
Angry	Furious	Enraged	Bitter	Provoked
Anguished	Agonised	Tormented	Heartbroken	Distraught
Antagonistic	Contentious	Ill-disposed	Opposed	Averse
Anxious	Fretful	Distressed	Overwrought	Troubled
Appreciated	Valued	Understood	Admired	Cherished
Apprehensive	Disquieted	Uneasy	Concerned	Worried
Ashamed	Humiliated	Guilty	Remorseful	Humbled
Bitter	Hostile	Antagonistic	Spiteful	Malicious
Bored	Apathetic	Stale	Weary	Flat
Confused	Mixed up	Baffled	Bewildered	Perplexed
Delighted	Pleased	Triumphant	Cock-a-hoop	Jubilant
Depressed	Dismal	Downcast	Melancholy	Dejected
Devastated	Destroyed	Disconcerted	Demolished	Desolate
Doubtful	Indecisive	Dubious	Sceptical	Uncertain
Energetic	Vigorous	Alive	Overflowing	Active
Envious	Green-eyed	Jealous	Invidious	Malice

Embarrassed	Disconcerted	Abashed	Mortified	Awkward
Empty	Destitute	Bleak	Devoid	Hollow
Exasperated	Irritated	Aggravated	Riled	Annoyed
Excited	Elated	Exhilarated	Stimulated	Inspired
Grief	Sorrow	Heartache	Mournful	Agony
Guilty	Blameworthy	Wicked	Sinful	Wrong
Helpless	Powerless	Defenceless	Unprotected	Impotent
Hopeless	Despairing	Despondent	Giving up	Beaten
Hurt	Injured	Wounded	Aggrieved	Outraged
Inadequate	Defective	Lacking	Incapable	Inferior
Inferior	Poor relation	Second class	Lower	Menial
Lonely	Friendless	Isolated	Solitary	Forlorn
Lost	Bereft	Lonely	Deprived	Empty
Miserable	Sorrowful	Woeful	Wretched	Low
Numb	Stunned	Paralysed	Immobilised	Dazed
Overwhelmed	Swamped	Aghast	Dismayed	Unsettled
Rejected	Excluded	Rebuffed	Cast aside	Dismissed
Sad	Cheerless	Dejected	Dismal	Downcast
Shocked	Traumatised	Disturbed	Numb	Paralysed
Silly	Foolish	Absurd	Stupid	Idiotic
Stifled	Suffocated	Suppressed	Quashed	Smothered
Tense	Edgy	Nervy	Uptight	Uneasy
Tired	Drained	Worn out	Fatigued	Exhausted
Trapped	Ensnared	Cornered	Caught	Tangled
Useless	Worthless	Ineffective	Good-for-nothing	Inept
Vulnerable	Exposed	Sensitive	Defenceless	Weak

Exercise 6.5 *Reflecting feelings*

Case study 1 – Mary

Key words and phrases: success, hard work, long hours, suffer, end results.

The counsellor says: 'You're on the ladder of success, and very determined to reach the top. So desperate is your desire to succeed that no matter what it costs, you're going to slave away and, if necessary, burn the midnight oil to get what you want. You fully realise that this stiff climb could be painful and that you may put your relationships at risk, yet so strong is the drive that you won't let anything stand in the way.'

Case study 2 – Sam

Key words and phrases: time, enjoyment, work, chores.

The counsellor says: 'Sam, it seems that no matter what you do, other people always find something else for you to do. It's really bugging you, to the extent that you feel life is just one long chore. You long for some recreation, to have time to enjoy yourself doing what you want for yourself, yet all the time you're being driven into the ground by the pressure from Bill and Susan.'

Exercise 6.6 Open questions

Case study 1 – Joe

1. By the sound of it this has happened to you a few times before, Joe.

2. There seems some doubt in your mind that you're in love with Emma.

3. It's happened so many times before and you don't really know why.

4. You feel fairly sure how you feel, Joe, but not so sure how Emma feels.

5. You don't want to end up hurting girls or getting hurt yourself.

Case study 2 – Amanda

1. The prospect of going to America doesn't appeal to you.

2. You don't like the idea of being separated from Charles.

3. There's a fear within you that holds you back.

4. Both the money you will earn and being with Charles are equally important.

5. Your own work is important to you and Charles's work is important to him.

Exercise 6.7 Summarising

Case study 1 – Tom

Andy says: 'The last thing you want me to do is to lecture to you like your dad did when he was alive. The memory of his constant nagging to do well, and not to let the family down, still haunts you, and because you didn't make the grade in his eyes, you feel you let him down, which he never forgave you for. You think that being an only child brought certain privileges perhaps, but instead it has left you feeling pretty worthless and as if you don't fit in.'

Case study 2 – Tom

Andy says: 'You have disclosed some very painful memories and feelings about parents, and your parentage. There was a lot of venom in your repetition of "bastard" and yet that seemed to unlock some dark and sinister secret that had been eating away at you for years.'

Exercise 6.8 Focusing – summarising issues

Case study – Sally

'Sally, would you mind if I recap? You are sharing a house with four other students, two of whom are untidy and inconsiderate. This is causing arguments and an unhappy atmosphere to live in. You need a car because you live quite a distance from the college, and recently you had a prang in your car. Because you are only covered by third party insurance you have to meet the cost of the repairs yourself, and these are going to prove expensive. The bank is putting pressure on you to pay back past debts, and is already deducting a large chunk of your pay, which is leaving you with very little money to live on. This means that you are not eating properly and are rapidly losing a lot of weight. As if all this isn't enough to cope with, your work is suffering too, and you are now faced with having to redo your last college assignment. You feel completely exhausted and desperate and don't know what to do.'

Contrast response

'Sally, it seems as if things have deteriorated since you moved out of residential accommodation at the hospital, and I'm wondering whether it might be helpful to look at the differences between living in and living out.'

Choice-point response

'Sally, it seems as if there are many issues we could talk about:

1. The stress of sharing a house with four students, two of whom are noisy and untidy.

2. Needing your car to get to work, and how you are going to pay for the repairs.

3. Being in debt with the bank, and being pressed to pay the money back.

4. Insufficient money left to feed yourself properly, and losing weight rapidly.

5. Having to resit your last assignment when you are feeling so drained and worried because of everything else that's going on. Which one of these issues is the most urgent to explore first?'

Figure-ground response

'Sally, looking at what we've identified, it seems to me that the most urgent issue is how to balance your account. How would you feel about exploring that first?'

Exercise 6.9 Being concrete

Case study 1 – Adam

Adam says: 'I don't talk to my wife, except when I want something. When I come in from work I just sit in front of the TV and wait for her to bring my meal on a tray. I do talk a little at bedtime, but usually only when she speaks first. I never ask her how her day has gone. Yet I expect her to have sex with me whenever I want.'

Case study 2 – Judith

Judith says: 'I'm all right if I'm just listening to others, and I really can listen, but when I'm asked for an opinion, or even when I want to give something that I think is important, I just want to curl up and die. I just freeze, I start sweating and my mind might well be a bag of cotton wool. I feel so embarrassed.'

Case study 3 – Bill

Bill says: 'She really winds me up, and how! Whenever she rings me it's, "You don't know how lonely I am, Bill, why can't you visit me more often." Whenever she rings off – after pounding my ear for ages – I feel really depressed, yet guilty that I feel like strangling her with the telephone cord, except it's a mobile! I feel really weighed down by her, and even when I am able to get over to see her, it's no better.'

Chapter 7

Exercise 7.1 Confronting

Case study 1 – Vanessa

The counsellor says: 'Vanessa, you say you want to lose weight, and you realise that your lifestyle probably works against that, yet the way you talk it seems you've a "couldn't care less" attitude. Something will turn up, you say, almost as if you're happy that it's out of your control.'

Case study 2 – Dan

The counsellor says: 'Dan I want to challenge you on what you've just said. On the one hand you said you have no problems with your children, and on the other you said that Bill swore at you. You also said you give them responsibility, yet refused to respect Bill's responsibility by giving him a key. What do you think about those contradictions?'

Case study 3 – Keith

The officer says: 'You say you don't feel up to handling this change in your life. Yet you are clearly a resourceful chap. You're intelligent and persistent and have coped well with changes in the past. Your Record of Service is first class. Your men speak highly of you, as do the officers. Apart from your coping skills, you relate well to people. I've watched you, and your outgoing personality is one of your assets. Had you considered that?

'Another strength is your loyalty. Your family life is sound, and I know that your family think you're a great guy. One of your other strengths is that you have managed the Mess accounts for four years, so your honesty is above question. Yes, you are scared of such a dramatic change, and maybe you need to think of this as yet another opportunity to show that positive side of yourself in Civvy Street just as you did in Northern Ireland.'

Exercise 7.3 Advanced empathy

Case study 1 – Nigel to Brenda, a counsellor

Expressed facts:	Likes entertaining. Likes meeting people. Family don't appreciate his jokes.
Implied facts:	Likes his drink. Is more at home with others than with his family.
Expressed feelings:	Puzzled, hurt, unappreciated.
Implied feelings:	Rejected, left out, misunderstood, childish.

Brenda says: 'Nigel, it seems that you feel hurt by the reaction of your family to your jokes and story-telling. In fact, you get more appreciation at the pub than you do from your family. You've become so used to playing the entertainer that perhaps it's wearing a bit thin for the family who have probably outgrown your humour. Maybe they would rather have you as a husband and father, not a pub entertainer. At the same time, being an entertainer gets you into company with people, but that entertainer doesn't fit too comfortably with the family.'

Case study 2 – Kate, a senior nurse teacher, talking to Simon, a colleague

Expressed facts: Nurse teacher. Works hard. Twelve years. Her own choosing.

Implied facts: Lacking enjoyment. Self-imposed. Stressed. Driven.

Expressed feelings: Regrets, tired, fear, joyless.

Implied feelings: Trapped, no future, desperation, never getting anywhere, wasted life.

Simon says, 'Kate, it seems that you've pushed yourself all these years to get somewhere, and now the driving force has caught up with you. You've put work first in your life and you've forgotten how to relax and enjoy yourself. There seems to be a desperation in your voice as you think about the immediate future, for you can't see any way out of this feeling of being caught like a helpless mouse on some endless conveyer belt of work and more work, and never seeming to get anywhere.'

Case study 3 – Karen, talking to Joan, one of the counsellors in attendance at the church coffee morning

Joan says: 'Karen, what I'm hearing is that on the one hand you say you are content with your lot, and on the other I hear a big question mark. For most of the time what you do satisfies you and it's rewarding, yet within that there are moments of boredom. You say you don't miss going to the office, yet I hear a certain wistful longing there for change, something to relieve the boredom and routine. It seems as if there's also a certain feeling of "I'm not sure that I should be saying this, perhaps I'm being disloyal". It seems that you may be feeling that you've reached a stage when you would like to think about something else than just being a mother and a housewife, something to relieve the staleness, yet just thinking about that somehow feels wrong.'

Case study 4 – Andrea's fourth counselling session with Martin

Martin says: 'Andrea, you feel so totally disillusioned with me and with counselling that you want to give up. You feel angry that I misunderstand what you say and that I even don't hear what you say. It seems to you that we're caught on a roundabout, getting nowhere. I also hear a desperation that seems all mixed up with hopelessness. Part of you wants to call it a day, yet another part seems to be yelling out quite loudly, "Where else can I go?". I also hear a plea for me to understand you and what you are saying today.'

Exercise 7.4 Immediacy

Case study 1 – Alan

The facilitator says: 'Alan, I feel a bit uncomfortable in what I'm going to say, as I'm not sure how you'll take it. Over the past few weeks I've become increasingly frustrated and irritated. You are obviously very knowledgeable and have a lot of insight into counselling, and what you say is often to the point. There are times, however, when you've cut across me, as if what you have to say is more important than what I am saying. There are times when the group lapses into silence, as if we're all struggling with some deep issue, and you break the silence with a comment that doesn't seem to be relevant to what is happening. I just need you to know how I feel right now, for it's possible that this is the effect you have on other people. How do you feel about what I've just said?'

Case study 2 – Jenny

'Jenny, I would like you know how I am feeling right now, bloody angry. When you got up and walked out I felt as if you were cutting right across what was happening in the group. Cathy was talking about her pain, something I thought we all felt, certainly I did. I would like to have heard your feelings about what Cathy was saying, for what you have to say is important to me. Yet what you did stopped the action, at least for me, and now I feel angry at what you did. I would like to hear what you think about what I've said.'

Glossary

Acceptance. The feeling of being accepted as we really are, including our strengths and weaknesses, differences of opinions, or whatever, no matter how unpleasant or uncongenial, without censure. Not judging the client by some set of rules, values or standards.

Active listening. Accurate and sensitive listening that indicates to the client that the counsellor is truly listening. Includes non-verbal responses such as gestures, body posture, facial expressions and eye contact. Involves listening at a 'head' level to the thoughts behind the words, and a 'heart' level to the feelings and emotions behind the words.

Advising. Telling other people what they *should* do, rather than enabling them to find their own solutions. To recommend; suggest.

Attending. Being physically and emotionally available to the client.

Advanced empathy. Works almost exclusively with implied feelings, those that lie below the surface and/or hunches. Helps clients see their problems and concerns more clearly and in a context that enables them to move forward.

Affect. A subjective emotion or feeling attached to an idea, to some aspect of self or to some object. Common affects are euphoria, anger and sadness. Affect may be flat, blunted, inappropriate, labile (shifting).

Affirmation. Positive self-talk. Affirmations are useful for changing a negative self-image to a positive one.

Ambivalence. Simultaneous and contradictory attitudes or feelings (such as attraction and repulsion) towards an object, person or action; continual fluctuation between one thing and its opposite, uncertainty as to which approach to follow.

Anxiety. Apprehension, tension or uneasiness from anticipation of danger, the source of which is largely unknown or unrecognised.

Attitude. A pattern of more or less stable mental views, opinions or interests, established by experience over a period of time. Attitudes are likes and dislikes, affinities or aversion to objects, people, groups, situations and ideas.

Availability. Where we make ourselves emotionally available to another person. It demonstrates our willingness to be involved.

Behaviour therapy. A method of treatment designed to modify observable behaviour and thoughts that relate to behaviour. Aims to help clients alter maladaptive, or self-defeating, behaviour patterns using rewards such as praise, and negative reinforcements, such as withholding attention or disapproval. Also teaches clients strategies for calming the mind and body (relaxation techniques) so they feel better, can think more clearly and can make effective decisions.

Body language. Non-verbal communication by largely unconscious signals. The principal elements of body language are: gesture, touch, eye contact, facial expression, posture and non-verbal aspects of speech: tone of voice, volume, etc.

Boundaries. The ground-rules for counselling. Necessary for the comfort and safety of client and counsellor.

Brainstorming. Generating a free flow of thoughts and ideas that might assist with developing new ideas for solving a problem.

Catharsis. (from the Greek *katharsis*, to cleanse, purge) A purification or purgation of the emotions (e.g. pity and fear) primarily through psychology, fantasy or art. A process that brings about spiritual renewal or release from tensions or elimination of a complex by bringing it to consciousness and affording it expression.

Child psychologist. A person who studies the development of the mind of a child.

Clinical psychology. A branch of psychology concerned with the understanding and application of psychological techniques to a variety of clinical and health problems.

Clinician. A physician, psychologist or psychiatrist specialised in clinical studies or practice.

Coaching. A method of directing, instructing and training a person or group of people, with the aim being to achieve some goal or develop specific skills.

There are many types and methods of coaching. Direction may include motivational speaking. Training may include seminars, workshops and supervised practice. http://www.certifiedcoach.org/

Co-counselling. A self-directed, peer approach, where two people work together to help each other deal with problematical situations or traumatic experiences. Each person, for an agreed length of time, acts as counsellor to the other, supporting that person while he or she works through the problem and/or expresses their emotional pain.

Cognitive behavioural therapy. CBT combines two approaches: cognitive therapy and behaviour therapy. This therapy is based on the premise that we are all conditioned by our upbringing to behave and think in certain ways. CBT involves guiding clients through experiences that will change the way they think so that they can change behaviour, and encouraging clients to challenge their negative thought patterns.

Concreteness. Encouraging the client to be concrete or specific about events and feelings, rather than making vague, woolly or generalised statements, and responding in a clear and specific way.

Confidentiality. Maintaining trust with the client by not passing on personal information about them without permission being granted.

Conflict. The simultaneous presence of opposing or mutually exclusive impulses, desires or tendencies. Conflict may arise externally or internally.

Confrontation. Anything the counsellor does that invites the client to examine his behaviour and its consequences. Done with sensitivity and caring, it can be a powerful gift to the client and can open up possibilities for change. Pointing out discrepancies to the client, for instance, between what they do and what they say. A bold challenge.

Congruence. Agreement, harmony, conformity, consistency.

Contract. Terms on which counselling is offered. Agreement may be written and signed by client and counsellor, or may be verbal.

Control. The need to feel appropriately in control in a relationship, without either feeling the need to dominate or be dominated.

Core conditions. Relationship qualities embraced in most therapies, and considered to be crucial in person-centred therapy.

Dialectical Behaviour Therapy (DBT). A treatment method developed by Marsha Linehan, University of Washington, to treat patients displaying features of borderline personality disorder (BPD). Treatment includes: individual therapy, group skills training (comprising four modules – core mindfulness skills, interpersonal effectiveness skills, emotion modulation skills and distress tolerance skills), telephone contact and therapist consultation. The key strategies in DBT are *validation* and *problem solving.*

Defence mechanisms. Unconscious adjustments made, through either action or the avoidance of action, to keep from recognising personal qualities or motives that might lower self-esteem or heighten anxiety.

Delusion. A delusion is a persistent false belief that is both untrue and that cannot be shaken by reason or contradictory evidence, and which is inconsistent with the person's knowledge or culture.

Depression. A disorder of mood marked especially by sadness, inactivity, difficulty in thinking and concentration, a significant increase or decrease in appetite and time spent sleeping, feelings of dejection and hopelessness, and sometimes suicidal tendencies. Reactive depression is said to be attributable to a specific event, such as a death. Clinical or endogenous depression: both these terms have been replaced by mood 'disorders', although some people still use them. Clinical depression refers to a depression that is serious enough to need treatment by a doctor. Endogenous means arising from within. In older textbooks the distinction was made between reactive and endogenous, the latter being more serious.

Eclectic approach. The eclectic counsellor does not adhere to any particular school of therapy or counselling. She or he chooses what is most appropriate from the complete gamut of therapeutic approaches. The approach chosen takes into consideration the client's individuality and identified needs.

Emotion. A mood, attitude, frame of mind, state of mind, strong feeling, particular mental state or disposition.

Emotional freedom techniques (EFT). A modern and growing form of personal development and therapy. EFT is one of a number of recent concepts increasingly used for improving and developing people. As a psychotherapeutic tool, EFT can be effective for various purposes, including personal and self-development, attitude and behaviour development, resolving personal problems, reducing stress and restoring life balance.

Empathic responding. Understanding, or striving to understand, the thoughts, feelings, behaviours and personal meanings from another person's frame of reference, and responding with sensitivity and caring.

Empathy. The ability to step into the inner world of another person and step out of it again, without identifying too closely with (becoming) that person. Trying to understand the thoughts, feelings, behaviours and meanings from the other person's frame of reference (to feel *with*, to be *alongside*). Should not be confused with *sympathy* (feeling *like*), or pity (feeling *for*).

Euphoria. An exaggerated feeling of physical and emotional well-being, usually of psychological origin, not attributable to some external event.

Eye movement desensitisation and reprocessing (EMDR). EMDR is a therapeutic technique in which the patient moves his or her eyes back and forth, hither and thither, while concentrating on 'the problem'. The therapist waves a stick or light in front of the patient and the patient is supposed to follow the moving stick or light with his or her eyes. The therapy was discovered by therapist Dr Francine Shapiro while on a walk in the park. It is claimed that EMDR is useful in treating many emotional and behavioural difficulties but its main application has been in the treatment of post-traumatic stress disorder (PTSD).

Family therapy. Counselling more than one member of a family in the same session. The assumption is that problems in one member of the family affect all other members to some degree, and the interrelationship between family members. Particular attention is paid to the dynamics; how to mobilise the family strengths and resources; how to restructure dysfunctional behaviour. Family therapy should only be carried out by counsellors skilled in working with different family systems.

Feedback. An essential mechanism in any interpersonal communication. It gives one person the opportunity to be open to the perceptions of others. Giving feedback is both a verbal and a non-verbal process where people let others know their perceptions and feelings about their behaviours. Without effective feedback, communication will flounder.

Fight/flight response. The term given to the action of certain hormones within the body that prepares the person to fight or run away from danger.

Flashback. A past incident recurring vividly in the mind, often associated with previous taking of hallucinogen-type drugs, but also with traumatic experiences.

Focusing. Helping the client explore a specific area in depth. Focusing helps client and counsellor find out where to start, and in which direction to continue.

Force-field analysis. A decision-making technique developed from Lewin's field theory. Designed to help people understand the various internal and external forces that influence the way they make decisions.

Frame of reference. Hearing and responding in such a way that you demonstrate that you are trying to see things through the other person's eyes.

Genuineness. The degree to which the counsellor can be freely and deeply herself with the client. Also referred to as congruence and authenticity.

Gestalt therapy. Gestalt, a German word, does not translate easily into a single English phrase. Loosely, it means: the shape, the pattern, the whole form, the configuration. Gestalt therapy aims to increase a client's awareness of the whole – shape and pattern, and integration of incongruent parts. Gestalt therapists assist clients to work through 'unfinished business' that is interfering with present-day functioning by helping them gain insight into what is happening within the self in the here-and-now.

Goal setting. Working out a satisfactory solution. A highly cognitive approach. Takes account of the affective and behavioural factors as well as the creative potential of the client.

Grief therapy. There is no single approach to dealing with grief and bereavement. What people have concentrated on are the various types of grief, and how grief can interfere with normal living. There are various models, such as Kubler Ross and her five phases of grief. A second, and for many, more acceptable, is William Worden's stages model: to accept the reality; to experience the pain; to adjust to the new environment; and to withdraw emotional energy from the deceased and re-invest it in new relationships. These are tasks to be worked at.

Humanistic approach. The humanistic psychological, or phenomenological, approach to counselling emphasises the uniqueness of each individual. It stresses the subjective experience of the client, rather than trying to fit the client into some predetermined model or theory. Carl Rogers's person-centred approach is probably the definitive example of this approach. One of the emphases is self-actualisation.

Hypnotherapy. Hypnosis produces a dream-like or trance-like state. Hypnotherapy is used to help clients achieve specific, achievable short-term goals – reduction, or cessation of, nail-biting, bedwetting, smoking, weight, stress levels – relieving pain and depression or overcoming phobias. For many years a controversy has been raging concerning the possibility of hypnotic techniques creating 'false memories' in trauma survivors (memories believed to have been repressed, but in fact fantasised). These memories (whether real or imagined) can cause considerable distress or retraumatisation. Therefore, hypnosis with trauma survivors should be used with extreme caution, and only administered by a qualified and experienced practitioner.

Immediacy. The skill of discussing your relationship with a client. Also referred to as 'here-and-now', or 'you-me-talk'.

Insight. In psychological terms, the discovery by an individual of the psychological connection between earlier and later events so as to lead to recognition of the roots of a particular conflict or conflicts. A clear or deep perception of a situation.

Integrative approach. Integrative counsellors do not subscribe to one therapeutic approach. The term 'integrative' refers to either the integration of two or more approaches to therapy, or an integration of both therapies and counselling techniques.

Intellectualising. Avoiding gaining psychological insight into an emotional problem by performing an intellectual analysis. Using the *head* rather than the *heart*.

Internal frame of reference. The subjective world of a person. When we view another person within the internal frame of reference, that person's behaviour makes more sense.

Intervention. Intervening with the aim of preventing or altering the result or course of actions.

Judgmentalism. Where we judge people according to our own self-imposed standards and values, and impose them in a way that condemns and criticises.

Mentoring. A relationship in which one person – usually someone more experienced, often more senior in the community – helps another to discover more about themselves, their potential and their capability. It can be an informal relationship, where an individual leans on someone else for guidance, support and feedback, or a more formal arrangement between two people who respect and trust each other. Mutual respect and trust is the essence of a successful mentoring process.

Mood. A prevailing and sustained emotion or feeling.

Neuro-linguistic programming (NLP). An interpersonal communication model and an alternative approach to psychotherapy, based on the subjective study of language, communication and personal change. It was co-created by Richard Bandler and linguist John Grinder in the 1970s. The initial focus was pragmatic, modelling three successful psychotherapists, Fritz Perls (Gestalt therapy), Virginia Satir (family systems therapy) and Milton H. Erickson (clinical hypnosis), with the aim of discovering what made these individuals more successful than their peers.

Non-judgmental attitude. Suspending own judgments and standards and not imposing them on others.

Non-possessive warmth. An attitude of friendliness towards others.

Openness. How prepared we are to let other people see beneath the surface; to let them be appropriately aware of our feelings, secrets and innermost thoughts.

Open invitation to talk. Demonstrating to the client that you are ready to listen.

Open questions. Keep conversation going and create greater interest and depth. They seek clarification, elaboration and encourage exploration.

Paraphrasing. Restating the client's thoughts and feelings in your own words.

Person-centred approach. This approach emphasises the quality of the counsellor and client relationship. Genuineness, warmth, honesty, unconditional positive regard and empathy are considered essential 'conditions' to a growth-producing climate between client and counsellor.

Pharmacotherapy. Treatment of disease with medicine.

Post-traumatic stress disorder. An anxiety disorder in which exposure to an exceptional mental or physical stressor is followed, sometimes immediately and sometimes not until three months or more after the incident, by persistent re-experiencing of the event, with its associated feelings and behaviours.

Problem-solving. Helping someone, or ourselves, to resolve some difficulty by working to a model or plan, the aim of which is to generate positive action.

Psychiatry. A branch of medicine concerned with the diagnosis and treatment of psychological disorders. A psychiatrist is a doctor of medicine who has received postgraduate training in psychiatry.

Psychoanalysis. A theoretical system of psychology based on the work of Sigmund Freud. Psychoanalysis may be defined as human nature interpreted in terms of conflict. The mind is understood as an expression of conflicting forces – some conscious, the majority unconscious. A deeper and more intense form of treatment than other forms of psychotherapy.

Psychodynamic. The study of human emotions as they influence behaviour. Psychodynamic theory recognises the role of the unconscious, and assumes that behaviour is determined by past experience, genetic endowment and current reality. A psychodynamic counsellor works toward the client achieving insight.

Psychotherapy. Any form of 'talking cure'. The treatment of psychological problems through the use of a variety of theories of personality development, specific techniques and therapeutic aims. Aimed at relieving psychological distress. Psychotherapists use talk and thought, rather than surgery or drugs. May be superficial, deep, interpretive, supportive or suggestive.

Rational emotive behaviour therapy (REBT). REBT is a comprehensive, active-directive psychotherapy that focuses on resolving emotional and behavioural problems and disturbances and enabling people to lead happier and more fulfilling lives. REBT was created and developed by the American psychotherapist and psychologist Albert Ellis. REBT is one of the first and foremost forms of Cognitive Behaviour Therapy (CBT) and was first expounded by Ellis in the mid-1950s.

Reflecting feelings. Understanding the client's emotional world and mirroring their emotional content with empathic responses.

Self-awareness. An awareness of our inner experience – what goes on inside our heads – how we think and feel – knowing how we function emotionally. A continuous and evolving process of gathering information about ourselves. A basic need in effective helping.

Self-disclosure. Disclosing personal information, thoughts and feelings to clients. Used to serve the needs of the client, not the needs of the counsellor.

Self-esteem. A confidence and satisfaction in oneself: self-respect, self-worth, self-pride. Self-esteem is the value we place on ourselves. A high self-esteem is a positive value; a low self-esteem results from attaching negative values to ourselves or some part of ourselves.

Stereotyping. Pigeon-holing, putting people into a mould, typecasting, making assumptions – not making allowances for a person's individuality. Stereotyping is typically negative, and is often rooted in prejudice, ignorance or irrational fears.

Stress. An imprecise term, but generally taken to mean a state of psychological tension produced by the kinds of forces or pressures (stressors) that exert force with which the person feels unable to cope. The feelings of just being tired, jittery, or ill are subjective sensations of stress.

Summarising. The process of tying together all that has been talked about during part of, or all of, the counselling session. It clarifies what has been accomplished and what still needs to be done.

Supervision. Concerned with the emotional development of the counsellor, and developing the counsellor's skills. Focus is not therapy for the counsellor. Supervision falls between the polarities of counselling and tutoring.

Syndrome. A group of signs and symptoms that occur together and characterise a particular abnormality.

Therapeutic alliance. A collaborative relationship between counsellor and client. A strong therapeutic alliance (client–counsellor bond) is considered a necessary condition for effective counselling.

Transactional analysis. Transactional analysis (TA) is a system of analysis and therapy developed by Eric Berne (1910–70) and popularised in his book *Games People Play* (1964). The theory is that we have various ego states, Parent, Adult and Child (PAC), all of which influence our behaviour. Counsellors using TA work with the client to get more harmony between the three ego states.

Trust. Faith in one's own integrity (confidence in oneself), and reliance on the integrity, ability and character of another person (having faith in).

Unconditional positive regard. A non-possessive caring, valuing, prizing, acceptance of the client, regardless of how unpleasant the client's behaviour might be.

Unconscious. According to Freud and psychoanalysis, the unconscious is that part of the mind or mental functioning which is accessible only rarely to awareness. The aim of psychoanalysis is to bring into the conscious mind what has been repressed into the unconscious. We repress painful memories and wishes, and unacceptable drives. Counselling does not work directly with the unconscious, and that is one of the major differences between counselling and psychoanalysis.

Values. Deeply held principles, standards or beliefs that we consider good or beneficial to our well-being and which influence our behaviour, thoughts and feelings and how we relate to people.

Useful addresses and websites

British Association for Counselling and Psychotherapy

1 Regent Place

Rugby

Warwickshire CV21 2PJ

Tel: 0870 443 5252

Email: bacp@bacp.co.uk

Website: http://www.bacp.co.uk

Description: The association's aims are to promote understanding and awareness of counselling throughout society, increase the availability of trained and supervised counsellors and maintain and raise standards of training and practice. Produces a range of publications and a quarterly counselling journal. The United Kingdom Register of Counsellors (UKRC) is part of the British Association for Counselling and Psychotherapy.

British Association of Psychotherapists (BAP)

37 Mapesbury Road

London NW2 4HJ

Tel: 020 8452 9823

Email: mail@bap-psychotherapy.org

Website: http://www.bap-psychotherapy.org

Description: Specialises in individual psychoanalytic psychotherapy for adults, adolescents and children and is one of the foremost psychoanalytic psychotherapy training organisations in the country.

British Association of Sexual and Marital Therapists (BASRT)

PO Box 13686

London SW20 92H

Email: info@basrt.org.uk

Website: http://www.basmt.org.uk

Description: Objectives are to advance the education and training of persons who are engaged in sexual, marital and relationship therapy, promote research in the field of marriage and other intimate relationships and advance the education of the public about sexual, marital and relationship therapy.

British Psychological Society (BPS)

St Andrews House, 48 Princess Road East

Leicester LE1 7DR

Tel: 0116 254 9568

Email: enquiry@bps.org.uk

Website: http://www.bps.org.uk

Description: Aims to encourage the development of psychology as a scientific discipline and an applied profession, to raise standards of training and practice in the application of psychology and to raise public awareness of psychology and increase the influence of psychological practice in society.

Institute of Family Therapy

24–32 Stephenson Way

London NW1 2HX

Tel: 020 7391 9150

Email: info@ift.org.uk

Website: http://www.instituteoffamilytherapy.org.uk

Description: Provides a range of services for families, couples and other relationship groups, family mediation service, training courses, conferences and workshops.

Relate: The relationship people

Central Office, Herbert Gray College

Little Church Street

Rugby

Warwickshire CV21 3AP

Tel: 0300 100 1234

Website: http://www.relate.org.uk.

Description: UK's largest and most experienced relationship counselling organisation. Whether you are having problems getting on with your partner, your kids, your siblings or even your boss, Relate can help. Local branches can be found by entering a postcode on the site.

The Samaritans

10 The Grove

Slough

Berkshire SL1 1QP

Tel: 08457 909090 (calls at local rates)

Email: jo@samaritans.org

Website: www.samaritans.org.uk

Description: Provides confidential and emotional support to any person who is suicidal or despairing (twenty-four-hour-a-day service – all year round). For details of your nearest branch consult your local telephone directory.

United Kingdom Council for Psychotherapy

167–9 Great Portland Street

London W1W 5PF

Tel: 020 7436 3002

Email: ukcp@psychotherapy.org.uk

Website: www.psychotherapy.org.uk

Description: Promotes and maintains the profession of psychotherapy and high standards in the practice of psychotherapy for the benefit of the public, throughout the UK.

Westminster Pastoral Foundation Counselling & Psychotherapy

23 Kensington Square

London W8 5HN

Telephone 020 7378 2000 (counselling enquiries)

Email: reception@wpf.org.uk

Website: http://www.wpf.org.uk

Description: Exists to extend access to high quality, professional counselling and psychotherapy and to strive for excellence in the training of counsellors and psychotherapists. Provides a list of UK affiliate training centres.

Distance learning courses in counselling skills and related subjects

National Extension College

The Michael Young Centre

Purbeck Road

Cambridge CB2 2HN

Tel: 0800 389 2839

Email: info@nec.ac.uk

Website: http://www.nec.ac.uk/courses

The Open University (Course Information and Advice Centre)

PO Box 724

Milton Keynes MK7 6ZS

Tel: 01908 653231

Website: http://www.open.ac.uk

The Institute of Counselling, Clinical and Pastoral Counselling

40 St. Enoch Square

Glasgow G1 4DH

Tel: (44) (0)141 204 2230

Email: admin@instituteofcounselling.org.uk

Website: http://www.collegeofcounselling.com

Description: The Institute offers a wide range of tutor supported correspondence courses, videos, audio cassettes and books; specialising in counselling skills training. The Institute is a non-profit organisation established in the UK in 1985 to provide quality home study training and education at affordable costs.

USEFUL WEBSITES

Cruse Bereavement Care

Website: *http://www.cruse.org.uk*

Description: Exists to promote the well-being of bereaved people and to enable anyone undergoing bereavement to understand their grief and cope with their loss. The organisation provides support and offers information, advice, education and training services.

Mind

Website: http://www.mind.org.uk

Description: The leading mental health charity in England and Wales. Mind produces a wide range of publications. Useful booklets include: *Making sense of counselling, Making sense of psychotherapy and psychoanalysis, Making sense of cognitive behaviour therapy* and *Understanding talking treatments.*

The Royal College of Psychiatrists

Website: www.rcpsych.ac.uk

Description: The professional and educational body for psychiatrists in the United Kingdom and the Republic of Ireland. The RCP website contains several informative factsheets including: *Psychotherapy, counselling, and psychological treatment in the NHS: FAQs for professionals and service commissioners; Psychotherapy in the NHS: 25 FAQs for service users; Professionals involved in the care of people with mental health problems* and a *Glossary of Terms.*

Further reading

APPROACHES TO COUNSELLING AND PSYCHOTHERAPY

A Practical Approach to Counselling, Margaret Hough, Longman; 2nd revised edition (2001).

Cognitive-behavioural Counselling in Action, Peter Trower. SAGE Publications (2015).

Four Approaches to Counselling and Psychotherapy, Windy Dryden and Jill Mytton, Routledge (31 Mar 1999).

Integrative Counselling Skills in Action, Sue Culley and Tim Bond, SAGE Publications; 2nd edition (2011).

Psychodynamic Counselling in Action, Michael Jacobs, SAGE Publications; 4th edition (2010).

ASSESSMENT AND INTERVIEWING

Client Assessment, Stephen Palmer and Gladeana McMahon, SAGE Publications (1997).

CARL ROGERS

A Way of Being, Carl R. Rogers, Houghton Mifflin; new edition (1995).

Client Centered Therapy: Its Current Practice, Implications and Theory, Carl R. Rogers, Constable and Robinson; new edition (2003).

On Becoming a Person, Carl R. Rogers, Constable and Robinson; new edition (2004).

The Carl Rogers Reader, H. Kirschenbaum, Houghton Mifflin (1996).

CONTRACTS

Contracts in Counselling and Psychotherapy, Charlotte Sills, SAGE Publications; 2nd revised edition (2006).

COUNSELLING IN A NUTSHELL SERIES

Cognitive Therapy in a Nutshell, Michael Neenan and Windy Dryden, SAGE Publications 2nd revised edition (2010).

Counselling in a Nutshell, Windy Dryden, SAGE Publications 2nd edition (2011).

Person-centred Counselling in a Nutshell, Roger Casemore, SAGE Publications 2nd edition (2011).

Psychodynamic Counselling in a Nutshell, Susan Howard, SAGE Publications 2nd edition (2011).

GERARD EGAN

The Skilled Helper: A Problem-Management and Opportunity Development Approach to Helping, Gerard Egan, Thomson Learning; International edition; 8th edition (2006).

INTRODUCTORY TEXTS AND NEXT STEPS

An Introduction to Counselling, John McLeod, Open University Press; 3rd revised edition (2003).

Counselling for Toads: A Psychological Adventure, Robert De Board, Routledge (1997).

First Steps in Counselling: A students' companion for basic introductory courses, Pete Sanders, PCCS Books; 3rd revised edition (2002).

Next Steps in Counselling: A Students' Companion for Certificate and Counselling Skills Courses, Alan Frankland and Pete Sanders, PCCS Books (2008).

LEGAL MATTERS

Counselling, Psychotherapy and the Law, Peter Jenkins, SAGE Publications; 2nd edition (2007).

Therapists in Court: Providing Evidence and Supporting Witnesses, Tim Bond and Amanpreet Sandhu, SAGE Publications (2005).

MEDICAL AND PSYCHIATRIC MATTERS

Medical and Psychiatric Issues for Counsellors, Brian Daines, Linda Gask and Amanda Howe, SAGE Publications; 2nd edition (2007).

PERSONAL AND PROFESSIONAL DEVELOPMENT

Counsellor's Workbook: Developing a Personal Approach, John McLeod, Open University Press 2nd edition (2009).

Personal Development in Counsellor Training, Hazel Johns, SAGE Publications 2nd revised edition (2012).

PERSON-CENTRED COUNSELLING

Being Empathic: A Companion for Counsellors and Therapists, Steve Vincent, Radcliffe Publishing (2005).

Congruence: Rogers Therapeutic Conditions: Evolution, Theory & Practice, Gill Wyatt, PCCS Books (2001).

Contact and Perception: Rogers Therapeutic Conditions: Evolution, Theory & Practice, Gill Wyatt and Pete Sanders, PCCS Books (2002).

Developing Person-Centred Counselling, Dave Mearns, SAGE Publications; 2nd revised edition (2002).

Dictionary of Person-centred Psychology, Keith Tudor and Tony Merry, PCCS Books (2006).

Empathy: Rogers Therapeutic Conditions: Evolution, Theory & Practice, Sheila Haugh and Tony Merry, PCCS Books (2001).

Learning and Being in Person-Centred Counselling, Tony Merry and Bob Lusty, PCCS Books; 2nd revised edition (2002).

Person-centred Counselling in Action, Dave Mearns and Brian Thorne, SAGE Publications; 4th edition (2013).

Unconditional Positive Regard: Rogers Therapeutic Conditions: Evolution, Theory & Practice, Jerold Bozarth and Paul Wilkins, PCCS Books (2001).

Skills in Person-centred Counselling and Psychotherapy, Janet Tolan, SAGE Publications (2003).

RESEARCH AND STUDY

Doing Counselling Research, John McLeod, SAGE Publications; 3rd edition (2013).

Step in to Study Counselling, Pete Sanders, PCCS Books; 3rd edition (2003).

SKILLS, THEORY AND PRACTICE

An A–Z of Counselling Theory and Practice, William Stewart, Cengage Learning; 5th edition (2013).

Counselling Skills and Theory, Margaret Hough, Hodder; 4th edition (2014).

Theory and Practice of Counselling and Therapy, Richard Nelson-Jones, SAGE Publications; 6th edition (2014).

STANDARDS AND ETHICS

Standards and Ethics for Counselling in Action, Tim Bond, SAGE Publications; 4th edition (2015).

SUPERVISION

Person-Centred Counselling Supervision: Personal and Professional, Richard Bryant-Jefferies, Radcliffe Publishing (2005).

Supervision in the Helping Professions, Peter Hawkins and Robin Shohet, Open University Press; 4th edition (2012).

Index